MW00774810

Ma a Fakai Futuna

For the People of Futuna

Nokonofo Kitea
We Keep On Living This Way

A Hkai ma a Tagi i Futuna, Vanuatu
Myths and Music of Futuna, Vanuatu

Collected, Translated and Interpreted
by Janet Dixon Keller
and Takaronga Kuautonga

UNIVERSITY OF HAWAI'I PRESS
HONOLULU

A CHP production

First published in the United States of America and Europe by
University of Hawai'i Press
2840 Kolowalu Street, Honolulu, Hawai'i 96822

Designed and published in Australia by
Crawford House Publishing Australia
14 Dryandra Drive, Belair SA 5052

Library of Congress Cataloguing-in-Publication data has been applied for.

ISBN 978-0-8248-3113-4

Cover by TLC Design, Adelaide

Printed in India by Thomson Press Limited

10 09 08 07 1 2 3 4

A Fesao Uai Ta Koro / Table of Contents

A Farigoi / List of Figures

Tano Uai Moa ma Fafetai / Preface and Acknowledgements

This project was conceived and developed collaboratively by Janet Dixon Keller, an American anthropologist and linguist, and Takaronga Kuautonga, fieldworker from Futuna (also known as West Futuna) and curator of museum collections at the Vanuatu Cultural Center. We share an enduring interest in the customs of West Futuna, a small island in the south of the Republic of Vanuatu in the southwest Pacific. Throughout our collaboration we served together and independently as authors, fieldworkers, interpreters, translators. At times Takaronga also acted as narrator. As scribe for the English language passages of the book, I, Janet, write in the first person singular or plural as appropriate to reflect our respective or mutual contributions. When aspects of the research are developed directly from Takaronga's insights I use his name and third person reference to make this attribution clear.

Against a background of field research initiated by me in the 1970s, and more recent fieldwork undertaken independently by Takaronga beginning in the 1990s, our cooperative efforts began in 1998 when I visited Vanuatu for the first time since the post-independence moratorium on expatriate scholarly research had been lifted in 1994 (Bolton 1999). During this visit we were introduced by Ralph Reganvanu, Director of the Vanuatu Cultural Center. He encouraged us to co-design a project that would build on our common interests in cultural heritage while also contributing to the West Futuna community and to citizens of Vanuatu more generally. Both of us had experience with oral narratives and music. We turned our attention to these forms of artistry and undertook the tasks of creating a written literature and providing interpretive context for it. Subsequently we spent time together working on the project in Vanuatu in 1999, in Canberra, Australia in 2000, in the United States in 2001 and in Auckland, New Zealand in 2002. Throughout these years we each attended to our respective tasks and interests relevant to the project when we were separated by the Pacific Ocean keeping in touch by postal and electronic mails as possible.

Shortly after Takaronga and I were introduced, we began reviewing texts collected in the 1970s. Eventually Takaronga narrated an expanded version of one tale and edited others. We developed interpretations gradually, discussing particular passages with their presuppositions, exploring inter-textual relations and establishing connections among texts and the world. As ambiguities were identified we gathered more information from both past and present vantage points and elicited alternative versions of narratives from members of the West Futuna community. In this process Takaronga gradually became increasingly comfortable articulating his insights regarding unspoken significances. I found it easier over time to read between the lines of a given text, to imagine connections among texts and to suggest possible interpretations for Takaronga's consideration. As a result our exegeses as presented here reflect a process of emerging consensus. Yet our agreement is never absolute. Our interpretations are accentuated with occasional differences and these we take care to note.

The actual writing process involved time together and time spent independently editing and reworking passages. I am more at ease writing in English. Takaronga prefers West Futuna. The final pages reflect these preferences. English language sections including translations were drafted by me, vetted collaboratively in discussions with Takaronga and others from West Futuna, presented in scholarly arenas and then revised. The West Futuna versions of the narratives are based on texts recorded from a number of people of West Futuna including Takaronga. In each case, transcriptions initially prepared by me were collaboratively reviewed with Takaronga line by line. *Ta Pasiesi ma Majihjiki* was presented for a public audience in the United States. Takaronga spun the tale in West Futuna and I translated. Subsequently Takaronga polished and honed not only this tale, but all the materials written in the language of West Futuna. He has aimed throughout to produce a secular literature in his native tongue, one that we hope will resonate in West Futuna or in English with a wide variety of readers.

Entwined within the pages to follow are narratives, songs, memories and perspectives from many sources. Raconteurs, musical performers and audience members from the community of West Futuna, Vanuatu provide the primary materials. Our understandings of local philosophies linked with western scholarship allow us to interpret the texts and to encompass oral traditions within expanding spheres of significance. We owe an enormous debt of gratitude to the people of West Futuna who have assisted in this research now over thirty years and we extend our thanks to many living around the island and elsewhere today. At the heart of this project are a few who gave of their time, energy and resources over a very long term. Napausi Teifisou, Naparau Naora, Popoina Magau and the late Iawoi Seiake, Liji Sore and Teikona Nuaita, all contributed significantly to the original texts and translations on which this interpretive study is based. Niau and the late Vaega Liji, Serei and Yama Natuka, Niani and Natuka Liji, Matilta and Popoina Magau, and Napausi and the late Teifisou graciously provided a home and shared their meals with me when I was on Futuna or in Vila. We hope this publication takes a small step toward giving back to the community in a new form some of the wisdom so many have shared with us.

This project is also indebted to many supporting institutions, colleagues, friends and family members. The University of Illinois, Urbana-Champaign has given financial support over the years for travel and equipment to keep the research active. The William and Flora Hewlett Foundation sponsored one summer's travel and research in 1998. The National Institute of Mental Health supported initial phases of the study in the 1970s. Director Ralph Reganvanu of the Vanuatu Cultural Center has created an atmosphere in which collaborative research like that we have contributed here can flourish. His constant support and warm humor have been much appreciated. The Center for Cross-Cultural Research, Australian National University and The British Museum sponsored a conference in Canberra in 2000 that provided an occasion to bring initial interpretations to an interested audience well informed about Vanuatu. Lissant Bolton designed the conference, creating a welcome forum for exchanging ideas and constructing common goals among participants. Comments from many who attended helped us revise and continue to develop our ideas for this book. And it was in this context that we were first introduced to our publisher, Tony Crawford, who has patiently guided us through the final stages of manuscript preparation.

Edward M. Bruner, Alma Gottlieb, Andy Orta, Derek Pardue, Jennifer Shaffer and others offered critical insights on this work during a University of Illinois Urbana-Champaign departmental workshop in the late 1990s. Whenever we could take advantage of their insights this work has been improved. An Association for Social Anthropology in Oceania seminar on Pacific Seascapes held in Vancouver in February 2000 generated helpful commentary from Gene Ammarrell, Rick Feinberg, Per Hage, Tony Hooper, Judith Huntsman, and Patrick Kirch. A number of people including Giovanni Bennardo, Marion Dixon, Brenda Farnell, Rick Feinberg, David Herdrich, Kirk Huffman, Charlie Keller, Lamont Lindstom, Tzu-kai Liu, Steve Maas, Margaret Rodman, Pamela Rosi, and Brenda Farnell read early drafts of parts or all of this work and offered insightful and encouraging commentary. Kirk Huffman also contributed a photograph of a contemporary musical performance.

We also thank The Field Museum of Chicago, especially Carolyn Schiller-Johnson, John Terrell, and Alaka Wali for an opportunity, in February 2001, to tell some stories to a large audience of schoolchildren from whom we learned much, especially during the question period following the performance. The Spurlock Museum at the University of Illinois, especially Christa Deacy-Quinn, Tandy Lacy, Kim Sheahan, and Stephanie Stout offered us additional opportunities to tell these stories and work with artifact collections. Dan Keding, professional raconteur, constructively critiqued our early story telling practices.

Takaronga wishes to acknowledge his grandfather, Breisa, now deceased, whose virtuosity as a raconteur has inspired some of the narrative passages recorded here. I wish to thank Peter Morris of Traralgon, Australia who has been more than generous with his time, insight and research from mission archives. I hope he may find the history and translations here worthy in some small way of his interest even when our perspectives differ. William R. Dougherty, who spent much of the time in 1973-74 with me on the island of West Futuna, has generously granted permission for some of his photographs to be reproduced here. Tom Schleis originally transcribed all the musical texts that appear within these pages and others for which the lyrics remain untranslated. He attended to this labor over an extended period and for this we offer him our deepest gratitude. Eva Pajuelo has converted Tom's handwritten transcriptions into digital form. Lauren Sieg digitized the information we gathered on cultural geography and created base maps. Steve Holland prepared many of the graphic illustrations working with us as our ideas changed over several years. His insights have created more perspicuous visual representations than we could have constructed on our own. Jim Stanlaw worked on the earliest linguistic materials associated with this project creating a database connecting West Futuna with other Polynesian languages.

Our families have been at the heart of our enthusiasm for this work. Takaronga and I greatly value the opportunities we have had to share stories with our children and spouses. I wish to give special thanks to my husband, Charlie Keller, who has supported my travel to Vanuatu in every way possible, assisted me in welcoming Takaronga into our home, listened to numerous translations at various stages and commented on their accessibility. He has always seen the possibilities that might come from this research.

1
Ta Kamata / Introduction

From village to town, gardens to computers, traditions to global influences, everyday life in the Republic of Vanuatu reflects a commingling of peoples, a profusion of places, a mélange of possibilities. Our project was conceived in the midst of this diversity to address one of the many constitutive threads: oral literatures and musical lyrics bridging past and present. From this vantage point we looked to the future to envision a library of ancestral narratives where the pages of volumes are soft and wrinkled from constant use. We imagined modern citizens inspired to reflect on their heritage, to reminisce, retell, critically discuss and ponder their legacy. The narratives collected here are, today, a part of the fabric of voices in the archipelago of Vanuatu, but they are fading. Their value as resources for creating community, addressing challenges of modernity and bridging differences goes largely unrecognized. Our hope, as authors of this work, is that re-presentation of oral literatures and musical lyrics from one community in Vanuatu will facilitate novel engagements with these genres, promote comparison with the verbal arts of others, and legitimize assessments of relevance for events unfolding now within Pacific island life ways.

Traditional stories and musical performances are often unwittingly stigmatized within contemporary Vanuatu. Performed in tourist arenas or in displays of ethnic pride, or imagined as symbols of national heritage, the verbal arts are seldom plumbed for textual meanings. These kernels from the past are viewed as quaint residues, mismatched with current circumstances, irrelevant in detail for addressing issues of modernity and international politics. At the same time that local leaders seek uniquely inspired roads to progress and strive to articulate Melanesian principles for development, society has largely forgotten the power of narrative to embody wisdom (Miles 1998; Rakau n.d.; Reganvanu 1999). The stories, songs and reflections committed to writing in the pages to follow are reminders that words from the past glimmer with perspectives that transcend time. These histories and mythologies carry seeds for living in the moment and for cultivating the future, if only readers will uncover and replant them (Bolton 1999; Facey 1988; Kenzo and Associates 1992; Lindstrom and Gwero 1998; Mageo 2001; McLean 1999; Nero 1992; Sherkin 1999; Wan Smolbag Theater 1996, 1997).

In this volume we introduce five stories and two songs from Futuna, Vanuatu (subsequently referred to herein as West Futuna to clearly distinguish the island from the French Overseas Territory of Wallis-and-Futuna). The island is photographed in Figure 1. Discussions of geography and cultural associations are taken up in Chapter 3. Individuals who identify today as descendants of an ancestral community from this place are dispersed throughout the archipelago of Vanuatu and the larger region of Oceania, but West Futuna is still their homeland. Their collective compositions represent a single community, yet these are indicative of the rich heritage of verbal arts associated with the many languages and culturally differentiated peoples of Vanuatu. To orient our introductory discussion we offer capsule summaries of the compositions. The narratives, not generally titled in local parlance (Facey 1988), are here given labels that will serve to reference each piece throughout the book.

Ta Pasiesi ma Majihjiki, 'The Monster and Majihjiki', is a great myth of conflict between evil and right. The story, initiated as the population of West Futuna is annihilated, culminates in triumph for moral order. At the denouement evil is destroyed

Figure 1: West Futuna on approach from the west. William R. Dougherty 1973.

and proper placement of villages around the island is established once again. The fundamental order of society is re-affirmed.

Majihjiki ma Fafine Tonga, 'Majihjiki and the Women of Tonga', is a story that questions indigenous gendered constructions of women who move and men who are rooted in place. It is a tale of marriage by trickery that ultimately results in a challenge to normative residential practices.

Sina Fine Ariki, 'The Princess Sina', is also a tale centered on marriage. It focuses on disruption in the natal family as daughters mature and leave home. Conflicted associations for women and men with land and sea are symbolized in the episodes.

Rufei Soa, 'Two Brothers', is an allegory reflecting on the fundamental principles of brotherly co-operation and spousal loyalty. Violations to the norms for kin based relationships become life-threatening challenges to individuals and the social fabric.

Samaine, 'Samaine', is a fable of abandonment and incorporation. The development of episodes reaffirms the connectedness and reciprocity essential to human existence.

Tiata, 'Tiata', is a humorous song derisively mocking the plight of a man without a mate.

Nahjeji, 'Lobster Trap' is political commentary set to verse. The composer offers local perspective on mid-nineteenth century evangelism. Comparing convert seeking to lobster trapping the song lyrics document resistance to early Christian influences.

Framing an Approach

Takaronga and I share a conviction that these quite localized narrative productions offer the potential to 'stimulate thought, to assure us there are things we do not know, things we must know, things capable of unsettling the world we inhabit' (Glassie 1982:13). We come to this conviction from a profound sharing of intellectual perspectives despite differences in background and experience. We were both surprised to be able to draw connections between our disparate starting points: western scholarly theory and West Futuna cosmology. Yet connections emerged prominently for both of us as we worked together, allowing us to interrelate our respective views. In the process we posited analogies between indigenous, West Futuna conceptual frameworks on meaning and western scholarship on narrative. In drawing these correspondences we found that we were each motivated to ask similar questions of the material before us. It is these questions that guide our interpretations and discussions of the literature and lyrics to follow.

West Futuna Semiotics

The people of West Futuna interpret spoken discourses by reference to a local theory of semiotics. I first encountered this framework in learning word meanings as I recorded utterances like, *Tano hkano gatatasiana*. Said of synonyms this indicated 'Their meanings are just the same'. A similar expression occurred in discussions of illocutions embodied in conversational utterances. *Tano hkano i ai pekua*? This question refers to an opaque utterance and asks, 'What does it really mean?' Later the word *hkano* coupled with the word *ata*, emerged in accounts of metaphorical speech. Instances of this pairing came to my attention as parishioners assessed the moral of a sermon or villagers sought significance beyond the literal episodes in a story.

As I pursued the semantics of these expressions examples of their use multiplied well beyond the realm of language. Gradually it became clear that fundamental cosmological principles as well as a basic theory of signification were signaled by the terms *hkano* and *ata* (Keller and Lehman 1991). In its broadest sense *hkano* refers to the essence of some living thing; *ata* to an echo, shadow, image or reflection of that essence. *Hkano* and *ata* are inherently and efficaciously linked. *Ata* are gifts of the supernatural offering magical connections to living *hkano*. As material repositories of the invisible power of the supernatural, *ata* serve as ritual conduits for enhancing the fertility and vigor of individual members of the species they resemble (see also Bonnemaison 1994; Codrington 1891; Sherkin 1999).

These ideas are aptly extended and metaphorically transformed by the people of West Futuna in the construction of an indigenous theory of meaning. Like living things, speech embodies complementary facets. Spoken discourse, referred to as *ata*, constitutes an observable reflection, an image of underlying meanings. Hidden meanings, themselves, are the real essence, *hkano,* of a tale or conversational exchange. Spoken utterances, *ata,* portend deeper significances, but the links connecting discourse with its import are indirect, open to interpretation and debate. It is only through proper attention to observable *ata* or spoken words that one can discover implicit significances. Up to a point, the more well developed the *ata* of a story, the richer a listener's insights into its *hkano* will be. The *hkano* itself, however, must remain unstated. Meaning should never be directly captured by explicit prose. A speaker's task is to construct intriguing discourses, episodic developments or figurative tropes that reflect unspoken wisdom. A listener's task is to decipher and (re)construct meanings hidden in the proffered utterances.

This theory applies to musical compositions as well. The verses of a song are referred to as *ano jino*, 'its image'. Lyrics constitute a surface indirectly referring to a deeper *hkano* or meaningful essence of a composition. The chorus is called the *ata* of a song. Choruses are usually composed of meaningless syllables thought to represent words of the supernatural no longer directly intelligible to humankind. In the repetition of these meaningless sounds, the choral refrains offer supernatural legitimacy for the accompanying lines of each stanza. The choral *ata* direct the audience to seek the underlying *hkano* of a song through careful listening to its verses.

Relevant to this perspective on meaning are ideas about metaphor referred to as *furi fesao,* 'turned words', used as a way of coding communications historically. Today *furi fesao* remain particularly vital in musical compositions. As in other Pacific societies, 'turned words' are a device employed richly in song lyrics (Feld 1990:106; Firth and McLean 1990; Kaeppler and Love 1998; Luomala 1955; Nero 1992). The tropic process offers a space in which composers may present what might otherwise be unacceptable commentary or political criticism. The verses of a song create an aura of ambiguity engendering curiosity and speculation regarding the connections between the lyrics and what they signify. In the past traditional songs were decoded in the whispered reflections of an audience. Today decoding musical texts of a former time requires studied attention to figurative language and rests heavily on recognizing indexes that may reveal the typically unmentioned identity and interests of a composer, his or her subjects, and the era referenced.

Jikai ta hkano i ai 'There is no meaning in it. Where is the sense in it?' might be asked of a misunderstood utterance, or muttered with respect to a story or narrative passage that seems no deeper than its surface episodes. The sentence might also be articulated in frustration by someone hoping to conceal the significance of a song or again, when lyrics rich in historical metaphors, seem to resist interpretation in the present. Such remarks embedded in the larger framework constructed by reference to *ata*, *hkano* and *furi fesao* have directed Takaronga and me to pursue connections between meaning and discourse, to seek implicit themes of tales and lyrics through reflection on explicit statements.

The West Futuna theory of meaning suggests we should expect ancestral or supernatural wisdom to be embodied in stories and songs. Like *ata* given in the physical landscape, narrative *ata* are gifts from the deities. On their surface the words entertain, but beneath a story line they have the power to convey what can't be said. Speaking, therefore, directs a listener to take heed, to link utterance, events and sage council. Neither such supernatural gifts nor the verbal compositions of the ancestors are designed to apply exclusively to distant moments of the past though they may be rooted there. They offer instead insights worth recovery and reflection as time takes its course (Bakhtin 1981; Tedlock 1983).

Meaning and Narrative: Views from Anthropology

> These West Futuna ideas are far from foreign to anthropology. There is … a familiar understanding among anthropologists that the semiotic nature of myth lies in the paradoxical fusion of reality and irreality: the literal embedded in the nonliteral, fact implicated in fiction. As cultural representation, myths talk obliquely and most usually in the language of symbols and are recognized to be an amalgam of mimetic, poetic and ludic intentionalities. Mythmakers thus constantly manufacture a slippage between the various modalities of 'what is', 'what was' and 'what if', … These oral artifacts inform us equally about the knowns of this world as well as what can potentially be known. … This quality of imaginal potentiality imbues myth with the unique capacity to transform tradition and make sense of ever-changing social conditions. [Goldman, Duffield and Ballard 1998:3]

Such anthropological discourse rephrases and reproduces the West Futuna directive to interpret texts richly, to seek underlying significance and experiential connections for bald words. In pursuit of the links between said and unsaid (Tyler 1978), in deciphering the senses conveyed by myth or song, Takaronga and I approach our texts with convergent expectations. We seek to reveal cultural values and symbolic logics constituting both subjects and mechanisms of the narrative process, not as reified orders but as imaginal and integrative potentials (Agar 1980; Biersack 1991; Keller and Keller 1996; Sahlins 1985; Shore 1996). Our goal is not an essentialized vision. Each narrative builds on perspectival variance and conjunctures that we explore (Bakhtin 1981; Ortner 1989, 1995). And we recognize each text is incomplete, open to imagined links with other discourses (Hanks 1989). Ultimately we seek not to create a privileged archive (Baumann and Briggs 2003), but to reveal the potential for conflict, harmony and consensus as reflected in heteroglossic dialogues within and among the narrative texts, and as evidenced from strategic and flexible variations in interpretive stances (Firth 1998:853).

Our analysis aims to bring narrative and the world together (Bakhtin 1981). As Hanks has noted,

> understanding a text requires situating it in a context. This means that inference, background knowledge, and extralinguistic features of the communicative situation must be brought to the work in order to make it semantically whole. [1989:104]

We articulate narrative events with patterns in everyday life implicated by the tales and songs in order to reconstruct tacit, encompassing conceptual frameworks and points of discord from which these verbal arts were fashioned (LeRoy 1985). We also ask what verbal passages themselves might keep available for reflection where individual memories fail. Firth has pointed out that in Tikopia 'since a song may endure for several generations, it may give a clue to history, as in the doings of a chief or noted ancestor' (1998:853) and in this way evoke culture memories by re-presenting for reconsideration events people may have forgotten or never witnessed (Connerton 1989; Mageo 2001; Stewart 1996).

The narratives collected here are offered as resources, good to think about and good to think with. Traditional tales relinquished by one generation as the social milieu around them shifts may well be reclaimed by younger generations. Reclamation, however, often involves changing relevance. A traditional discourse may be heralded in contemporary circumstances 'not as a validating resource for specific institutions but as a validating resource for … general continued existence as a society' (Firth 1961:171). This is already occurring in West Futuna and in Vanuatu more broadly where ancestral wisdom and customary history are revered as *kastom* heritage of ethnic and national communities, though the same practices are ignored as foundations for contemporary social institutions. But such a reclamation process need not be only an honorary acknowledgement of shared cultural roots. The past has the potential to stimulate debate, focus dialogue, and envision possibilities for complementarity and consensus in a continually developing social fabric (see discussions in McLendon 2003). When tradition is open to figurative as well as literal renderings, to analogic as well as direct applications, ancestral insights can have a privileged place in transforming social conditions and sponsoring conversations about the future (Jolly 1999; Mueggler 2001).

Emplacement

It has been noted by many that Oceanic peoples (among many others) construct their identities using geography (Bonnemaison 1984; Feld 1990; Kaeppler and Love 1998; Kirch and Sahlins 1992; Gifford 1924; Lindstrom 1990; Luomala 1955; Merlan 1998; Myers 1986; Sahlins 1981, 1985; Weiner 1991). The people of Vanuatu are no exception. They take from the land, reef and seascapes a sense of belonging that derives from participation in or recountings of experiences memorialized in specific places (Bonnemaison 1984, 1994; Jolly 1999:286; Rodman 1992, 1985:68; Sherkin 1999). Narratives, sung or told, create and link meaningful sites (Kaeppler, Crowe, Chenoweth and Lindstrom 1998:707). The discourses connect these sites not only to events but also to personalities, families and the supernatural. Tales and songs from West Futuna, in particular, are notable for 'the way each is precisely located geographically, and often associated with a certain area on the island, usually with prominent landscape features, especially large boulders or stones' (Thomas and Kuautoga 1992:17). Enduring kinship-based ties to places established through residence, subsistence and reciprocity ground ownership of narrative discourses while those very discourses infuse new significances into places and reshape islanders' associations with the landscape. Complex identities such as ni-Vanuatu (belonging to Vanuatu), Polynesian, Pacific islander, member of a West Futuna community, male or female, young or old are forged and transformed in well known locales where the episodes of narratives and life are joined.

The late anthropologist and geographer, Joël Bonnemaison, commented (1984:117-18; see also Bolton 1999):

> Cultural identity in Melanesia is a geographical identity that flows from the memories and values attached to places. Membership in a clan or social group, individual or collective identity, is inherited through a network of places, the sum total of which constitutes a territory. Each local group is thus a kind of 'geographical society,' defined in relation to the space within which it resides, or a 'territorial society,' deriving its identity not only through appropriation of a common territory but also from identification with that homeland.

What Bonnemaison has captured here is half the dynamic involved in narrative contributions to identity construction for the people of West Futuna. This is the half so critically tied to local places embedded in lived experience and serving as mnemonics for culturally and biographically significant events. Bonnemaison has aptly recognized here the role of spatialized practices in engendering social relations (Mueggler 2001:54). Yet paradoxically these places gain much of their meaning from their associations with the movements of people not only within a territory but as they come and go, crossing boundaries and creating a rich consciousness of alliance and connection. The other half of identity then is revealed in place making through appropriation of encounters that expand local horizons and shape homelands into travelogues (Sherkin 1999).

From the anthropological literature we take the position that a dynamic relationship holds between places, people and ideas such that a landscape provides its residents with a sense of belonging and an historical consciousness derived from the memories of situated events (Basso 1996; Bonnemaison 1984, 1994; Merlan 1998; Mueggler 2001; Rodman 1992; Stewart 1996). Narrative plays an important role in this process by grounding history and supernatural encounters in the landscape. An association of locality with a stable tradition or identity is, however, challenged by the very episodes that create it. Reproduction of a territory and its community entails ever-expanding, external linkages (Strathern 1998:37). Travel becomes a process through which locale is simultaneously produced and reproduced. Places are constant and constantly changing, ever-transforming repositories of history, reminders of the past in the present, and co-constructors of current and future affairs (Goodwin 1990; Sahlins 1991).

The complementarity of enduring geography and ever-changing positions of human actors and actions in the tales at issue in this volume creates landscapes richly imbued with dynamic, multiplicitous significances. Bonnemaison (1994:113) points out that on Tanna, 'there is hardly any mountain, spring or large rock that does not refer to a myth. Between space and mythology, places and culture, the symbiosis is complete'. In West Futuna narratives, problems arise at well-known sites only to be resolved by movement from one place to another, a process that offers resolution while inevitably introducing novel quandaries. As spoken and sung, narratives capitalize on tensions between travel and place, disruption and stability. Reflecting from the present moment it is clear that these are dynamisms of the '*long durée*' (Braudel 1958; Sahlins 1981:8). Episodes themselves and the places entailed endure over time offering resources for considering identity and difference, isolation and connections, homelands and peripheries, emplacement and mobility, heritage and innovation, and ethnicity within the Republic of Vanuatu.

The dynamic role of place in our orientation led Takaronga and me to map narrative episodes and the directions in which activities and movements of people transpire. We include with all but one of the stories and histories a map of episodic developments and landmarks (Corr 2000; Feld 1990; Perez 1999; Sullivan 1988). Outlines of cultural geography or cosmography (Ballard 1998) emerge from this narrative cartography and allow us to suggest in the volume's final chapter a cosmological scheme constructed from the tensions of places and people in flux.

The narrative maps were essential in our interpretive process. Locating events and directions of activity explicitly, often elicited discussions that would not have been forthcoming from the verbal material alone. The need for detail to complete the maps and the process of visually scanning spatial information provided welcome insights. Hypotheses about the significance of directions, relations among places, and connections among people and the landscapes referenced, naturally arose in the process of mapping events. As Takaronga and I made concrete the spatial relations entailed by stories' episodes, the maps gave visible confirmation to nascent ideas that remained vague or slippery when we focused on words alone. Although the spatial relations charted were never articulated in full in the texts, we gradually recognized that narrative mood and flow were co-constructed from verbal *ata* that evoked spatial information. As a result the maps presented here are an essential complement to the verbal texts. Visual, kinesthetic and emotional associations with the land, reef and seascapes are held in mind by members of local audiences and serve in making sense of narrative. While many readers will lack this depth of associations, specific places as indexed by features of the maps herein are drawn upon in interpretive discussions to give at least an inkling of the saturation of text with topography and of topography with text.

Organization of the Volume

The narrative chapters 5 through 11 are the center of this work. Each text is introduced with prefatory discussion to create 'contexts around ... [the words] to make them meaningful' (Glassie 1982:xvi). This information is designed to fill in blanks that shared experience would have provided for past audiences when listeners were all members of small neighborhoods on West Futuna. We introduce narrators, performers, themes and ethnographic settings for each recorded text. We also discuss related literature and musical lyrics from throughout the Pacific building a foundation for further comparative study. We concentrate, however, on thematic developments (e.g., Feld 1990; Firth and McLean 1990; Monberg 1974). Gender and kin relations; authority; gluttony; confinement and engagement; community; reciprocity; transformation and continuity; cosmological orderings of people, places and directions are each at issue at various points.

We surround the textual core with interpretive reflections. The present chapter frames our approach. The second chapter sets out our philosophies and practices for transcription and translation. The third chapter of the book sketches geographic contours for West Futuna and discusses cultural practices in contemporary and historical perspectives. We explore here the political, social and cultural conditions that simultaneously generated the narratives, and in turn, were influenced by the very discourses they inspired (Basso 1979, 1996; Bauman 1986; Drummond 1981; Farnell 1995; Feld 1990; Hymes 1981; Tedlock 1983). The fourth chapter focuses specifically on the characteristics of the verbal arts genres represented by the texts. In the twelfth and final substantive chapter of the book we return to the narratives, this time examining them as a corpus. We address inter-relationships, overlaps and contradictions that lead us to cultural first principles and a cosmology encompassing island life. It is with these distillations in mind that we again suggest contemporary relevance for the narratives, traveling via enduring words of wisdom to unprecedented times of change.

2
Ta Serea ma Ta Furusia / Transcription and Translation Issues

The narratives we present here are literary versions of oral performances and the first in what could become a rich, written tradition. For the people of West Futuna these are bedtime stories, entertainment for the long nights, tales to share with a group of friends, inspiration for music to perform together during special events, or sometimes the idle pastime of elders and anthropologists. They are part of a rich cultural heritage rooted in centuries past and toward which people of West Futuna have varying attitudes today. For people of Vanuatu who are not from West Futuna the collected narratives represent a bit of local *kastom* with resonances in the traditions of other local groups. Stitching together commonalities is a task hardly begun, but one that might be possible were a series of collections of indigenous lore to be published. For readers outside Vanuatu these tales will be exotic. Yet the diligent foreign reader will find the unfamiliar intriguing and sensible, offering novelty, but also refreshing vantage on the familiar.

'The life of a literary text begets imaginative life' (Hymes 1981:383) and the narratives collected here should inspire interpretations constrained only by readers' abilities to construct them. Associations and moral weight will vary from reader to reader. How West Futuna readings will diverge from the interpretations constructed by other ni-Vanuatu or foreign readers is an open question, but as Hymes reminds us, good literature will touch its readers differently (1981; see also Pinsker 1992). We expect a diverse audience and anticipate that the variety of perspectives from which our readers will approach this volume will promote debate over relevance, significances and specifics of these texts. This potential for interpretive variety accentuates the responsibility Takaronga and I feel to the people of West Futuna, to scholars and to other readers to convey as accurately and fully as possible the form of West Futuna stories and songs through their literal *ata,* versified prose and English language renditions (Feld 1990). For it is through precise renditions that the local idiom may serve to inspire readings anchored in culture and history yet commensurate with global settings.

Making meaning from the stories and songs re-presented in this volume has been limited recently to a very few, to those with knowledge of the particulars of language, customs and culture history informing the discourses. While this excludes outsiders of every stripe, such conditions also often preclude even the children of urban migrants, thereby restricting their access to a vital narrative heritage. Having grown up in the city, educated in English or French, and usually fluent in Bislama, the local variety of Melanesian Pidgin, youthful migrants have mastered town life and relinquished pathways more familiar to their elders. Their West Futuna speech is punctuated with foreign loans and flows in exogenously blended syntactic forms. Such young people, adept in classrooms and professional settings, struggle to conjure the contexts for turns of phrase that give entrée into the imagined and recounted worlds of these narratives.

We see in this an importunate clash: audience reduction at a time of expanding relevance for discourses that might connect peoples, places, temporal and cultural scapes. The West Futuna texts and English translations collected here are, therefore, intended as a first step in establishing a secular literature that might circulate widely. We don't claim to have captured ideal forms, nor is this an unveiling of authoritative versions from antiquity (Bauman and Briggs 2003). Rather with these texts we aimed for stories readable in each of the two primary languages in which they appear. We hope to have provided texts accessible to knowledgeable locals who are as likely to remodel as to reproduce these versions. And we aimed to provide engaging and provocative legends that would entice foreign readers for whom 'understanding the simplest folk tale [can be] a major undertaking' (LeRoy 1985:ix). We aspire through our efforts to enlarge the arena in which the verbal arts can be centered for discussion.

The present volume presents a single version of each tale or song. The versions of stories and songs we report are primarily derived from recordings I made in the 1970s. These are narratives that were compelling for residents of West Futuna then and that still seem to have the power to create community, stir reflections on identity and generally engage local audiences. In order to arrive at a suitable literary form, Takaronga and I examined the recordings and early transcriptions and translations I had done. We compared these transcriptions with other versions of the narratives we heard, in most cases deciding to reproduce a text from the 1970s but with some augmentation or revision made possible from exposure to other versions and our interpretive insights. Each text we intended to publish was edited repeatedly to enrich contextual associations. Oral presentations in face-to-face encounters among community members allowed for assumed background knowledge that would be lacking for readers of written prose. Original recordings may have missed an orienting paragraph, garbled a text with audience laughter or incorporated momentary negotiations over partially forgotten lines. In such cases, in preparing a story in written form, Takaronga and other consultants fashioned the final version to suit the novel venue in which it would appear.

At points while he was telling or clarifying one of the tales I could see Takaronga imagining an audience of children he was regaling. He would reflect on the surface episodes essential to convey humor or unspoken significances and then provide details or rephrase, so that his imagined audience could find a passage funny or sinister, so that they could share in the listening pleasures he, himself, had known as a child. At times I would press Takaronga, querying passages that made little sense to me until he unveiled the tacit or taken-for-granted knowledge that I lacked. Much of this added detail is incorporated into the introductory discussions provided for each story or musical piece. Some appears parenthetically in the translations. A few alterations make their way into the texts themselves: a word added here, performance errors corrected there or a brief rationale for plotted events provided in yet a third place. For all this, with one exception, the original recordings from the 1970s remain largely intact in written form.

Ta Pasiesi ma Majihjiki, however, was retold by Takaronga for this volume. His rendition is thematically consistent with other versions that we recorded or were otherwise familiar with. His re-narration was motivated by a desire to hear the episodes told in ways he remembered them from childhood rather than in the form they were reconstructed by other narrators. Takaronga's version grew through several editing cycles. In the end it is considerably revised and expanded in detail by comparison with other recorded versions including his initial telling. Working in a written medium provided an unprecedented opportunity for Takaronga to critique his own productions building cumulatively and critically on the narrative forms. He was relentless in this process until he felt he got it right.

It is often said that Western authors are inevitably bound by Western discourses (Borofsky 2000; Lindstrom 1992; Salmond 1991). This is, of course, true. Takaronga and I, aware of this problem, have tried to minimize interference on my part as we worked with the texts. We have probed my confusions but ended with tellings he commends. I have tried as much as possible to shed expectations and to listen to the voices of Pacific islanders in reporting these tales. Over thirty years that have ensued since I first heard the tales and lyrics, I have gradually come to appreciate local significances in ways I could not have done naively. Yet inevitably my influence as co-collector, co-translator, and cointerpreter must be reckoned with. Takaronga has tried to keep me on track, making the most of my ignorance by preparing clearer explanations to address my confusions in anticipation of others who might display misunderstandings similar to my own. His hand in our collaboration guided us to the final versions of our texts while still leaving the evocative process open.

Takaronga also helped me to achieve understandings and local details on which he felt confident the translations into English must rest. With his prose and exegesis as directives I adapted methodologies from Tedlock (1983) and Hymes (1981) to render West Futuna into a foreign tongue. I worked to create

> areas of plausibility as spoken [or sung] English, [aiming] never [to] sound ... broken where the original storyteller sounded perfectly smooth, while at the same time opening the [reader's] ear to the possibility of new economies of means ...

and of meanings (Tedlock 1983:13). I struggled to avoid 'embroidery' (Tedlock 1983:35; Hymes 1981:39-41) or be seduced by aesthetics of English and yet to reproduce forms with an artistic impact that might enable readers to engage productively in constructing potential import (Lindstrom 1999).

The translator's task is in some ways a contradictory one for while 'perception of depth depends on perception of detail' (Hymes 1981:10), making West Futuna experiences comprehensible for a diverse readership also requires contextualization of those details. To this end we maintain textual particulars of style, episodic development, figures of speech, and cryptic reference to the world. Yet we augment the texts with interpretive discussions that place particulars in larger frames of reference. We address turns of phrase, tropes and indexes that reference cultural themes, signal emplacement or directed action, and pose dynamic tensions. We touch on inter-textual themes seldom explicit in performances themselves, and we use the order of presentation of the narratives to accentuate relative chronology and mark genres and their differences.

Our motives for presenting and translating the narratives in this book include what are probably usual ones for many folklorists, anthropologists and translators. We want to bring West Futuna into the schools and urban centers of the Republic of Vanuatu and to add these tales and lyrics to Vanuatu's cultural resources and to the world's literatures. We also hope to represent the narratives so audiences of many backgrounds will be able to imagine the characters, envision their adventures, and grasp the deeper, enduring messages conveyed (Firth and McLean 1990: viii). In reaching to attain these goals we rely on usual methods: an appreciation for ancestral insights; awareness of both ancient and contemporary relevance; cognizance of perspectival divergences among narrators, audiences and original composers; identification of alternative voices; and comparisons among alternative versions and genres.

Perhaps foremost in our awareness throughout our collaboration has been the tension inherent in the dual, conflicted yet synergistic goals, for which we have aimed. Our efforts to produce in a single volume both a secular written literature in the endangered language of West Futuna and a discursive resource of global import forced us into a constant balancing act. We discussed potential pitfalls: creating a presumed narrative canon; fomenting dissent over conventions for orthography, grammar, style or meaning; channeling the interpretive process by virtue of decisions we were forced to make in writing down oral events; failing to convey particulars; or closing off evocative potentials by failing to transcend obscurities. At each step of the way we considered the implications of our choices in light of these risks. We address the specifics of this process by attending to Sense and Semantics, Sound and Orthography, and Syntax more specifically below.

Sense and Semantics

I use sense and semantics in what follows to refer respectively to 1) a general context referenced or constructed by narration and 2) the meaning of specific words or phrases. With respect to the former, original texts rely on cryptic indexes to events, conventional values and symbolic associations. We found at many points it was necessary to 'probe ... for more specificity' (Ortner 1989:88) in order to give passages their contextual import. Critical in the process of reconstructing sense were discussions of the tales and lyrics between us and with community members. Probing was typically a matter of finding a way to center a text placing 'linguistic symbols against ... [their] cultural background' (Malinowski 1978 [1935]:18; Hanks 1989). As our own purchase on significances improved we would then consider options for making essential background knowledge apparent. Sometimes this was a matter of providing ethnographic relevance for narrated episodes. Eventually, for example, following lengthy discussion of the possible motivating factors behind one brother's intent to murder another, Takaronga expanded the textual onset of *Rufei Soa,* 'Two Brothers', adding several preliminary paragraphs to elaborate the version I had recorded earlier from Napausi Teifisou. The tale as Napausi told it began with a cryptic reference to strife between brothers and detailed, without explanation, a series of attempts by one man to kill the other. Takaronga subsequently provided an orientation clarifying the normal expectation of co-operation among male siblings and parallel cousins. He identified jealousy over marital status as the motive behind one brother's murderous intent, putting subsequent events explicitly in a context of social interdependence and normative kinship ties gone awry.

Figurative tropes used to evoke connections complicate the process of recovering sense further. In the case of the last song, *Nahjeji*, where creative metaphor, known as *furi fesao* or 'turned words', governs the entire composition, translation became particularly thorny. We interviewed people around the island gathering accounts of the composition and historical significance of the lyrics. Ultimately we found it necessary to construct two English language versions in translation. The first of these stays close to the original West Futuna as a roughly literal rendition of lobster trapping, the ostensible subject of the song. The second aims to convey the historical context for the musical piece by reconstituting the metaphorical target, early evangelism, and making the unsaid explicit.

More conventional metaphors are embedded within local perspectives and pose difficulties for conveying sense in translation as well. One must decide in each case the virtues of numerous possible renderings for recreating imagined and emotional contours of the narratives. For example, *Neiragona e sa hmafi tiona roto* (Tense-feel tense bad very article-his heart) from *Ta Pasiesi ma Majihjki,* 'The Monster and Majihjiki', might be translated variously. And in paragraph 60 of the tale we use two of many alternative possibilities. The initial version, 'He felt terrible', adopts a narrator's perspective and aims to convey a self-indulgent and quasi-intellectual reaction of anger and foreboding as the monster contemplates the unknown. More literally this might have been translated as 'He felt very badly inside'. However, the more literal translation is awkward in English and as a stilted passage it fails to encourage the reader to envision the monster's anticipatory distress. Perhaps the English word 'upset' might also have captured the monster's conflicted feelings in this passage, and indeed, we employ this option in translation much later in paragraph 91 where frustration is centrally at issue. Note, however, that for the second occurrence in paragraph 60, the West Futuna phrase is rendered in English as 'His heart ached'. This translational shift marks a shift of narrative perspective. The second instance represents the monster's reaction in the face of known and, to his eyes, disastrous events. The translation 'His heart ached' aims to offer a sense of the character's genuine anguish as he, himself, might have experienced it. For this purpose the more literary form conveying an organic seat of emotional feeling seems appropriate.

In another example, ... *jikai saha nifakea* (negative indefinite-impersonal pronoun tense-emerge/be exposed) from *Ta Pasiesi ma Majihjiki*, paragraph 110, the passage is translated as 'Nothing was revealed'. *Fakea* is used commonly to describe someone appearing in the open from a path or home that had shielded him or her from view. It is in fact, so used when the monster describes Majihjiki's anticipated trip to the village to see children there, paragraph 36. However, in the later passage the West Futuna construction emphasizes an outcome of the monster's search not the process of emerging itself. Using 'appear' or 'emerge' in translation here, as in something like 'no one appeared' would fail to capture the scene intended. 'Nothing was revealed' comes closer we hope to evoking the ongoing action imagined by the verbal and pronominal elements of this passage.

The translations throughout do not preserve the gestural, paralinguistic and extra-linguistic characteristics of voice quality that would further support reconstructions of sense. I have focused over the years on understanding textual meanings and indeed neglected to record or investigate many nonverbal components of performances. Then too, elicitation often involved dialogue and interaction rather than independent performance as such. To complicate matters further when narratives were told or sung in the 1970s the preferred choice of temporal setting on West Futuna was after dark and the social setting had a clandestine aura that discouraged intrusive video and film recording even had such equipment been available. Had I been able to note gesture and movement originally the final product would be different, but to attempt now to reconstruct these dimensions of performance would mislead. The opportunity remains to capture such aspects of musical performances as they co-contribute to sense making in productions of the 21st century, but for now, this book must focus on words, the primary 'means used by the authors of the texts' (Hymes 1981:5), to communicate received wisdom or their own ideas and opinions.

In relying so completely on words, issues of semantics become foremost in the process of translation. Rendering specific words, phrases and oral speech practices from West Futuna into

English, mimics the problems of reconstructing sense and implicates in more focused ways the inherent intertwining of language and culture and the gaps between utterances and ideas. Morpheme-by-morpheme renderings were developed as a first step in the process of creating English language texts and serve as a basis for subsequent translations. We attempted a number of formats in which this information might be incorporated in the published texts, but ultimately decided that too much was sacrificed in terms of readability to justify the logistical complications.

In any case it is a long way from morphemic correspondences to colloquial translations. Two primary features of language use tie words inextricably to cultural practices and ideologies simultaneously complicating the translation process and directing us in strategic choices. First is situational variation. Word meaning shifts with context and emphasis. Such nuanced variation is difficult to capture in a second language inevitably governed by alternative norms for speech. To recreate the principled bases for word meaning shifts requires a repertoire of translation equivalents for each word. Every occurrence of a given word requires a translation that evokes in the target language elements of context and style appropriate to the source. The match is seldom perfect but the full compendium of translation equivalents for a given expression offers a glimpse of intended relations between a piece of language and its applications. The second primary challenge we faced in translation was evoking unspoken conceptual frameworks in which word meaning is embedded. The cultural ideologies and local theories within which West Futuna ideas are positioned are not replicated by foundational assumptions from which English word meanings are derived (Keller and Lehman 1991). Strict word-for-word correspondences, therefore, fail to evoke alternative frames of reference essential to comprehension of original texts. Short of interpretive annotation, on which we must rely to a large extent, we find that the most successful approach to translation is again a diversity of English forms for significant West Futuna expressions such that, when taken together, the many intersections among local and foreign meanings may suggest to readers the cultural and conceptual perspectives with which speakers of West Futuna may receive the world or reconstruct it. We offer some examples below to illustrate these translation strategies.

a) The translation of *pasiesi* as 'monster' illustrates some of the problems we faced. Early translations by others designate *Pasiesi* as the proper name of an evil demigod character (Capell 1960; Gunn 1903; Ray 1901). However, the word *pasiesi* usually occurs in the narratives we recorded with the definite article, a combination not appropriate for proper names otherwise. Also as I discovered rather late, West Futuna is inhabited by numerous *pasiesi* of both genders making translation as a common noun fitting. I have heard *pasiesi* locally translated as 'devil', and used that word in early versions, but the Christian associations seemed to cause confusion for some audiences. 'Goblin' was another possibility and one used in translations of other Pacific literature, but this word fails to encourage a vision of a truly evil character, one with enormous size and reprehensible habits. Should future publications make the array of *pasiesi* apparent perhaps 'goblins' will become a viable translation option. 'Monster' seemed the best alternative available to convey the qualities attributed to the *pasiesi* of the first tale including his gluttonous demeanor, huge proportions, astonishing habits and evil intentions. The word emphasizes the terrifying and deviant qualities of such a being. As a result we finally settled on this word as the primary translation. We use 'ogre' occasionally in translation as well. As an alternative, 'ogre' should encourage the reader to imagine a dreaded and hideous giant. Taken together the two English expressions offer access to local visions of evil personified.

b) The expression *foi* occurs throughout the story of 'The Monster and Majihjiki'. This expression is difficult to translate. Firth refers to the morpheme as an 'individualising categorizer' in Tikopia (1985:128). It is used in West Futuna similarly to designate something unusual or unique. Takaronga indicates that this word marks something as distinctive, special. Many qualities or entities can be so designated. So, for example, *ta foi pasiesi* emphasizes the especially reprehensible character and grotesque appearance of the monster. I translate *ta foi pasiesi* as 'A/the horrid/horrible monster', 'the/that incredible monster', 'the evil monster/one', 'the incomparable monster', 'the special monster'. Occasionally we translate the phrase simply as 'the monster' or 'the ogre'. Perhaps in encountering these distinct phrasings throughout a story English-speaking readers will make many of the associations locally attributed to the *pasiesi* character.

Foi is also used in reference to a magical breadfruit, one conjured up by the culture hero, Majihjiki, and so large it can accommodate children as its seeds. I translate the phrase *ta/sa foi kuru* as 'the/a magic(al) breadfruit', 'that special breadfruit', 'the fine breadfruit', or 'an exceptionally large breadfruit'. *Foi eture* in *Ta Pasiesi ma Majihjiki* is translated as 'magical mackerel' and *foi paua* as 'magical snapper'.

c) Some very common words such as *mate*, *mrae* and *nofo* resist easy translation for lack of conceptual equivalents in English. *Mate* refers generally to someone whose spirit has fled the body, in English parlance a person in this state might be either 'dead' or 'unconscious'. English does not conceptually or lexically unite these possibilities. In fact, quite the contrary for 'life' turns on the distinction. Yet at times in the narratives we relate, the loss of one's spiritual life force and the potential to be revived critically merge life and death and so drive episodic developments. For example, in *Rufei Soa* a character's drowning leads him to the underworld. Yet in the possibility of returning to consciousness lies the drama for his spirit is available to be reclaimed and his life regained. The possibilities entailed by *mate* compel the outlines of the denouement. In translation I use both 'death' and reference to a brother's spirit having left his body. Perhaps taken together these variants begin to open the foreign imagination to *mate* as a reversible state entailing loss of one's life force. However, at other points, such as the final passages of *Ta Pasiesi ma Majihjiki*, one English sense or the other is appropriate in translation. At the end of this narrative *mate* (*oji*) ultimately refers to 'death', a state from which a monster will not recover, and is so translated. Associated meanings of this expression are in use in the narratives as well. For example, *mate* may refer to pain, hurt and discomfort and, where appropriate, is thusly represented.

Similarly, *mrae,* a common Polynesian word, has numerous possible renderings when translated into English from West Futuna. The word can be used to refer to 'home', 'neighborhood', 'familiar place', 'hearth', or 'village'. We use all of these and related expressions. However, there is an underlying conceptual unity to these ideas in West Futuna that I find missing in English. *Mrae* conveys a place where one lives with family and kin. The boundaries of the place and its connotations vary. What is central is the idea of kinship associated with physical space. 'Home' is the closest English equivalent, but it tends to suggest a physical abode not always intended by *mrae*. There is no single English word or phrase we are aware of that conveys this meaning and so we use the closest approximation for each setting in which the West Futuna word arises.

With respect to *nofo* we face a similar problem. *Nofo* refers to 'living in the customary way'. Depending on context this word can be best translated as 'pass the time', 'stay', 'dwell', or 'live'. In West Futuna both duration of the activity and its customary character are important elements of the meaning. Yet without contriving awkward or stilted passages we found it difficult to capture both senses within a brief English expression. We resort to using the contextually most appropriate English word or phrase for separate occurrences.

The title of book itself is one example. 'We keep on living this way' relies on markers of tense and aspect with the core meaning of *nofo* to emphasize enduring lived practice.

d) Vocabulary items may also refer to local scenarios by metonym. In such cases our translation of a single word is sometimes expanded to capture the richer context implied. For example, *fujia* refers to 'pulling someone or something'. The object is usually heavy and the process a strenuous one. Where the object is apparent or explicitly stated we translate *fujia* simply as 'pulling' but where broader reference is left implicit we may expand the translation. For example, in *Samaine, fujia* is translated as 'went deep sea fishing and pulled in' [a tuna]. *Fujia* is a conventional expression for 'deep sea fishing', an activity that crucially involves drawing in a catch by hand. Although the translation above doesn't capture the full experience of fishing with a hand line, or the strenuous process of pulling in a large fish this way, or the subsequent honor in giving a prized gift of a tuna, the expansion at least clarifies the specific activity at issue. The simpler and more literal 'pulled in' [a tuna] is less evocative especially for the foreign reader. Deciding how much expansion is appropriate was difficult and we found ourselves minimizing this strategy, and drawing attention to wider contexts of action in prefatory discussions.

e) Synonyms in English are useful in capturing situational variation. So, for example, *tau* is translated at various points in *Ta Pasiesi ma Majihjiki* as 'dangled' or 'hang'. *Kaina* is effectively rendered as 'devour' or 'eat' depending on context. Throughout the stories *kanieni* is variously translated as 'want', 'be excited', 'be happy', 'affection', 'desire', 'wish', 'appeal for', 'feel driven' and in other ways as best suits the linguistic and cultural associations. As should be clear from this example translation options not infrequently include changing parts of speech. *E rufie* literally 'present tense good' can be translated as 'It's good', 'You're kind', 'It's time', or

'Okay' among other possibilities. And as a final illustration, *tukua* can be translated distinctly as 'to say', 'to reply', 'to respond', 'to speak', 'to warn', 'to call', as best reflects the intentions of a speaker or character.

Longer passages too may be translated with roughly synonymous yet nuanced alternatives. ... *pe eia kahmai kameitaru i ta fano i ai* (if third-person tense-come tense-come-be-prohibited preposition article go article there) is a line in *Ta Pasiesi ma Majihjiki* (paragraph 76). This might be translated as '... so that if he approaches he'll find it difficult to go there'. Or alternatively as '... so that if he approaches his progress will be impeded'. Each reflects the original a little differently and each conveys the semantics paraphrastically. I chose the second construction in this case because it gives a more specific meaning to the word *fano,* translates *taru* in a word rather than a constructed phrase, and creates a passive syntactic form that appropriately emphasizes the obstruction of progress rather than the agency of the monster. Sometimes making such decisions becomes at best a matter of intuitive feel.

In addition, variation occurs in the translation of certain stylistic devices. Repetition, for example, is used commonly in the stories to indicate emphasis, duration, and/or iteration (see Dougherty 1977). Where this pattern occurs shifts from telling to telling. It is not used by rote but creatively as a literary device. Translations of repetition from West Futuna into English include repeating a word or phrase to replicate the original form or rephrasing slightly to add connectives or insert prepositional indicators of continuing action. Examples of the latter include, 'He kept on gardening and gardening, gardening and gardening ...' used to translate *Novere vere vere vere* ... or 'He lived on and on' used in several places to translate *Eia konofo nofo* which would be rendered word for word as 'He lived and lived'. Some support for the variations in English alternatives for translating repetition may be found in the diversity of forms used by speakers of West Futuna themselves to convey duration, emphasis or iteration when they shift into English.

f) Occasionally words are inserted in English to convey meanings derived from word order or affixes in West Futuna phrases. For example, in *Ta Pasiesi ma Majihjiki* (paragraph 100) one of the culture hero's utterances expresses a conditional concern. *Kahmai ta foi pasiesi kairikofiamai kitea kunei kaitaia kitea kaikaina* (Tense-come article particle monster tense-third-person-reach-transitive-to-us we-all here tense-third-person-kill-transitive us-all tense-third-person-eat-transitive). The conditional, conveyed by word order, verbal affixes and context in West Futuna is expressed using these devices as well as 'if' in translation. 'The monster is coming and if he reaches us here he will kill us all and eat us.' A few pages later in the same tale (paragraph 121) the sentence *Tanofajaga mehlou eia noipapai nohsara hfie, kitea kafura* (Article-possessive-time now third-person tense-third-person-far tense-seek firewood, we-all tense-flee) is translated as 'Now while he is far away gathering firewood, we must flee', English uses a lexical item, 'while', to convey the relative timing communicated through word order and verbal affixes in West Futuna.

g) Parentheses distinguish commentary by Takaronga or myself from the narrative texts. In addition I translate proper nouns parenthetically as possible in the English version within the first text passage where such a name occurs.

h) A few words in the narratives collected here are said to be meaningless, representing the words of ancestors. As Malinowski would have it (1978 [1935]:vol 2) their force comes from their presumed connection with the ancestral and spirit worlds (see also Dougherty 1983). '*Tawianiso*', chanted in *Ta Pasiesi ma Majihjiki*, is one example, and the choruses of musical compositions contain others.

i) For all save the final song, the original texts and translations are presented adjacent to one another: the left column is West Futuna and the right is the English language translation. The final song is presented in three columns with the center representing a more literal translation and the third column a free translation. For the stories utterances are grouped into paragraph blocks that make sense as conceptual, stylistic or performance units. These are not definitive and other groupings would be possible. There seemed considerable freedom of arrangement as we converted oral tellings into written texts. The songs, by contrast, are translated by melodic line and in these cases the phrasing directly reflects the musical as well as textual structures.

Sound and Orthography

In 1983 I published a dictionary and grammar of the language of West Futuna-Aniwa from which two summary charts are adapted here as Figure 2. More detailed discussion of the rationale for the symbols chosen to reflect phonemic distinctions appears in that volume along with basic introductions to the grammar and vocabulary of the language (Dougherty 1983). As Takaronga and I reworked the narrative texts and lyrics for the present anthology it became clear that an orthography for the present texts warranted some revisions to earlier phonemic alphabets. We have, therefore, modified conventions from my dictionary slightly to match orthographic practices developed in recent years as children and their teachers, literate in French and English, have shaped spelling practices for West Futuna.

Although there is no previously published secular literature in West Futuna, islanders write in their native language frequently. E-mail and phone messages are composed and letters written. The local language is used in contemporary song compositions and sermons. In addition, people from West Futuna read biblical passages and sing hymns that have been translated into their native language or composed for Sunday service. Practical literacy among the people of West Futuna is, therefore, quite

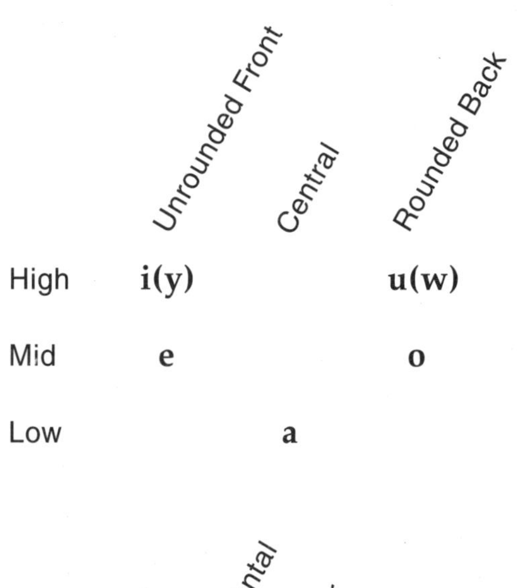

	Unrounded Front	Central	Rounded Back
High	i(y)		u(w)
Mid	e		o
Low		a	

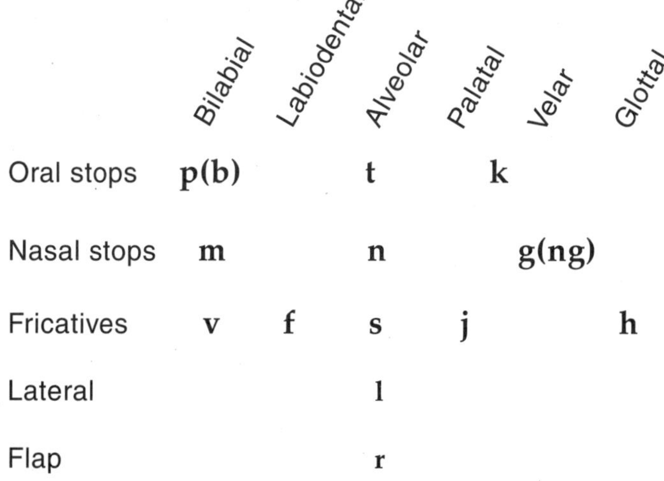

	Bilabial	Labiodental	Alveolar	Palatal	Velar	Glottal
Oral stops	p(b)		t		k	
Nasal stops	m		n		g(ng)	
Fricatives	v	f	s	j		h
Lateral			l			
Flap			r			

Figure 2: West Futuna phonemic alphabet adapted from Dougherty 1983 to create an orthography reflecting current spelling practices.

common and we have taken advantage of this in developing our orthography here.

The alphabetic conventions used in my own 1983 publication were informed by analysis of phonemic distinctions that I represented by the International Phonetic Alphabet modified to suit letter options easily available on a typewriter. The earlier transcription systems developed by the Gunn (n.d.) and Capell (1958, 1984) also influenced my choices. For the present volume we tried to adapt this scholarly tradition to enhance accessibility for a range of audiences. The orthographic conventions stay close to pronunciation, but as older generations of speakers of West Futuna are familiar with one set of spelling conventions and younger generations are more familiar with another, we have expanded the list of symbols in use. The full West Futuna alphabet as used in this volume is: a, (b), e, f, g, h, i, j, k, l, m, n, (ng), o, p, r, s, t, u, v, (w), (y).

The symbols noted in parentheses above are restricted to limited environments. They are used primarily to reflect currently preferred spellings of proper names for individuals and places. The symbols 'b', 'ng', and 'y' are used exclusively in proper names such as Breisa, Takaronga and Yama. Some who write West Futuna today use 'w' and 'y' interchangeably with 'u' and 'i' especially when the represented sound takes on an extended glide. In the absence of a standardized convention we have chosen not to use 'y' in this way due to its rarity. We do use 'w' at a few points in transcribing our West Futuna texts to reflect contemporary practice for place names such as *Naweji* and in common nouns such as *weiwaha* 'quickly' where 'w' is preferred by most writers to 'u'. The symbol 'sh' appeared in some early texts to designate the palatal fricative and is used optionally in some contemporary, personal scripts for West Futuna, but is not incorporated in our transcriptions. We use 'j' for this sound.

We aim for consistency in spelling conventions. However, a few word stems are spelled distinctively depending on their linguistic environment. Stress shifts with respect to affixation are one factor in pronunciation. For example, *takákea* 'to fall down', *nitekáifo* 'they went down'. The root morpheme, *taka-* 'to step or fall' is the same in both cases. In the first example stress falls on the second syllable. The stem vowels are pronounced homophonously. In the second, the stem follows a prefix. Stress is on the second stem syllable but the first stem vowel is reduced in pronunciation. Takaronga reflects such changes with the spelling conventions available to us. Note also the alternation of the future time, incomplete action marker between the forms *ka* (*kaforikage*) and *ke(i)* (*keitukage*) (paragraphs 10 and 11) of *Ta Pasiesi ma Majihjiki*. The phonemic environments condition pronunciation. Takaronga's preference was to reflect this variation in our spelling and we followed his inclinations. Alternative pronunciations of other morphemes may also result in variable spellings. For example, 'now' is transcribed as *mehlau* or *mehlou*. The alternate forms reflect possible pronunciations of the final syllable. In the absence of a standard we have distinguished such pronunciations orthographically where Takaronga found it useful to do so.

In still other cases, by following contemporary practices, we have incorporated orthographic conventions that vary from strict transcription accuracy. Such variance is to be expected in a language that is gradually developing a standardized written form. For example, Majihjiki is the spelling we ultimately decided upon for the name of the culture hero of several of these stories. Yet my own earlier transcriptions reflect a pronunciation closer to /*moujijiki*/ and versions represented in the work of others often used Moshishiki (Gunn 1903; Capell 1960) or even Moshikishiki (Ray 1901)

In addition, vowels in musical passages may take on a different quality than in spoken dialogue. Such differences are typically reproduced in the transcriptions here. However, in comparison to the phonological variation recorded for other Pacific island musical genres (Feinberg 1998b; Firth and McLean 1990; Moyle 2003, n.d.), intentional shifts in vowel sounds are relatively uncommon in West Futuna. Abbreviation of morphemic structure and contractions occur in West Futuna lyrics to match text and melody and are so recorded here.

We have done our best to remove unaccounted-for spelling inconsistencies throughout this work but suspect some remain. There is much variation in current spelling practices and we hope any lingering evidences of this here will reflect the dynamic state of the orthography and not detract from the readability of these texts. Capitalization and punctuation marks are used in both languages on the model of English usage. Titles of narrative compositions and foreign words are italicized within English language text sections. Individuals' names and place names, however, are excepted and appear in standard typeface. The West Futuna narratives themselves appear in standard typeface.

Syntax and Discourse

Creating syntactic units and discursive segments for the written narratives involved close assessment of content, form and extra-linguistic cues evident in the oral presentations. As mentioned, fixing sentences and paragraphs in writing calls for somewhat arbitrary decision-making from a transcriber's or translator's perspective. Alternative arrangements for paragraph blocks or sentences are almost always possible. Even native speakers' intuitions are not definitive. We rely on the meaningful substance of utterances, on continuity of topic throughout a given passage, on nonverbal indicators of pace and rhythm in speech, and on breaks or continuities in flow in order to determine the syntactic and discursive arrangements in which the West Futuna narratives appear.

In addition, we recognize oral communication involves elision and contraction resulting in the deletion of grammatical particles in spoken discourse. We replace such particles in the written texts as possible. The dedication of the book is such a case. The plural article, *a*, is inserted where it would be elided in pronunciation with the preceding vowel.

West Futuna speakers use a variety of word orders, case

markings and other affixes in utterance construction that do not translate directly into English (Dougherty 1983). In rendering passages I aimed on the first pass to preserve intra-sentential relations and word order of the original West Futuna while also striving for naturalness in the target language. When ergative structures and other verb initial or object initial phrasings occur in West Futuna, this ordering is preserved if it is possible to do so without sounding too awkward or stilted in English. If such patterns do not result in a likely English sentence, or skew interpretation, then word order is modified in translation. Balancing syntactic form, content and style was a constant task.

Below are examples where final translations do not reproduce the order of elements in the original West Futuna text. A few other examples were introduced above.

Example 2 below illustrates alternative English translations for one West Futuna utterance. In this case virtually the same utterance appears at several different points in a given narrative. For the English I choose a clause in one place and a full sentence in somewhat different versions for two subsequent occurrences. The variations reflect the developing mood of the story and connections with surrounding linguistic segments.

Example 5 uses an idiomatic English expression to translate an equally idiomatic West Futuna expression although there is not a word-for-word match nor is ordering preserved. In this case the original utterance is a colloquial first person plural pronominal reference to a group of people excluding the hearer but including others in the speaker's reference group. No exact phrasal or semantic equivalent in English exists but the chosen idiom comes close to reflecting the entailments of this plural form in West Futuna while preserving common usage.

1. *Anopogi oji nomivere akitaua …*
   Plural-day all tense-aspect-come-garden we-two …
   Everyday the two of us come and garden
   (paragraph 11 *Sina Fine Ariki*)…

2. … *katagi (a) muma kanragona.*
   … future-singular (personal article) my-mother future-first-person-singular-hear-it
   … so I may hear my mother's song
   (paragraph 18 *Sina Fine Ariki*).
   … My mother entreats me and I will hear her
   (paragraph 21 *Sina Fine Ariki*).
   … My mother will call out and I can listen to her
   (paragraph 24 *Sina Fine Ariki*).

3. *Koromai a mentua rehresia pe kaitia tano soa.*
   Present-come article thought/idea intensify-deceitful that future-third-person-singular-kill his brother
   Gradually the vicious idea that he would kill his brother took shape (paragraph 5 *Rufei Soa*).

4. *A fijikaunga nipena oji kitea ta fura ta foi pasiesi.*
   Article work past-do completely us-all article run away/escape article particle monster.
   We have accomplished our escape from the monster
   (paragraph 102 *Ta Pasiesi ma Majihjiki*).

5. … *akimea ma gatama* …
   we-all-exclusive with/including plural-children …
   the children and I
   (paragraph 92 *Ta Pasiesi ma Majihjiki*) …

6. *Ta kanieni e sorekage i akirea.*
   Article love present-tense big-away-from-speaker preposition they-all
   Their love for him was great
   (paragraph 6 *Ta Pasiesi ma Majihjiki*).

7. K*aie a gatamaraua e nalupai.*
   conjunction article plural-children-of-they-two be many

Her parents had many children
(paragraph 1 *Sina Fine Ariki*).

8. *A gatama noinage i ai.*
Art plural-children tense-third-person-singular-put preposition there
He put the children there
(paragraph 24 *Ta Pasiesi ma Majihjiki*).

Directional elements as free or bound morphemes are common and may have a range of productive semantic effects (see Bennardo 1996). These are translated diversely, as pronouns, demonstratives or directions, or otherwise as best suits the context (Dougherty 1983).

For example, utterance 6 above illustrates the use of the directional particle *kage* 'out, away from speaker' to modify an adjective and create a quasi-superlative structure.

Tense and aspect are indicated in West Futuna primarily by particles pre-posed to the verb stem. Several particles may be used together to create a combination of temporal sequence and manner with pre- and post-verbal markers indicating orientation of an event relative to other events narrated, time of narration or biographical associations of the speaker or hearer. Both relative and absolute time frames are used in the narratives. Shifts in temporal reference are as common as linear progressions (Tedlock 1983:142-43).

Example 9 below illustrates the translation ultimately used to convey a combination of temporal, aspectual and directional markers in several connected sentences. Given the limitations for Takaronga and me with regard to our respective competencies in each others' first languages we simply could not produce translations that rendered the framing of activities in this passage in West Futuna consistently with time or manner designations in English.

In Sentence 9 below distinct markers (*ni, no, ko*) that typically convey past time and completed aspect (*ni*) and alternative forms for the present are collapsed in temporal reference. In addition the aspectual marker, *ro*, indicating a departing orientation, is only explicitly translated in the first sentence. We are guided by our sense of the narrative flow and timing as much as by the explicit affixes in these cases to recreate the integrity of the narrated event sequences.

9. *Kofanifo korofori ta mrae. Nirofori ta fare. Norofori ta fare nofori fakarua fakatoru.*
   Tense-go-down tense-aspect-circle article area. Tense-aspect-circle article house.
   Tense-aspect-circle article house tense-circle cause-two cause-three.
   He went down going to circle the area. He circled the house. He went around the house circling twice, three times (*Ta Pasiesi ma Majihjiki* paragraph 40).

Where no temporal or manner indicators appear I translate passages to fit an encompassing temporal sense as in *Neitaia nei-kaina, kaina, kaina, kaina kopuni* (Tense-third-person eat-transitive, eat-transitive, eat-transitive tense-gone ...). 'He killed them and ate them eating and eating and eating until he had consumed everyone ...' (paragraph 2 *Ta Pasiesi ma Majihjiki* or similarly but with some variation paragraph 8).

Translation of tense and aspect in the song lyrics is further complicated by fluctuations in perspective entailing shifts in sequencing and voice. For example, in the initial verse of *Nahjeji* I have translated *noko-,* which often indicates incomplete or ongoing action in the present, by using the past instead in order to accommodate the combination of other verbal modifiers in the same and following stanzas. The narrative past seems more natural in English in this first verse as the speaker sets the scene for commentary to emerge. However, by the third verse, where the narrator is quoting Taina, use of present time in translating *noko-* is more appropriate. It is clear that translation inconsistencies such as these await the careful ear of West Futuna scholars able to publish confidently in both English and West Futuna. I hope the inadequacies in my renditions will not detract from the readability of the songs and tales presented here but may ultimately encourage local attention to such matters.

3
Fatuana / Just a Rock

West Futuna, those who live there often say, is 'just a rock'. In fact, the West Futuna expression, *fatuana,* 'just a rock' is by one account the source of the island's present name. As the local story goes, Captain James Cook sighted the island from Tanna in 1774. Upon asking the name of the place he could see in the distance, it is said he was told, tongue-in-cheek, *Fatuana*, 'It's just a rock', and the name, modified somewhat, apparently stuck (Futuna – the Rock Island 1917:2). This is a remarkable parable. *Fatu* 'stone or rock' in West Futuna carries an association with supernatural powers from which influence radiates. This idea is emphasized in the meaning of *ata* to which we turned our attention in the first chapter. Given this association, the claim that the name Futuna derives from the phrase *fatuana*, is a claim as much about power and influence radiating outward from the small island as it is a statement about physical geography (see Lehman and Herdrich 2002).

Cook's journals themselves tell a different story, however. He remarks that the island was originally called Erronan, or Arronan, by neighboring islanders (Beaglehole 1961:495, 504).[1] These are appellations he elicited on sighting West Futuna from the *Resolution* anchored near Tanna in 1774. George Forster, who accompanied Cook, reported both Irronan and Footoona as appellations elicited for the island they could see in the distance (2000:523). More recently Lindstrom recorded Ivaronan from an elderly Tannese man who recalled this name in reference to the island of West Futuna (Lindstrom 1986, pers. comm.). The name Erronan and its variants are still remembered and occasionally used by others on Tanna and by people of West Futuna themselves.

A third story goes like this:

> Nowadays many people believe that they [the first settlers to West Futuna] came from some small islands in the Polynesian sea. At any rate, at first the appearance of our people was like the people of Tonga [*toga*],[2] but the common name for our land of [West] Futuna was given by the [East] Futuna people from abroad. The people of our land believe that Captain Cook gave it the name Varonan, but the name Futuna was given by people from abroad, from the island of Futuna [French overseas territory of Wallis-and-Futuna]. [Charlie Nimoho cited in Capell 1960:26]

In tracing the history of the Pacific prior to European contact, Kirch (2000:143) gives credence to this third tale.

Perhaps all these accounts contain a bit of truth. The *fatuana* versions capture well the indirection of West Futuna speech. The surface phrase constitutes *furi fesao* indicating by implication a deep respect for and pride in the island homeland. The expression *fatuana* inevitably evokes laughter. As *ata* used to educe underlying *hkano*, diffidence at the surface elicits humor by evoking its opposite; the tremendous, autochthonous power of the land. Through this use of local idiom, understanding is circumscribed, foreigners hear only the mundane 'just a rock'. By contrast, Nimoho's argument for naming by distant islanders serves to emphasize links among Pacific peoples and connects West Futuna regionally. This discourse is a direct, literal one that mimics and perhaps derives from Western pedagogy. Erronan and cognate terms refer to West Futuna as designated by neighboring islanders. Each of the positions reflects community entanglements. Taken together the diversity of names is indicative of the contemporary multiplicity of voices constituting intertwined discourses in Vanuatu.

Similarly heteroglossia is characteristic of most conversations even among people of West Futuna. Diverse knowledge, interests and experience promote kaleidoscopic arrays of opinions and discursive practices. Consensus is elusive. Negotiation and contestation constitute principled dynamics of social interaction. Past and present circumstances, European and indigenous ideologies are co-mingled. It is into this cauldron that we wish to take you briefly in order to contextualize the narratives to follow.

Political Geography and Culture History

However it came to acquire its present name West Futuna is today commonly referred to within the Republic of Vanuatu as Futuna. Outside the Republic the common appellation is West Futuna to distinguish the island from East Futuna of the French Overseas Territory of Wallis-and-Futuna. We have chosen to refer to the island of our focus as West Futuna as well to avoid confusion.

The Republic of Vanuatu is depicted in Figure 3, with West Futuna in the southern Tafea district. The island lies at 170°13' East and 19°32' South near the southern extreme and easternmost edge of the archipelago where the tropics meet the sub-tropics. It is one of approximately eighty islands politically united as Vanuatu. The peoples of the republic represent over a hundred ethnically and linguistically distinct communities networked across the islands. West Futuna constitutes the homeland for one of these communities. No longer localized, people of West Futuna reside on their home island, or in settlements throughout the Tafea district, especially on Tanna and Aneityum, or in neighborhoods of Port Vila, the capital city of Vanuatu. Smaller groups and individual representatives of the West Futuna community have settled temporarily or permanently elsewhere throughout the country and the Pacific. The people of West Futuna are mobile and aspiring, proud of their heritage yet expansive in their reach to their horizons. As they move about Vanuatu and elsewhere,

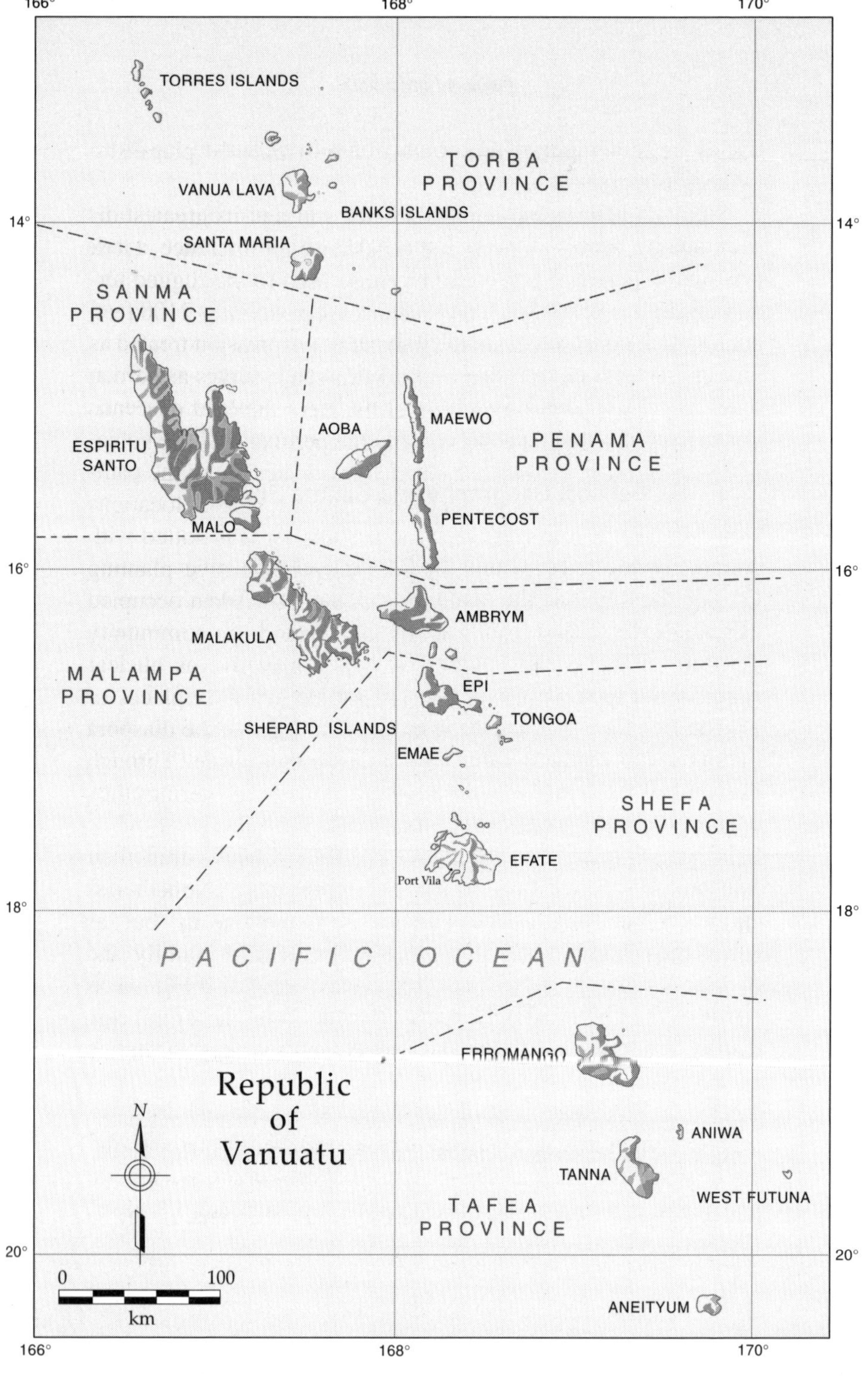
166°
168°
170°
14°
16°
18°
20°
TORRES ISLANDS
TORBA
PROVINCE
VANUA LAVA
BANKS ISLANDS
SANTA MARIA
SANMA
PROVINCE
ESPIRITU
SANTO
MALO
AOBA
MAEWO
PENAMA
PROVINCE
PENTECOST
AMBRYM
MALAKULA
MALAMPA
PROVINCE
EPI
TONGOA
SHEPARD ISLANDS
EMAE
SHEFA
PROVINCE
EFATE
Port Vila
PACIFIC OCEAN
ERROMANGO
Republic
of
Vanuatu
N
ANIWA
TANNA
WEST FUTUNA
TAFEA
PROVINCE
0
100
km
ANEITYUM

they mingle and collaborate productively within the pluralistic contexts of contemporary life.

The island of West Futuna is about 2 miles at its greatest diameter and some 13 miles as one walks the circumference, a trek that can be completed in a day by those used to the rugged terrain. The uplifted interior is 643 meters, approximately 2100 feet, above sea level. Centered in the plateau is a depression treated as sacred ground. The land surrounding this space serves as garden plots that reach to the encircling cliffs. Here the land descends abruptly to an irregular brim shaping the perimeter of the volcanic core. Villages today are located at level sites along the pathways that circle the brim. Historically, steeper, coastal locations also served as residential sites[3] and the interior was dotted with temporary places of habitation used during intensive planting or tending to the gardens. Such sites, although seldom occupied today, are frequently remarked in conversation. As community members move out to other islands they may live as nuclear families woven into the residential patterns of other places or establish neighborhood concentrations. Throughout the diaspora people know where others from West Futuna reside. Through constant dialogue, visits and occasions for larger gatherings they continue to constitute a social circle.

The people of West Futuna are distinguished within their archipelago by particulars of history and language. Nonetheless they do not perceive themselves as homogeneous but as differentiated internally by neighborhood, district, family and ancestral moiety affiliations. The island of West Futuna is divided into a number of districts radiating from the central core and conceptualized as roughly equal sized, wedges extending

Figure 3 (opposite): Republic of Vanuatu locating West Futuna at the southern extreme of the archipelago. Adapted from Republic of Vanuatu, Republique de Vanuatu Directorate of Overseas Surveys, Institute National Geographique, 1973. Edition 4 revised by Director of Surveys, Survey Department, Vanuatu, 1995.

from the plateau to the sea. Figure 4 offers an illustration of this political geography. The districts were initially recorded in 1858 when Reverend Copeland, the first European missionary assigned to the island, began to document local practices and conditions. At the time seven major districts (Gunn 1914:18) including Mouga[4] (with upper and lower sections), Iasoa, Iakana, Matagi, Iraro, Ipau, and Hsia were noted. (A preceding locative marker, /i/, is formally incorporated into four of the names as recorded in the mission literature cited here. We follow these conventions throughout with one difference. Ipau is written Pau[5] in our text reflecting common practice today.) The same districts are still recognized with the upper and lower subdivisions of Mouga distinguished as Mouga i hluga and Taroumara respectively.[6] Hsia is sometimes included within the greater Mouga area and sometimes distinguished from it.

Surrounding the land is a fringing coral reef that narrowly lines the sheer coastal cliffs below the brim at some locations and extends seaward in other places for a significant distance most notably from the northeastern peninsula. Beyond the reef the ocean rapidly attains great depth and the color changes from lighter blues and greens to deeper hues of blue tending toward purple. The surface of the sea is usually agitated. White caps and high winds are typical. A smooth surface with calm conditions is a relatively rare circumstance appreciated for enhanced fishing opportunities.

Land, reef and deep sea are negotiable by foot and/or canoe although the topography and climate make itinerating by any means treacherous. Nonetheless people move around the island circumference and clamber up and down its sides constantly. In the dark, flashlight clenched between one's teeth so hands and toes can grip the rock, over land and reef with grandchildren securely tied on traveler's backs, and in canoes battered by surf and sun, the islanders maintain connections with one another and their places. Families have married children among many of the island's villages and visit back and forth regularly.

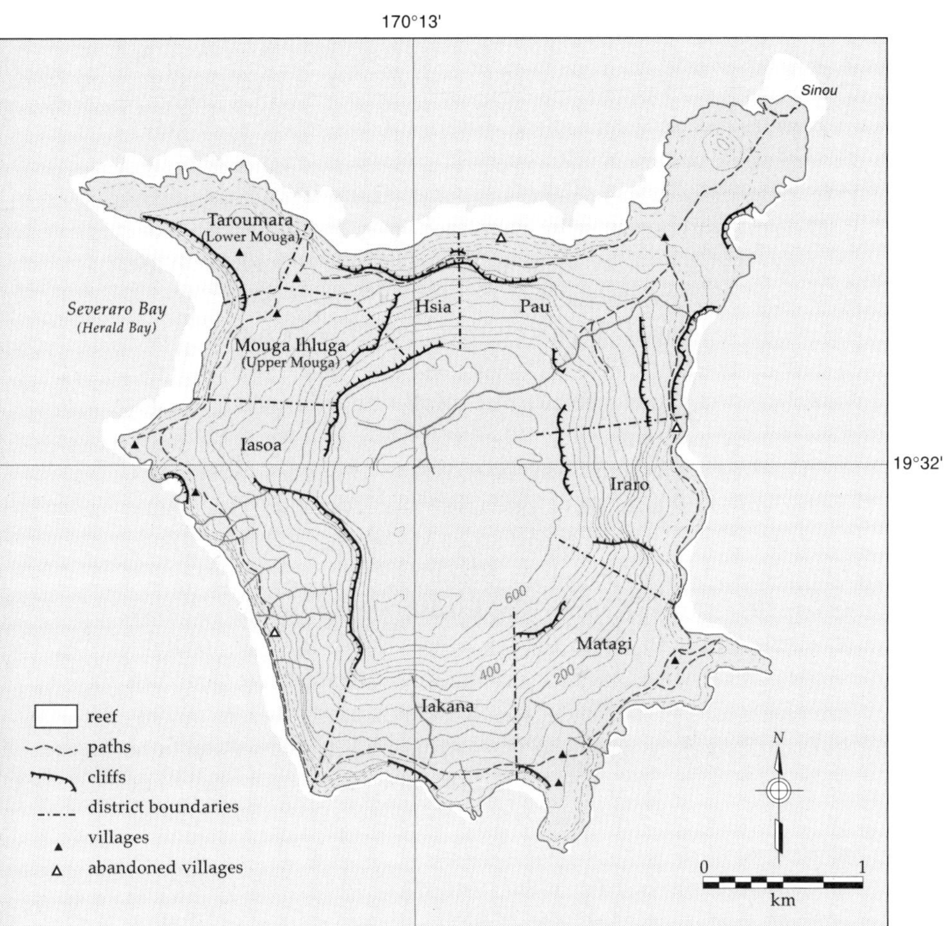

Figure 4: Wedge-shaped political districts of West Futuna, Vanuatu.[7]

Gardening, gathering and fishing activities take individuals to diverse locations around the island daily. At one time during the 1970s monthly feasting exchanges associated with Presbyterian services provided regular occasions for collective gatherings. Today, more commonly, irregular religious events associated with life crisis rites draw villagers together from around the island and bring migrants home from diaspora communities. Long distance navigation in local sailing or paddling canoes, while reported and remembered as a regular occurrence historically, is no longer practiced. Travel by ships (which visit several times a year although not on schedule) and by planes (which touch down several times a week) offer well-utilized modern options for coming and going.

The nearest neighboring islands are Aneityum, Tanna and Aniwa also of the southern Tafea district of Vanuatu. Ties among islanders living within this district are strong and have likely been so for several centuries (Bedford 1973; Capell 1958:27; Gunn 1914, 1924; Keller 1988; Lindstrom, pers. comm.; Lynch and Fakamuria 1994). Although other islands are not normally visible from West Futuna, orientations toward their positions are ensconced in the landscape. Residents easily and accurately indicate departure points to the surrounding islands. Directions to more distant places such as Fiji, New Caledonia and Efate can be similarly indicated. In establishing their own location relative to other places in the Pacific, the people of West Futuna envision themselves at a center from which the positions of other islands are projected as points along imaginary lines radiating out over the seascape (see Herdrich and Clark in preparation; Hutchins 1995; Lehman 1980; Lehman and Herdrich 2002; Monberg 1991:25). The region of reference is not the nation-state but familiar lands with which the people of West Futuna

Figure 5 (opposite): West Futuna in Pacific context. The bird's-eye view locates departure points around the island. The lower map represents the region from a western cartographic perspective.

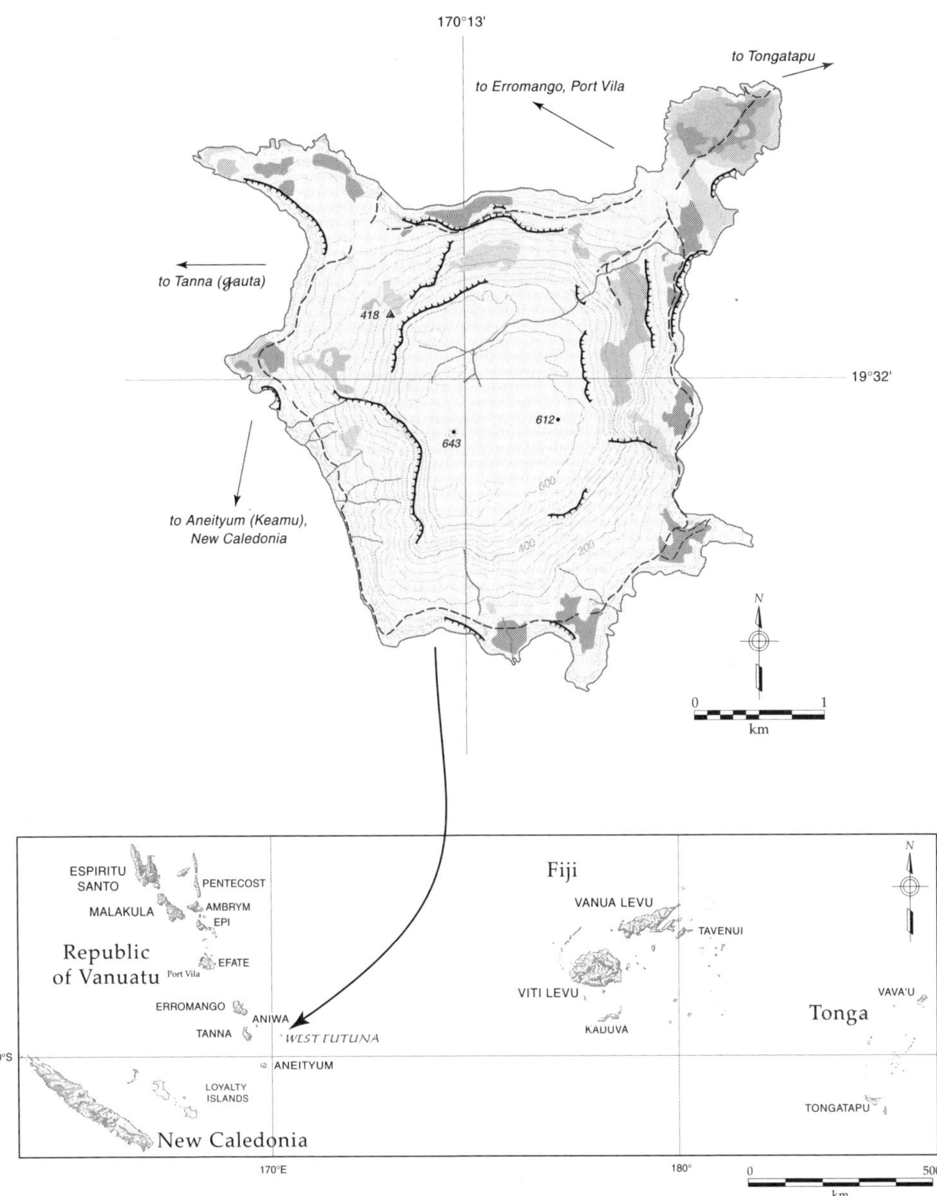
170°13'
to Tongatapu
to Erromango, Port Vila
to Tanna (ɡauta)
418
19°32'
612
643
600
400
200
to Aneityum (Keamu),
New Caledonia
N
0
1
km
ESPIRITU
SANTO
PENTECOST
MALAKULA
AMBRYM
EPI
Republic
of Vanuatu
Port Vila
EFATE
ERROMANGO
ANIWA
TANNA
WEST FUTUNA
ANEITYUM
LOYALTY
ISLANDS
New Caledonia
20°S
170°E
Fiji
VANUA LEVU
TAVENUI
VITI LEVU
KADUVA
180°
Tonga
VAVA'U
TONGATAPU
0
500
km

have historical and contemporary connections. Figure 5 depicts West Futuna centered in its larger Pacific context. A related conceptual centering is the basis of the wind compass shown in Figure 6 (see Feinberg 1988; Hooper and Huntsman 1991:15 for comparison).

In the past voyaging by canoe entailed life-threatening risk.

> The south and south-east winds which carry vessels to Fotuna and Tana, are in general steady winds; but the north-east and north-west winds which blow respectively from Fotuna and Tana to Aneityum are unsteady winds; and although canoes leave these islands with a fair wind frequently [it] either dies away or changes before they can reach the island and the poor natives sink into a watery grave. [Inglis 1860:57-8]

This hazard has been ameliorated by safer means of modern transportation, but the economics of inter-island flight pose continuing obstacles to maintaining connections today.

In the more distant past much of the founding settlement of the Pacific is understood in terms of movements of people in the general direction of west to east over a period of millennia. People left the Asian mainland and gradually dispersed into ever more remote areas of Oceania. Early settlers of West Futuna, however, probably arrived, directly or indirectly, from the central Pacific homelands region of Polynesia including Samoa, Tonga, and East Futuna. From the Central Pacific travelers moving back toward the west settled among established Melanesian communities (Bayard 1976; Feinberg 1998a; Green 1967; Kirch 1997, 2000; Lynch 1998; Shutler 1971; Ward, Webb and Levison 1973) sometime during the 1st millennium AD.[8] The language spoken by the people of West Futuna reflects this heritage and is distinguished within Vanuatu as one of only a few tongues with similar Polynesian affinities.[9] Such communities are referred to in scholarly literature as Polynesian outliers remarking the Polynesian contribution to their settlement history and reflecting the distinctive heritage of these peoples by contrast with the majority

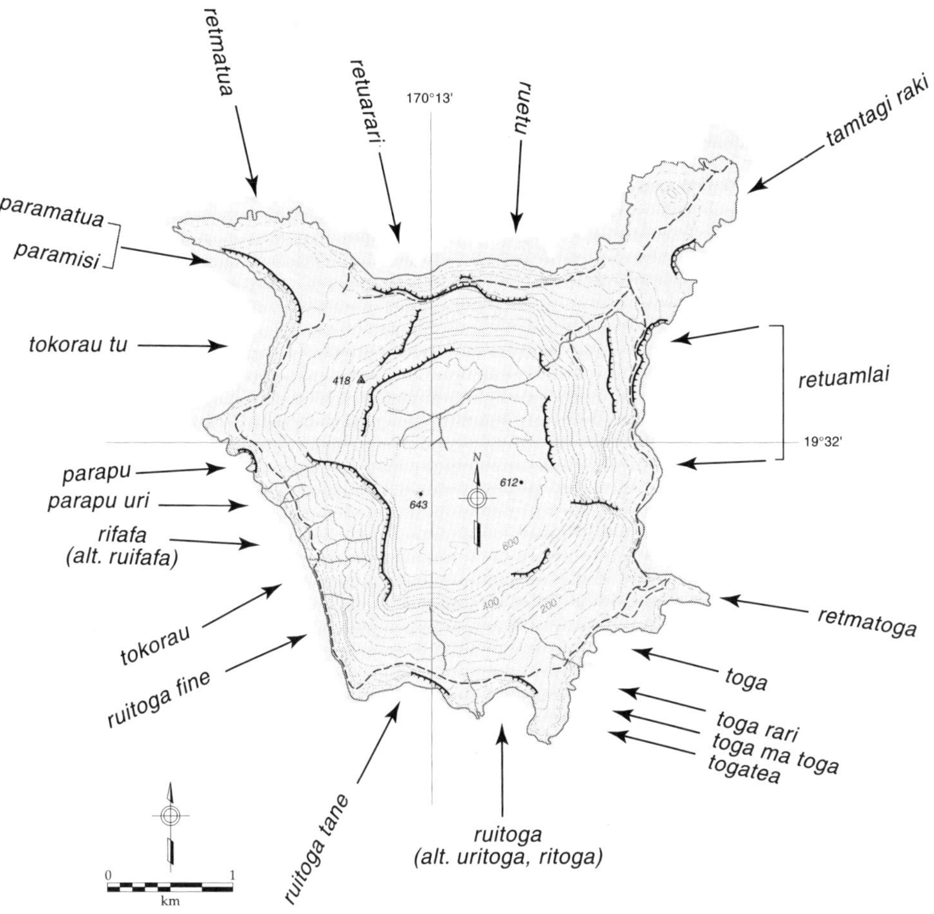

Figure 6: West Futuna wind compass adapted from Dougherty 1983.

of their immediate neighbors.[10] Figure 7 locates Polynesian Outlier communities of Oceania including West Futuna.

People of Vanuatu, however, seldom draw attention to this distinctive heritage for West Futuna or the few other small outlier communities in the republic. They prefer instead to see ethnic diversity within the republic as contributing to an overarching Melanesian mélange. Intermarriage, education, work experiences, migration and the project of building a nation-state have blurred ethnic boundaries and settlement histories somewhat. Ties among islanders are as significant as their differences. In the midst of this pluralism and emergent nationalism West Futuna represents just one of many local communities densely intertwined with others. While Polynesian influences are evident to scholars examining West Futuna *kastoms*, especially oral literature and music, affinities with neighboring Melanesians are equally apparent and perhaps more vital as these linkages are constantly renewed in the everyday contexts of performance and social interchange. In a few cases, even influences from more distant Micronesian, peoples can be posited for West Futuna.

This history of settlement and interaction, of bounded districts and blurred ethnicity, begins to suggest the braiding of influences, peoples and ideas constitutive of present day West Futuna. The community is neither isolated and unitary nor completely imagined (Anderson 1983). People of West Futuna descent are instead distributed and connected over the spaces of their republic and beyond. The homeland is still conceived of as a place at the center of the sea from which the community radiates outward. But the center is more porous and links to places beyond the original shoreline more extended, more diverse and denser than ever before. Processes by which the experience of

Figure 7 (opposite): Polynesian outliers in the Pacific. Outlier languages appear in italic font and underlined. Traditional culture areas are designated as Polynesia, Melanesia and Micronesia.

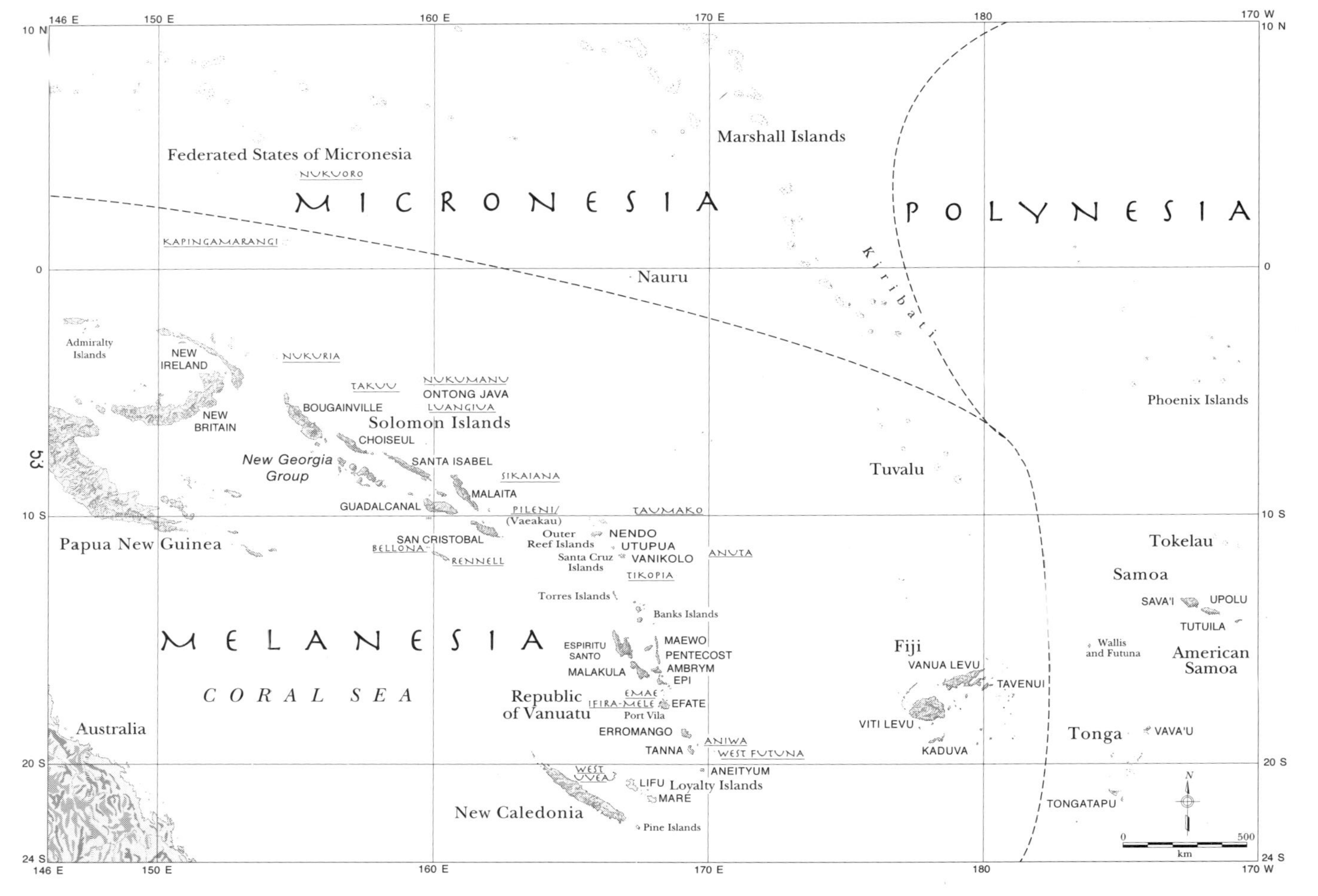
Federated States of Micronesia
NUKUORO
MICRONESIA
KAPINGAMARANGI
Marshall Islands
Nauru
POLYNESIA
Kiribati
Phoenix Islands
Tuvalu
Admiralty Islands
NEW IRELAND
NEW BRITAIN
NUKURIA
TAKUU
NUKUMANU
ONTONG JAVA
LUANGIUA
BOUGAINVILLE
Solomon Islands
CHOISEUL
New Georgia Group
SANTA ISABEL
SIKAIANA
MALAITA
GUADALCANAL
PILENI/ (Vaeakau)
TAUMAKO
Papua New Guinea
SAN CRISTOBAL
BELLONA
RENNELL
Outer Reef Islands
NENDO
UTUPUA
Santa Cruz Islands
VANIKOLO
ANUTA
TIKOPIA
Tokelau
Samoa
SAVA'I
UPOLU
TUTUILA
American Samoa
Wallis and Futuna
Torres Islands
Banks Islands
MELANESIA
ESPIRITU SANTO
MAEWO
PENTECOST
MALAKULA
AMBRYM
EPI
EMAE
IFIRA-MELE
EFATE
Port Vila
Republic of Vanuatu
CORAL SEA
Fiji
VANUA LEVU
TAVENUI
VITI LEVU
KADUVA
Australia
ERROMANGO
TANNA
ANIWA
WEST FUTUNA
ANEITYUM
WEST UVEA
LIFU
Loyalty Islands
MARE
New Caledonia
Pine Islands
Tonga
VAVA'U
TONGATAPU
N
0
500
km
146 E
150 E
160 E
170 E
180
170 W
10 N
0
10 S
20 S
24 S

community is reproduced intertwine conservative ideologies with transformative influences from outside. Personal biographies shaped by modern contingencies and traditional values offer novel configurations for public consumption and evaluation of potential life-ways.

Ethnographic Highlights: Past and Present

The songs and stories translated in this volume are embedded in past eras and in present moments, leading us to seek a wide temporal berth in which to situate them. We embark on this (re)constructive aspect of our project with caution. Bakhtin (1981) draws our attention to the inevitable processes by which literary works are re-accentuated and re-valued over time. He points out the risks of distortion attendant upon the task of recreating past discursive environments as literary contexts. Yet he also draws attention to the 'profound comprehension' (1981:420) that may emerge in the process of situating verbal imagery from one era within another. Ideologies within which enduring literary products were initially embedded are subject to transformation. As dialogic relations alter, conceptions of significance may be reformulated against the shifting backgrounds. It is this developmental potential that shapes the task ahead. We aim to reveal what we can of dialogues and practices, ideologies and influences that may have inspired composition of the West Futuna verbal arts and contributed to their interpretations at different historical moments.

We work from ethnographic observations over three decades and limited documentation of earlier times. We are sensitive to the many and refracted angles of entrée available to us. Still the ethnographic material allows us to glimpse past and present circumstances in which narrative production is enfolded. Taking inspiration from Bakhtin's history of the novel, we highlight narrative fusion of practices and places (1981:84-5, 131; Stewart 1996:93) through salient cultural memories recounted by people now living on West Futuna or those from the island who have recently emigrated. These are memories that resonate with local details yet reverberate in diverse commentaries, in a variety of practices, and in the intercultural jottings of missionaries and other outsiders (Mageo 2001:29; see also Sutton 2001).

Situating People in Places

As Figure 4 illustrates, West Futuna is currently divided into six, seven or eight districts depending on how one evaluates the Mouga area with Hsia and Taroumara, sometimes treated independently and at other times subsumed within it. Perhaps the proliferation of districts or subdistricts within Mouga and their non-concentric orientation is a modification of the typical district plan. Subdivision may have been necessary to accommodate a dense population concentration remembered for this region of the island or perhaps the areal organization reflects requirements of the most exalted among local family lines that resided here. Whatever accounts for the unusual arrangement in the Mouga area, all of the districts and subdistricts noted in Figure 4 contain or did contain in the recent past at least one and sometimes two or more villages, conceived of as encircling the island core.

Each village is home to several sets of related households whose members are intertwined through descent, marriage, shared labor, exchange and sociality. The people of West Futuna reckon kin relationships bilaterally with significant implications for cooperation and inheritance with members of both sides of one's family. The ideal of cross-cousin marriage, still frequently followed, creates dense networks around the island. Agnatic relations, and for selected men, ties to a mother's brother, are vital in insuring cooperation in labor, food exchange and transfer of rights and obligations. Especially important are the cooperative ties of those who call one another *soa* 'sibling of the same sex' encompassing children of the same parents and offspring of parallel cousins. This is true for both men and women but as a consequence of the normative patrilocal residence pattern brothers and male parallel cousins, in particular, have life-long opportunities and obligations to work together. The proper nature of social relationships constructed through ties of blood and marriage and problems that arise with transgressions of expected norms are frequently negotiated in the episodes of the narratives we have collected.

Residence after marriage in the vicinity of a husband's family is the preferred pattern, so wives customarily move from their natal communities to new homes (Capell 1958:8). From the perspective of a young bride, patrilocal or virilocal residence is an uprooting process only partially ameliorated by the inevitable presence of some of a wife's own relatives in her husband's village. Over time, however, as a marriage union matures a new sense of one's primary residence typically develops. Seen from the perspective of the parental generation located in a particular village, patrilocal residence creates patterns of alliance radiating outward to connect a couple with residents of all of the villages encircling the island. A family that places daughters with husbands in several different communities or one able to attract wives from other villages to their own thereby increases potential access to alternative resources. Ideally the parental generation would have ties through children's marriages to each of the villages encircling the island.

However, the preferential pattern with its perceived advantages does not preclude alternatives. Residence with a wife's natal family is also possible. This option is attractive to couples during times of resource shortage or even famine in a husband's locale. In the aftermath of extreme weather today people change residence for extended periods while they rebuild homes, canoes and gardens. Religious affiliations too may encourage shifting residential practices today, although such choices do not escape a critical public eye. In recent decades depopulation of village sites resulting from urban migration has encouraged isolated couples to join relatives living in places more densely occupied. The village of Iasoa, for example, was almost deserted in 1998 as a result of emigration. In such circumstances a wife's family may offer both sociality and economic possibilities while permitting continuing access to a husband's family resources from a distance. Residential options are much at issue in the social climate favoring mobility today. Similarly contested in the past, residential scenarios constitute the core of two of the narratives presented in this volume, *Majihjiki ma Fafine Tonga* and *Sina Fine Ariki*.

Within a village, neighborhoods and family homes called *mraes*, surround a center or sacred *marae* where community activities and religious events take place. The *marae* is a quiescent center associated with ancient and modern spirits who are inactive much of the time while daily activities transpire around the village circumference. On special occasions, however, the sacred quality of the *marae* is publicly emphasized. Feasts and exchanges were and are held on or near the *marae*. *Maka ufi* 'yam harvest' celebrations, *ta kai ta rua* 'mourning feasts', *kiripuga* and *rugaika* exchanges of foods, feasts for those journeying or returning, reciprocal hosting of island wide Christian services and festivities, and secular holidays like Independence Day are all celebrated in the space of the *marae*. Today village *marae* are sites for more mundane gatherings as well. Volleyball is played regularly on a centrally located court enjoyed by spectators who sit at the periphery under shade trees quietly watching and engaging one another in conversation. Occasionally athletic exchanges involving inter-island competitions are hosted on the *marae* as well.

In the nineteenth century an altar to the gods of the sun and moon stood on the periphery of most village *marae*s (Gunn 1914). A sacred banyon tree was also often located toward the edge of the *marae*. The altars and sacred tree were sites of worship prior to church building. Following the turn of the century, as one by one villages of West Futuna decided to build a Christian church, the problem of where to locate a place of worship associated with the new religion was typically solved by a gift of land. The locations inevitably associated with the *tapu* or sacred fringe of the *marae* continue to be recognized as hallowed ground today.

Well into the nineteenth century a *fare ariki* or chiefly house was constructed annually at the edge of the Pau *marae* and perhaps in other villages as well.[11] Construction was usually in March in Pau and the house when completed served as the site of island-wide dancing and feasting. This structure was reportedly an architectural triumph built with the cooperation of villagers from around the island. Residents of each community would contribute the best of raw materials from their respective territories for the structure. The *fare ariki*, sacred tree and altars from the past are no longer materially present at the *maraes* but memories of them are plentiful and the spaces where they stood are clearly noted and respected. Narrated events are frequently located where a sacred tree or *fare ariki* once stood. In *Ta Pasiesi ma Majihjiki* the *fare ariki* is a monster's home transformed into a prison. Today discussions in the Vanuatu Cultural Center in Port Vila critically reflect on such *kastom*s with a view toward selective renovation of communal architecture and events. Reviving the *fare ariki* is often mentioned in this light.

Beyond the residential areas of the village, land and reef become mosaics of kin group managed yet individually utilized property, each plot with a history of belonging to particular families and a history of use and sometimes abuse by particular individuals.[12] Everyone has a strong sense of rightful associations but constructions of those rightful associations are not necessarily shared. People keep track of each other's movements through the landscape constantly. Even typical greetings or departing comments ask from whence or to where a party comes or goes (see Duranti 1997).

Historically, as in other places in the Pacific resource management seems to have followed 'principles of flexibility that ensured all tenure [and use rights were] … a reflection of social dynamics at any specific time' (Foale and Macintyre

2000:32). Still disputes over subsistence use rights are legion. Disputants pursue resolution today through extended debates over privileged access by virtue of kin ties or formal grants of permission for use. Multigenerational kin charts, chalked on wallboards or penciled in notebooks, become the primary data for argumentation. Stalemate is not uncommon in the process and lands may be kept in production for years while claims are nevertheless under negotiation.

With respect to narrative, noted points in the landscape, reef and sea selectively authorize performances. There are a few 'great myths' that enfold the entire island (Bonnemaison 1994:114). *Ta Pasiesi ma Majihjiki* is one such encompassing tale. But these few grand narratives stand in stark contrast to the more usual and particular uses of geography in the verbal arts. An enduring association of places with families underlies narrative constructions. Named features of the land, reef or seascapes in a tale tie individuals of those places to the episodes. Responsibility for recollection and recounting of narrative discourses falls on those most closely associated by descent and residence with the pertinent geographical sites.

Often West Futuna consultants would feel ill at ease if questioned about a tale or the meaning of a text perceived as belonging to others. We were sent from one community member to another until someone who could properly speak to questions we raised was identified. Likewise original composers of songs sang of their own places and events that transpired in areas about which they had the authority to speak by virtue of proper kin and residential ties. Continuing this tradition young people today request permission from their elders to perform songs referencing places and events of old. The specific topology and toponymy entailed by myths and musical compositions thus reifies and continues rightful connections between people, places and knowledge (Bonnemaison 1994; Firth 1961; Jolly 1999:189) while simultaneously providing expanding performance rights through proper lines of communication.

Plaiting Lives and Creating Community

Complementarity is key to West Futuna social process. Gender differences, asymmetrically and symmetrically paired kin, families differentially associated with places, neighborhoods and districts, and ancient moieties recalled for the contrasting dispositions and inclinations of their members all constitute oppositional social elements plaited together in interactions, events and narrative. A man and woman when married co-create the foundations of domesticity (Keller 1988). Elder kinsman and youth reproduce knowledge and skill through apprenticeships. Siblings and cousins co-operate by virtue of diverse and complementary skills and resources. Families exchange produce, enhancing the variety of foods for daily subsistence and punctuating routine with extraordinary gifts.

Today exchanges of food with members of diasporic communities on Tanna and in Port Vila are as regular as the plane schedules. Bread, green vegetables and sweets come to the island while starchy puddings (*puri*) and sometimes pork are carried away. Prestige and industry of a donor family are simultaneously reckoned and indexed by such prestations. A gift confers respect, strengthens social bonds and creates the expectation of a future return, equivalent to but not identical with the original items. The continual circulation of foodstuffs of different types that results affirms a mosaic of social relationships.

Special events, village and island wide, are marked by community feasts to which groups bring produce associated with specific family or district resources. Each contribution is identified with its donors. Feast foods are displayed in church or on or near the *marae*. Everyone views the sumptuous array and subsequently, as each group tries to insure others are more richly compensated, equivalent shares (*rau*) are allocated.[13]

In this way ongoing reciprocity is enabled by enduring differences and mutuality of sacrifice (Biersack 1998:55). There is flexibility in the oppositional identities and complementary acts, enough to create tensions when expectations are violated or pleasant surprise as convention is reinforced through a forgotten gift repaid. But over the long term differences intertwined create equivalence. The larger community takes shape as individuals are plaited together in reciprocal interactions. It is thus that 'each man lives as he should' (Bonnemaison 1994:127).

The principle of complementarity also plays a role in the construction of social hierarchy.

In the nineteenth and early twentieth centuries authority and associated sacred or expert knowledge were organized within two opposing moieties, Kaviameta and Namruke. Each group was known collectively as a *vaka,* literally 'canoe', metaphorically 'a community of people'. Representatives of the two groups are 'found in each village, and each village has a Namruke and a Kawiameta marae [usually on opposite sides of a central *marae*]' (Lynch and Fakamuria 1994:85).[14] The moieties in the various communities were ranked internally. A high chief for each group was responsible to insure that norms of sacred and secular activities were followed. Responsible to him were experts who controlled the weather, sea and reef life, fruiting trees, domestic plants and animals, romantic involvements, illness, and the ancestral realm. These individuals were masters of protective, beneficial and destructive magic relevant to their domains. It was these individuals who would be consulted by members of their respective moieties when nature needed prodding or anticipated actions required supernatural assurance. The high chief for each group was consulted on serious matters and he alone could make decisions regarding the taking of a human life when required by social transgressions or authorize detrimental, black magic.

This organizational structure was part of a larger system referred to as *uka*, literally 'line', but with the extended meaning in this context of 'lines of authority and proper communication'. Mrs Copeland, wife of the Reverend Copeland who served as missionary to West Futuna from 1860 to 1881, described the leadership structure as like a 'chain ... of which every native

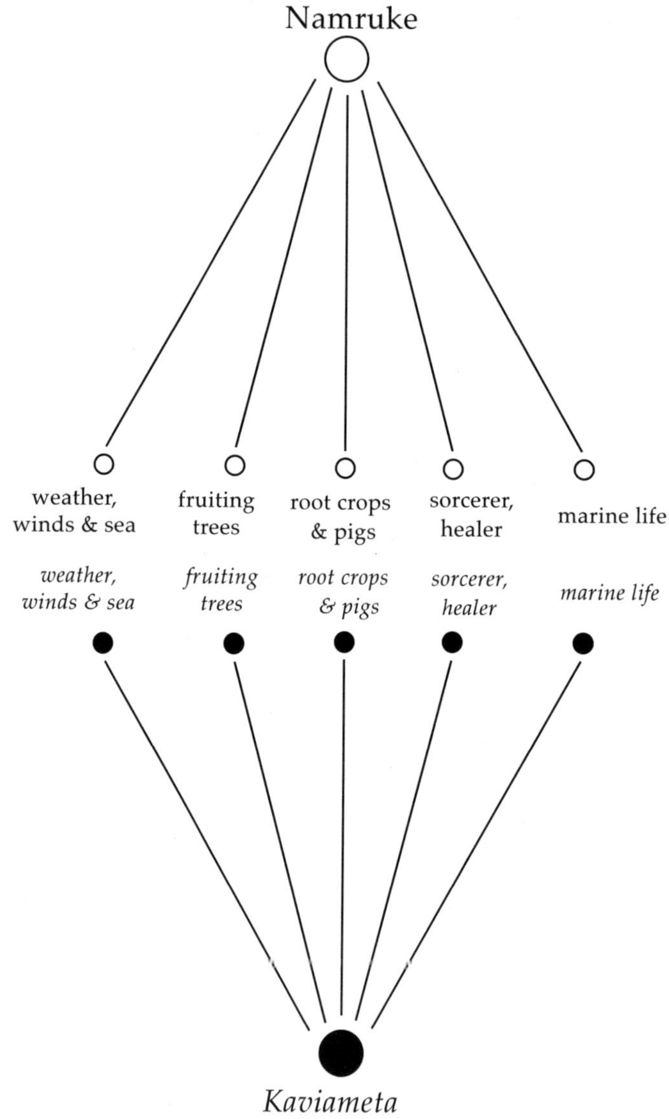

Figure 8: *Ta uka:* a model of customary distribution of local knowledge and expertise on West Futuna.

forms a link. Nearly all men and women have some office to perform' (Steel 1880:141).[15] Takaronga outlines some of the major responsibilities of traditional leadership in Figure 8.

Today community leadership resides with heads of families, church deacons and elders, and with an elected, island council of chiefs. Membership in Namruke and Kaviameta is no longer openly emphasized by the people of West Futuna and yet most members of the current generation of mature adults know what their membership would be if it were significant. There is a sense of uncertainty about the current relevance of these moieties, and yet a feeling of validity associated with the remembered collective identities. Attachments among individuals and expectations regarding people's characters persistently reflect would be moiety affiliations.

The original basis for moiety membership is not clear. However, in the remembered past, one's membership typically followed that of their biological or adoptive father. A sense of kinship among members is recalled, but mutual kin ties cannot be reconstructed for everyone known to have belonged to one or the other moiety. Intermarriage among members of the distinct moieties is common in recent times. A third group, Fana (sometimes Vana), gains its members from children of a family identified with one moiety who have adoptive or other significant kin ties with a member of the other moiety. Individuals who are the children of mixed marriages may be designated members of Fana as well. This intermediate group serves to mediate conflicts when they arise between members of the two primary moieties even today.

'Namruke are characterized as being quiet but evasive and calculating, thriving on the accumulation of wealth' (Lynch and Fakamuria 1994:85). They are said to be experts in the adept use of metaphor or *furi fesao*. Kaviameta are distinguished as direct and authoritarian in manner. They speak on the surface. These distinctions, reminiscent of the contrast between *hkano* and *ata,* are also represented by paired boulders near village sites. In the forested areas near Pau, for example, a huge rock formation juts out from a hillside area. Two boulders can be distinguished, one a top the second which lies partially buried underground. These boulders, Sura and Fatu, it is said represent the moieties. Kaviameta is represented by the boulder visible above ground on analogy with the clear and open speech of group members. The stone buried beneath the ground symbolizes the preference of members of Namruke for indirection and subtlety in their interactions. In times past when there was a conflict between the two groups it was said to be evident in an earthquake-like tremor of the boulder representing the group that would dominate. While the symbolism and overt conflicts of the past are not much in evidence today, the boulders stand as respected signs of ancestral principles not forgotten.

In the past proper lines of communication, *ta uka*, were specified according to these moiety affiliations, residence and directional orientation. *Notukua nofori,* 'it is spoken and it goes round', is one indigenous expression for the information circuit. All transfers of important information were restricted, involving specified links between authorities for each domain within each moiety. The Namruke leader with knowledge of weather patterns communicated with his Namruke counterpart in the next village moving to the right as one faced the central plateau. Communication continued in a circuit from one authority to another within the moiety. If a message was initiated by Namruke in Pau it would move through Namruke in Hsia, Mouga, Iasoa, Iakana, Matagi, to finally reach Iraro.[16] Similarly, high chiefs communicated only with high chiefs for each moiety from village to village. On a smaller scale within each village as well information passed to the right from neighborhood to neighborhood around the *marae*. Communication also relied on practices of coding messages in *furi fesao* to minimize eavesdropping. Illicit circulation of information was seriously punished. Such prescriptions are no longer formally adhered to, but there is still a lingering sense of propriety in the ancient patterns of authority and in communication transfers that move in the prescribed rightward direction around the island (counterclockwise as described from a bird's-eye view of the island with north at the top). This contrast between rightward and leftward orientations, as one faces the interior, is a structural feature of narrative creating shifting moods and expectations during performances.

The word, *uka,* has been extended to modern leadership hierarchies and communication networks of deacons and elders of the various Christian denominations and to information exchange in council circuits or among government officials. Finding a proper solution to a thorny problem is best pursued by *sara ta uka,* 'finding the right connection or link'. It is still commonly held that only designated authorities in a village can resolve conflicts among their members. Should exogenous institutions such as the police become involved in local issues many people believe that information ought to be channeled through a person of chiefly status, whose position as a pinnacle of leadership is appropriate for communication with outsiders.

As in the past much information is still considered private, valuable and closely guarded. Knowledge is power when properly held and disseminated (Lindstrom 1990). These attitudes, at least among members of older generations, are reflected in continuing concern over how and with whom information is shared. As a consequence working with narrative discourses can be sensitive. Ultimately the texts we present here are those shared with us as appropriate for dissemination. They constitute texts with the potential to facilitate continuing communication across the generations and from West Futuna with its margins.

Christianity: A Spiritual Canoe

Histories of evangelism in the Tafea district of Vanuatu are available from a variety of sources (e.g., Geddie 1855; Gunn 1914, 1924; Howe 1984; Inglis 1890, 1859; Miller, J.G. 1978, 1981, 1986; Miller, R.S. 1975). Our purpose here is not to repeat this history, but to address the intertwining of native life ways and

Christian religious values, as these may be pertinent to local narrative traditions. We aim to paint the outlines of a picture of entangled religious practices and beliefs set in historical perspective.

The London Missionary Society (LMS) took the lead in bringing Christianity to the New Hebrides (colonial designation for Vanuatu). John Williams, an early leader of the organization, sailed for the New Hebrides in 1839 anchoring at Severaro Bay, West Futuna on 17 November where he was met by Chief Koitiama of Mouga (Gunn 1906:113; Miller 1978:12, 26). Together, apparently aided by similarities of the language of West Futuna with Polynesian languages familiar to Williams, the two discussed the possibility of placing Samoan evangelists in West Futuna communities. Koitiama's response led Williams to promise that 'we should visit them again shortly … to settle teachers as soon as we can possibly spare them' (memoirs of Rev John Williams, Prout, p. 382-83 cited in Miller 1978:27). Although Williams was killed just three days later by neighboring islanders, the LMS leadership considered the exchange with Koitiama a pledge and arranged for the Christian message to be introduced to West Futuna (Miller 1978:27).

In March 1841 two Samoan teachers, Apela and Samuela, were brought to shore at Severaro (Miller 1978:27; Murray 1876:183-86) on the northwest side of the island. Koitiama was apparently less certain about the arrangements in the face of real personnel to be settled, but in exchange for an opportunity to travel to Aneityum and return to West Futuna on the mission vessel, … he promised to look after and protect the teachers (Inglis 1890:246-47; Keller 1988; Miller 1978:27).

From the West Futuna perspective settling teachers on the island may have been understood as a means for establishing long-term partnerships with the foreigners while simultaneously strengthening inter-island alliances through improved transportation (Miller 1981:13). This would have been a version of usual practice in the southern New Hebrides of the nineteenth century.

The foreign travelers were to be protected by a host community, in this case, Mouga. This village would serve as a point of entrée insuring a safe haven for the newcomers wherever they visited on the island. The people of West Futuna would benefit, in turn, from access to mission transport, more reliable than canoes for inter-island voyaging. This new access to transport would offer enhanced opportunities for exchange at usual ports of call.

The new partnership, however, was short-lived. Sickness struck West Futuna in 1842. The Samoan missionaries were blamed and murdered by people of Mouga (Miller 1978:28; Capell 1958:31). A decade then passed before a renewed attempt to evangelize the people of West Futuna was considered. This second attempt relied upon volunteer converts from neighboring Aneityum who felt their ties of friendship with the people of West Futuna would provide a foundation for exchanging religious ideals and moral values. The LMS leadership hoped that as chiefs numbered among the converted in Aneityum, the people of West Futuna might be impressed and willing to listen to their neighbors (Miller 1978:28).

> In 1852 a church was formed in Aneityum, and two of the converts, Waihit and Yosefa, were set apart as evangelists for [West] Futuna. ...They were landed at Futuna with their wives by the mission ship, *John Williams*, in 1853. [Gunn 1914:9; see also Steel 1880]

It is Waihit and Josefa who are the subjects of the final song included in this volume. They were stationed in Matagi and Iakana respectively, both populous districts on the southwest side of the island at the time. Early indications suggest they were received and treated well (Gunn 1914:10-11; Miller 1975:174, 183). Again, however, disease altered the willingness of islanders to tolerate outsiders in their midst, even outsiders well-known to the West Futuna communities. The Christian presence was blamed for epidemics that spread throughout the southern New Hebrides (Steel 1880). Waihit and Josefa had reported early in their stay that 'the work of God on Futuna is much less difficult than it was on Aneiteum [sic]' (Miller 1975:208). Nonetheless they soon found themselves treated as

> enemies and as slaves. The food which they planted in their gardens was stolen at night by both men and women, as soon as it was ripe … They [the people of Matagi and Iakana] almost sacrificed Waihit … One of the worshippers, a chief in Imatangi, who had gone on a visit to Aneityum, was so long away that his friends accused Waihit of raising a storm to drown him. Believing his life to be in great danger, Waihit was about to embark in a canoe for Aneityum when the mission vessel appeared, bringing back the chief. [Gunn 1914:10-11]

After three years of what the evangelists themselves saw as promise balanced by severe setbacks, in 1856 Waihit returned home to Aneityum with his sick wife and shortly thereafter Josefa followed (Gunn 1914:11; Miller 1975:222-23). In the three years they had had spent on West Futuna not a single resident had professed faith in Christianity, but a curiosity about the strange religion had been aroused.

In the years that followed, a number of Pacific evangelists were placed on West Futuna with little success at explicit conversion although the new religious teachings must have been becoming increasingly familiar at least to some islanders. During this period the mission establishment in the New Hebrides came to believe that the time was right for placing a European theologian on the island, someone who from their perspective could offer more detailed training in the scriptures than Pacific evangelists only recently converted (see Miller 1975:208; Inglis 1859:105-7). In 1860 the Reverend Joseph Copeland from the Reformed Presbyterian Church of Scotland visited West Futuna (Gunn 1914:14). Subsequently the Mission Conference of 1866 appointed him, together with his wife, Elizabeth Johnston (Miller 1978:190; Steel 1880), to West Futuna. They became the first European missionaries to settle on that island residing there until 1881 (Miller 1978:31, 1981:15).

By the end of his stay, Copeland had translated segments of the scriptures and a catechism. A small collection of hymns in the language was also available. Although no formal congregation had emerged alternatives to traditional narrative and spiritual practices had become accessible. While the population of West Futuna was declining, falling from about 1000 to under 500 during the years of Copeland's presence (Steel 1880; Miller 1981:13,18; see also Geddie 1855:86), and misfortune continued to be attributed to outsiders, the reverend felt that customary practices were changing, and he expressed optimism from his perspective about the future of Christian worship among the islanders (Steel 1880; Miller 1981:18-19).

After Copeland's departure a series of evangelists from Aneityum attended to the Gospel in West Futuna. In 1883, the best remembered of these, Habena/Hapina, a new recruit from Aneityum, arrived on West Futuna with his wife, Annie. He remained there for the rest of his life and, after losing his first wife, ultimately married a local woman, Laku, who was also the first convert (Miller 1986:168). In 1900 Hapina was ordained as pastor of West Futuna, a position he held until his death in 1916 (Miller 1986:183). Together Hapina and Laku founded a large family and are well remembered today. Their descendants are still numerous and include many who assisted in our project.

Another Scotsman, the Reverend William Gunn, was assigned to West Futuna as a medical missionary from the Free Church of Scotland the same year that Hapina arrived (Miller 1981:18). Most villages included a handful of worshippers at the time (Gunn 1906:127; Miller 1986:162-65) and internal tensions associated with the growing impact of religious and colonial influences must have been profoundly disturbing to islanders. Labor recruiting for plantations in Queensland and Fiji was ongoing and to remove themselves from increasing conflict at home many signed on.

The Gunns and Hapina began a campaign to destroy sacred stones used as *ata* in increase rites and remove other magical fetishes considered symbolic of the darkness of the past. Stalwart banyans located on village *marae*s fell to the fervor of the evangelists. In some villages the change was welcomed, but in other places residents predicted immanent disaster. Indeed, an epidemic of influenza followed shortly after the sacred stones of Pau had been destroyed. Hostilities re-emerged. In defiance of Christian morality a human sacrifice was carried out in the hope of ameliorating angered ancestors (Miller 1986:166).

An ambiance of resistance and embrace between Christian ideals and indigenous mores persisted. The population was continuing to decline rapidly as disease and labor recruiting took their toll. Amidst such tragic loss, survivors were finding reasons to attend to the new religion. The Reverend Gunn produced a growing number of scriptural translations and the people of West Futuna themselves began to write their own hymns or translate popular verses. These compositions were

> sung in and out of school and heard on the bush tracks … Children began to pray at home and to take their turn in prayer at school. They memorized Scriptures (and) … showed new understanding … [Miller (1986:167]

Five people were baptized in 1889. By 1890 with a population of 513 on the island, worship attendance was said to average 255 people (Miller 1986:170). The first church was soon built with local labor, the materials supplied by a sawmill in Aneityum and paid for by profits from the mission-introduced arrowroot crop. Worship in the new building began in 1892 and on New Year's Day of 1893 a crowd of 200 attended service there (Miller 1986:171). By 1898 Reverend Gunn gave the population of the island as 310 of whom he claimed 200 as regular worshippers (Miller 1986:177).[17]

Mouga was the last village to permit the building of a Christian place of worship, and even once a church had been established about the turn of the century there was continued resistance to attending worship. The Gunn's dedicated themselves to bringing this last village within their reach. In 1905 before they left for a long furlough in Scotland a successful farewell feast was seen as a sign of a change of heart among the people of Mouga with respect to the foreign teachings (Miller 1986:178-79). Although resistance continued in this region, gradually Christianity took hold even here.

In 1905 several West Futuna deacons were ordained and a new hierarchy of Presbyterian Church leadership involving pastors, elders and deacons began to replace and complement earlier forms of authority. Leadership was slipping away from family ensconced experts, moiety officers and chiefs to those most informed about Christian practices and beliefs. Traditions went underground or disappeared, including kava drinking, fertility rites involving customary stone *ata,* and *tafiri* or *kastom* dancing. The singing of hymns became the primary collective musical outlet. Traditional narrative and music retreated to memory. By 1917, when the Gunns took their final leave, the population of West Futuna was again climbing and Christianity had become at least a nominal way of life for many. Local leaders and trainees from other islands were prepared to continue Christian teachings, organize schooling and promote the development of new forms of community building, exchange and subsistence.

This history is celebrated today. And although introduced religious options and local theology has diversified, Christianity in some form or another is integral to local identities. Yet reflections on cultural heritage and contemporary practices are complex. The site of the mission in Pau and locations of the first churches around the island stand side by side with well known locations of sacred banyan trees, the site of *fare ariki* and emplaced reminders of narrative events. Traditional narratives are retold in religious sermons and musical arts from the past stand with choral performances among the pleasures of the present. Common among church leaders today is a desire to revisit *kastom* in order to reauthorize past practices that enhance community and reinforce Christian messages. At the same time *kastoms* are scrutinized to insure that those injurious to communal life are not revived (Jolly 1997; Rakau n.d.). Church leaders are firm in their beliefs that 'missionaries made an unfortunate separation between Christianity and local culture' in the past leaving them the 'task today to heal that separation' (Forman 2001:12).

The contemporary religious leaders of West Futuna are local men and women, educated in country and abroad to cultivate the spiritual lives of their families and friends. Christianity is firmly a part of islanders' contemporary traditions, but despite Gunn's observations that each of three generations of converts he witnessed was increasingly Western in their understanding of Christianity, the received systems today vibrate with local character. The Presbyterian Church, once the exclusive Christian force in the southern district of Vanuatu, is but one of several faiths practiced on West Futuna and among migrant communities. Numerous charismatic denominations have gained popularity in what has become an intense competition for congregations. Assembly of God, Holiness Fellowship, Seventh-Day Adventists, Pentacostalism, New Testament Ministries (NTM) and others offer a rich array of devotional possibilities. Personal commitments to one group or another often turn on the character of the associated musical culture. One woman of Mouga, torn between a longing for *kastom* and the collective rejoicing associated with Christian spiritual engagements, attends the Assembly of God services irregularly. She accounts for her conflicted interest in the following way, 'We no longer dance as we did (*tafiri*), but at least we have music in church'.

Folklore from West Futuna has been pressed into Christian service. Oral literature is explored for episodes and implicit meanings that convey Christian messages beneath the surface. Selected narratives appear in sermons, special programs and conversations affirming the presence of Biblical tenets in local ideology. One story of Tamalua and Paji, is about a fisherman and his wife. Tamalua, the fisherman, away from home for an extended period at sea, returns to find his wife pregnant. Initially angry, he learns that Paji believes he returned nightly to her bed. The beloved supernatural culture hero, Majihjiki, disguised as Tamalua, has slept with Paji in his absence. Tamalua gradually relents accepting that Paji's child is his responsibility too. This story is said to highlight Tamalua's indigenous Christian virtue. Explicit comparisons with Joseph's responsibility for Mary's child, the baby Jesus, are common. Several of the narratives included in this volume similarly portray values associated with communal life-ways identified as local precursors of Christian priorities.

Beyond folklore, Christ, himself, argues a US-trained theologian from West Futuna, must be considered as

> ni-Vanuatu [of Vanuatu]. He can walk to the village. He visits a woman in the community whose child was sick and healed her. He was at a wedding. He walked to the sea and found the fishermen and called them to follow him. He walks to people's home[s]; He tells stories to teach great men; little children were attracted by Him. [Rakau n.d.]

These are ancient practices of the people of Vanuatu reproduced in daily actions once also characteristic of the Son of God.

In reflecting on their past the people of West Futuna suggest that pre-Christian laws (*vaega*) embody the prescriptions of the Ten Commandments. Thou shalt not kill (arbitrarily), steal or commit adultery are said to have been ideals prior to European contact. Violations were handled very seriously. Such convergence is taken note of in Christian services and household conversations. Even practices such as baptism are thought by some to have *kastom* roots in West Futuna where customary meals involving sacred foods and anointing initiates' heads with water are noted. The name of one Namruke *marae*, Ta Fogarama, means 'The Light', and is associated with Christian references to this metaphor in their theology. These past practices, a selection from ancestral *kastoms* (Jolly 1997:139), provide indigenous justification for recognizing and adhering to Christian ways.

Church and *kastom* are increasingly indistinguishable.

Alliances and disputes among family members that would traditionally have surfaced in intrigue, sorcery and political realignments, are apparent today in the choices made regarding church membership. Disaffection, resisting authority, and the lure of the novel, spur youths, and even some of their elders, to use membership in a spiritual community to position themselves as they might have by other means in the past. It is not unusual for parent and child, brother and sister, to belong to opposing congregations, a fact discussed and often regretted openly, yet a mechanism that facilitates complementarity and redistribution of authority even while creating tension and discord.

Leadership today still involves one's descent, expert knowledge, wisdom and proper comportment. Taking responsibility for family and community are valued as they were traditionally and the church has become a primary arena in which such social involvement is demonstrated. From acts of traditional giving to contemporary program development, members' contributions are remembered and assessed. Seldom does one attain positions of authority without recognized achievements in a congregation. Local celebrations too have been hybridized. Christian holidays are as appropriate for customary feasting as the marking of the first of the yam harvest (*maka ufi*) or end of a mourning period (*kai tarua*). In death one's corpse is likely to be buried in a cemetery where graves are marked by headstones of Christian inspiration. Yet customary associations of the deceased with an area of the reef continue as the basis for traditional mourning restrictions on fishing. And *Rufei Soa,* a tale in which the Underworld (*i o tua*)[18] is associated with pathways in the reef, plays a crucial role in emphasizing contemporary social mores and perpetuating discourses of the supernatural.

With the relatively recent proliferation of religious alternatives, Christian doctrines have been linked with modernity and in this process have become openly subject to reflection, criticism and comparison in a search for a truly Pacific theology (Forman 2001:3). On West Futuna I have heard Christian notions of 'sharing' and 'forgiveness', debated. Do the principles undermine authority? Do they destroy traditional standards for respect or establish universal goodwill? Why forgive rather than punish a thief? Does forgiveness not encourage transgression? And doesn't universal sharing negate familial land rights and reciprocity?

According to Forman (2001:13) the process entails

> much criticism of Western culture and accusations that it [modernity] is incompatible with Christian life ... Pacific culture values cooperation, generosity, family loyalty, sharing and community life, [but] Western culture stresses money, violence, sex, sports and individual power ... Capitalism from the West is damaging the environment and deforming Pacific societies.

Takaronga noted with surprise during a visit to the United States that islanders are far better Christians than Americans. Fiama Rakau, a theologian from West Futuna who studied in Michigan, contrasts local and Western societies by analogy to canoes and motorboats.

> In the canoe concept, all people in the canoe do the paddling, and depend on each other as they paddle along the rough seas. ...[In the Western] speed boat concept all people depend on one captain who knows the way and the mechanics of the engine. [Rakau n.d.:87]

It is clearly the former model to which most people of Vanuatu today aspire at least ideally if not always in practice.

In this atmosphere of critical reflection Rakau has proposed that 'life affirming' values of *kastom* and the church should be united against 'life denying' values of Westernization and similarly against those ancestral practices, primarily sorcery and interpersonal conflict, that undermine community. 'Stories, myths and symbols', are part of the valued aspects of life that encourage convergences amongst past and present (Rakau n.d: 87-8). These practices it is said have a place in ongoing constructions of identity and in continuing spiritual development.

Independence and Life in the Republic

Christianity has become a cornerstone of governance as well as life-ways in the Republic. Nowhere is this more evident than in the symbolic foundations of the national flag and emblem. The flag divides red and green fields with a triangle and parallel lines in yellow and black. The yellow, representing Christianity, is simultaneously encompassed by and encompasses areas in black symbolizing peoples with dark skin. Displayed within the black triangle is a pig tusk and cycad leaves, indices of traditional authority and peace respectively. The yellow and black pattern further unites the blood red upper segment reflecting common descent with a lower panel of green representing the land. It would be difficult to imagine a more thoroughly syncretic imagery for the nation-state. The national emblem of Vanuatu is similarly inspired by local and introduced values. Featured is a man in indigenous attire with the motto *Long God Yumi Stanap,* 'In God we are independent' (Jolly 1997:139-40).

Vanuatu declared independence in 1980 to become an archipelago nation-state of eighty-three islands as *The New York Times* counts them (Kaufmann 1999), where a total population of about 170,000 in 2001 is networked across more than 100 ethnically distinct communities (e.g., Kaeppler, Crowe, Chenoweth and Lindstrom 1998:688). The first Prime Minister of Vanuatu was Father Walter Lini, a man who reflects the complex heritage of his people in his own biography. Born to a distinguished family on Pentecost Island, he was a leader in the Anglican Church. He studied in the Solomon Islands and New Zealand and married a woman from the Solomons. Lini strove during his years of national leadership to combine local and foreign, secular and spiritual practices selectively in guiding the new Republic of Vanuatu (Aaron et al. 1981; Forman 2001:11).

As we write this book, the recent past Prime Minister, Edward Nipake Natapei, a man of West Futuna descent and migrant to Port Vila, came to his position with a combination of achievements in the Presbyterian Church, foreign education and local government. He undertook the task set by those who preceded him, to seek 'ways to reconcile indigenous culture, Christianity and EuroAmerican values of materialism and progress …' (Hereniko 1997:437 cited in Sherkin 1999:238).

The colonial context immediately preceding independence had been one characterized by 'pandemonium', a condition that served to reinforce local disjunctions (Miles 1998; Van Trease 1987). From 1906 until 1980, France and Britain shared administrative control of the islands then called the New Hebridean Condominium. In what is often viewed as a foolish experiment, the British and French established a Condominium government through which they attempted to govern the archipelago jointly (Crowley 1990:4). 'Jointly', rather than collaboratively, is the appropriate expression here for the two imperial powers carried out activities often entirely independent of one another. Collaboration that might have unified the governing process was not an apparent priority. The expatriate colonialists augmented the local ethnic distinctions by two and were perceived as opposed to one another much as local ethnic groups defined themselves against a background of neighboring others or as traditional moieties positioned themselves in opposition to one another. Terry Crowley describes the divisive tenor of the colonial situation as follows:

> There were two currencies in free exchange, the *franc des Nouvelles Hébrides* "New Hebrides franc" and the Australian dollar. Some stores would post prices in one currency, some in the other; employees of some firms would be paid in one currency and employees of other firms in the other. The post office used its own artificial currency of gold francs and centimes, which had to be converted to dollars or francs depending on what day of the week it was, because on different days proceeds from the sales of stamps went alternately to the British and French treasuries. There were two base hospitals in Vila, one British and one French, while the outer islands cried out for decent health

> care. Melanesian policemen in different uniforms, one French-educated, the other English educated, patrolled in pairs (but spoke to each other in Bislama, the Melanesian Pidgin lingua franca). There were two education systems, each operating with its own language of instruction and its own educational philosophy. There were even two prisons in Vila, one staffed by French-educated warders, the other by warders who had been to school in English-medium schools. The number of such absurdities made eventual independence not only desirable, but essential. [1990:4]

Islanders were not only influenced by European powers during their colonial experiences, but also by an American presence in World War II. The Americans 'left two important legacies behind: a taste for material goods and a flirtation with freedom' (Miles 1998:19) that would exacerbate British/French rivalries in the face of persistent local movements toward independence. For three decades after the war ni-Vanuatu struggled to define themselves. Political factions proliferated and strategies for pushing independence ahead or delaying self governance were reflected in competing discourses as local alliances with colonial powers waxed and waned. Tensions intensified in the years just prior to independence and political parties that began to appear in the Condominium era proliferated in the early years of the Republic.

Still a parliamentary democracy has emerged and survived the turmoil. In the years since independence changes in government leadership have been frequent and approaches to issues of internal development and global integration have shifted as those in power come and go. Yet despite the constantly changing face of ni-Vanuatu politics, common goals derived from Walter Lini's 'doctrine of "Melanesian socialism" characterized by communalism, sharing and humanism' (Miles 1998:24) endure. As time passes a 're-Melanization' (Miles 1998:28) of governance is replacing colonial preoccupations. Land conservation, development of renewable energy resources, service delivery to rural communities and promotion of social harmony have taken their place with education and economic expansion as leading priorities (e.g., Dorney 2002). A National Council of Chiefs compliments the Parliament and is available for state level consultation on matters of customary traditions. Nationalism and *kastom*, selectively configured, are today joined in the production of the Republic of Vanuatu and in the making of its citizens (Miles 1998; White and Lindstrom 1997).

With independence, Bislama, a variety of the language linguists refer to as Melanesian Pidgin, became established as the national language (Crowley 1990:1, 6). The republic's official languages are three: Bislama, French and English. Today French and English are the languages of education while all three official languages are used in governmental and formal business contexts. Immigrant languages such as Vietnamese, Chinese and other Pacific Island tongues are part of the linguistic landscape. Vernaculars, including the language of West Futuna, flourish in rural settings and urban domestic contexts, while interesting patterns of language co-occurrence and shift are apparent in radio broadcasts and published newspapers, in markets and interactions on the street, in forms of transport including taxis, boats and planes, and during religious services.

Despite their continuity in rural areas and selected contexts of urban life, vernacular languages are threatened by the popularity of European or European influenced tongues in many arenas. One consequence of the predominance of English, French and Bislama in business, governmental and educational environments is a declining interest in the substance of traditional verbal arts or fluency in indigenous speech. It is in part the present emphasis on preferential use of colonial language standards and the resulting disinterest in indigenous language competence that motivates us to highlight traditional verbal arts.

The linguistic shifts promoted by post independence society in Vanuatu are associated with the increasing mobility of individuals and diversity within communities. The typical West Futuna residential community today includes neighbors who share competence in their native language yet speak a variety of other languages with varying degrees of fluency. These neighbors labor together and manage a combined cash and subsistence economy relying irregularly on copra and remittances from migrants for cash income. Their preferences for worship are diverse and personal histories create both ties and ruptures among kin. Customary heritage is simultaneously shared and individually constructed. Within each village are also residents who have married in or joined the group for professional reasons such as nursing, teaching or preaching. These extrinsic insiders tie the local community to other islanders, speak other languages and may find themselves more comfortable with practices unfamiliar to their neighbors than with recognized traditions of the island. In addition, even residents born and raised on West Futuna find themselves connected to other places in the nation-state by virtue of their ancestry, travels, and personal ties with kin who have married out or found work or opportunities for study elsewhere.[19] Similarly eclectic communities are the rule throughout Vanuatu.

Attitudes regarding present circumstances on the island and in the wider republic are diverse and often conflicted. One woman of West Futuna conveys her concerns in the following way, 'Those who take hold of the pencil are unable to learn skills of the land. Still those who school, win, for they learn the ways of money'. Paraphrasing Takaronga's reflections on current affairs, he argues 'there is no peace today because old systems have been supplanted and the new ways are suspect in local eyes'. Others volunteer, *Independence e sa. Nofakamata sore i ai.* 'Independence is deplorable. We must pay for everything now.' This is a common expression of frustration experienced by urban migrants over the costs of basic amenities such as water, food, and clothing that were traditionally derived from communal resources involving labor rather than financial investment. And in local discourses it is regularly remarked 'the ways of *tamatoga* "foreigners" have come. We've adapted and now we want things to be easy'.

It is in part this atmosphere of ambivalence and uncertainty that perpetuates urban-rural flows of people as they pursue roads to success. Village populations on West Futuna are currently low during much of the year leaving subsistence activities to the elderly, while a vital presence of the island's young adults is constantly growing in other places within Vanuatu and throughout the Pacific. Return visits to the homeland are common during holidays, for other special events, or in times of financial stress. The push-pull dynamics result from educational, professional and social opportunities provided in urban areas by contradistinction with a desired atmosphere of belonging experienced in one's home island. On West Futuna ancestral ties, a sense of correctness of cultural practices enacted in familiar places, and rights to land, reef and sea enable subsistence through labor and reciprocity rather than cash purchase. Such possibilities combine to create a sense of emplaced rightness that modern circumstances cannot sustain. As a result of these tensions a peripatetic life style is evidenced by many who choose an immediate place of residence by sifting through possibilities for a satisfactory existence in the moment given past and present links with others, current responsibilities, religious beliefs, opportunities for education or employment, avoidance of black magic, and ongoing involvements in disputes (see Bedford 1973 for extended discussion of circular migration).

One man offers glimpses of his biography illustrating frequent decisions to move from place to place. As a boy probably in the 1950s he went to school on Futuna for four or five years. Instruction mixed the languages of West Futuna, Bislama, and English. He says he completed his studies knowing English only *haf haf*. Before he had begun to shave he went to work for six months on Aneityum cutting *kauri,* sandalwood. The labor was strenuous. In the absence of power tools, two men worked together on one tree with one saw. If a boat arrived to pick up a load of wood and not enough was ready, the workers were assigned to twenty-four hour shifts in the interior until ample cargo was compiled. Exhausting himself in this effort, he went to Vila for several months and then came back to West Futuna only to return to Vila after a short stay. From Vila he worked on a ship and it was during this time that he learned Bislama well. After concluding this work probably in the early 1960s, the young man married. His chosen spouse is the daughter of his father's sister's daughter. In 1964 he established his family on Tanna where he worked in the copra plantations for a year or two. The family subsequently returned to West Futuna while the children were small. Here they could take advantage of gardens and the freedom of the island life. In the 1980s they moved back to Tanna while his children were attending schools there. In the 1990s, with his children grown, this man and his wife lived for various periods in Tanna or Vila residing in the capital city on the lands of family members who came to hold official positions in the national government. Recently a move to Aneityum has allowed him to take up residence with kin in communities there while his grown children continue to reside in Vila or on West Futuna.

Customs, values and language travel with people, transforming and mixing in new ways as their identities, interaction patterns and goals shift within the contexts of the new republic. Musical compositions and tales constitute a small but vital subset of the resources and ideologies that move with people. As national priorities have embraced local histories and created *kastom* as a symbol of the potential for unity in diversity, the verbal arts have become increasingly valuable. Past and present, familiar yet revisited from novel vantage points, these arts are implemented in the ongoing construction of the nation, its culture and practice for ni-Vanuatu, the people of Vanuatu in general, and *fakai Futuna*, the people of West Futuna (Donner 1992; Firth 1961:171, 174-75; Miles 1998).

Notes

1 A reference to Irromang among the appelations for West Futuna listed in Beaglehole (1961) is likely in error, the name more properly referring to Erromanga.

2 Tonga here may refer to the Tongan Islands but the expression *toga*, pronounced identically, may also refer to foreign peoples or peoples from the south (see also Capell 1960).

3 Rawlings (1990) notes that among the many transformations accompanying Christian conversion on Efate was the movement of villages from interior locations seaward. It is certainly the case on West Futuna today that villages lie as close to the sea as geography and climate allow. While there is a history of encampments in the interior that were occupied for extended periods of several days for gardening activities, the people of West Futuna do not remark on abandoned village sites in the interior nor is there any discussion of the movement of village locations in the mission literature.

4 Compare Maunga used in reference to prominent hill sites on both Tikopia (Firth and McLean 1990:xviii) and Anuta (Feinberg 1998a:47).

5 Note the similarity in the name of the West Futuna district Pau and the Fijian district of Bau (Sahlins 1991).

6 Taroumaro is not noted in mission records (Gunn 1914).

7 For discussions of similar district divisions on the Pacific islands see Bellwood 1979; Duranti 1994; Kirch 1994, 1996; Kirch and Sahlins 1992; Lindstrom 1990; Shore 1996 among many others. Note the reef is included within West Futuna districts, a pattern not necessarily typical in Polynesia (Feinberg 2003; Hooper pers. comm.). However, district divisions encompassing land and contiguous reef segments are common in other parts of the Pacific (Foale and Macintyre's 2000, Memmott and Trigger 1998; Peterson and Rigsby 1998).

8 Outlier populations may have originated in settlements from other outliers as well as from reverse migrations out of Polynesia. West Futuna, for example, may have been settled from Emae in Vanuatu (Bayard 1976; Besnier 1998:835).

9 The closest linguistic relatives to the outlier languages appear to be 'Samoan, Tokelauan, Tuvaluan, East Uvea, East Futuna, Niuafo'ou and Pukapuka' (Lynch 1998:50). Other outlier languages within Vanuatu include Aniwan, Emae and Ifira-Mele.

10 'In social structure and culture, outlier societies have few traits in common and other than for classificatory convenience they do not form a distinct culture area' (Besnier 1998:833).

11 Capell (1958:43) and Gunn (1914:219) describe a temple or cathedral to pagan deities which Capell labels as the *fare ariki*. Neither Capell or Gunn actually witnessed a building effort or subsequent festivities. These had apparently been discontinued as early as 1860 before Reverend Gunn arrived.

12 Compare to political mosaics remarked by Sahlins for eastern Viti Levu in Fiji (1991:79).

13 Emerging practices of self-service at collective gatherings and cash purchase at festival booths diminish the measuring and assessment of contributions as functions of identity. In these cases the principle of reciprocity, however, remains in tact in a novel form as the labor of hosts is reciprocated when guests or even shoppers later become hosts and entrepreneurs themselves.

14 My spelling of Kaviameta (also Kavimeta) differs from that of Lynch and Fakamuria's Kawiameta (1994). Perhaps this reflects variable pronunciations or perhaps my ears have played tricks on me. The two moieties are also recognized on Tanna and named with cognate expressions probably borrowed into West Futuna. However, the moiety system itself seems to have originated on Futuna and spread to Tanna (Lynch and Fakamuria 1994:79). Bonnemaison comments on the moieties in Tanna that 'the Koyometa race is one of warriors, while the Numurkuen race is one of powerful magicians' (1994:153).

15 The same metaphor probably characterized communication circuits in Tanna. Bonnemaison refers to 'ropes' in connection with dream links between humans and John Frum. Such 'ropes connected him [John Frum] with the rest of humankind' (1994:224).

16 It is unclear exactly how Taroumaro and Upper Mouga are ordered relative to one another in this circuit.

17 Bonnemaison (1994:43) notes that 'Futuna had 900 residents in 1871 and only 238 in 1905'.

18 See Capell's explanation (1958:9) of the linguistic ellipsis involved as *i ta fanua o atua* 'in the land of the spirits' becomes *i o a'tua* 'underworld,' and even more succinctly, *i o tua*.

19 For example, as noted the early pastor, Hapina, originally from Aneityum, and his wife, Laku, of West Futuna, are an ancestral pair from whom many in the present-day population of West Futuna are descended, closely linking communities on Futuna and Aneityum. (Whether Hapina may have had kin ties to the first ni-Vanuatu evangelists, Waihit and Josefa, who appear in the song Najeji discussed later is not known at the time of this writing.)

4
A Fesaoaga ma a Hgoro Feifakua / Genres of Myth and Music

There are a number of genres of oral and musical literature composed and performed by the people of West Futuna. These include memorial songs, political commentary, allegories, animal stories, epic ballads, church hymns, contemporary string band compositions and musical ditties for children's games (UNESCO 1996). The repertoire of compositions within each genre is enormous. We fully realize we have only arbitrary tips of the iceberg to work with at present. Yet even these bits and pieces serve effectively to allow us to begin to reconstruct a cultural geography and cosmology and to observe the interactions of historically shaped productions within their contemporary contexts.

The two genres we emphasize are *tagi,* memorial songs and political commentary, and *hkai*, mythical allegories of culture heroes and heroines. These are verbal arts rooted in antiquity yet still performed in the present. Just how far back these narratives reach is often difficult to determine. Translations of some of the *hkai* we present here and other *tagi* compositions, formally like the songs of Chapters 10 and 11 though differing in content, appear in mission records or scholarship dating to the turn of the century and before (Capell 1938, 1960; Gray 1909a, 1909b, 1891; Gunn 1903, 1914, 1924; Ray 1901). Specific reference to historical events and personalities in the lyrics of the songs Takaronga and I collected allow us to date the time of at least one composition to the mid-nineteenth century.

Intervening decades have altered texts and contexts rendering prose once clear, now often vague and indistinct, yet there are persistent continuities. Formal style, substance, and thematic significances endure allowing us a vantage point on a past that we will argue can be folded forward to offer perspective on the present. We have found we are working not with indigenous documents that constitute 'old prose' (Tedlock 1983:129), but with discursive encounters that constitute something old with something new.

Tagi

The texts of *tagi* are poetic forms set to music. Islanders have a clear notion that a correct version exists, and lyrical variations from performance to performance are indeed minor.[1] The verses take poetic form shaped in consort with the melodies to which they are sung (Neisser 1998). These lyrics are consistent over many performances we have observed spanning several decades. The versions we re-present reflect a conviction among many community members in West Futuna that each song has a proper lyrical text. Where change in musical performances has occurred, the novel elements surround the texts through alternations in settings, costuming and choreography.

The *tagi* genre includes songs that are performed today in public, usually festive settings as well as more solemn compositions probably performed in memorial or funerary contexts only in the past (see also Gray 1909a, b; Gunn 1914:240; Sore 1909). Historically the verses of *tagi* were sung to prominent rhythmic accompaniment and dance, punctuating the message with a visibly impressive display and forceful beat. As each song draws to a close the chorus is repeated several times and the tempo accelerates until the music is halted with a shout. These performances are known as *kafa* in reference to the sounding board percussive accompaniment. The associated dancing is called *tafiri*.

Today groups of young people, with the permission of their elders, perform *tagi* in touristic or festival contexts. In the midst of national debate over the sacrifice of traditional genres to syncretic performance the beat nonetheless goes on. Performers are guided by a conservative aesthetic canon and yet they are free to innovate. While the *tagi* genre as documented through mission records is clearly of considerable antiquity, and lyrics appear conservative, transformations in performance are extensive. Adapted to tourist contexts, for example, are forms of audience participation that create humorous finales, and offer a West Futuna encompassment of the foreign. In addition, choreography and costumes are being modified presently in many ways to take advantage of novel notions of staging for outsiders and insiders alike. Authenticity is continually redefined in the contexts of emerging, dialogic expressions of identity. Traditional and contemporary styles are juxtaposed and/or syncretized in variegated musical displays that reflect a temporal pastiche broadly characteristic of society at large.

For example, *Futuna Fatuana* is a string band that regularly entertains tourists and locals in the capital city. Their name incorporates the expression *fatuana* introduced in our discussions of island history. Like the supernaturally embued rock or *ata*, the band radiates influence. Their name accentuates the potential for disseminating local voices globally through musical productions. The group performs *tagi* with a view toward bringing the spirit and vitality of these compositions from the past into the present, and from local shores to the horizon.

Costuming for traditional performances has been in transformation throughout the twentieth century. In nineteenth century practice men would dance and sing in community events wearing the customary attire shown in Figure 22 that was the typical of the times. However, on the occasion of a mid-twentieth century visit of Queen Elizabeth II to Port Vila islanders from West Futuna developed a style of male stage dress to suit changing standards of modesty. In their performance for the Queen they wore plaited pandanus wrap arounds produced by the women of West Futuna.

The fabric was mid-thigh in length mimicking the length of western style shorts, popular everyday attire for men. Attached to the lower edge were a series of tassels that swayed as the men danced accentuating their movement. Ankle bracelets allowed them to keep the beat as they danced and performers carried fighting sticks as props. Figure 9 illustrates the plaited male stage dress popular in the 1970s.

Today, public performers, all of whom are men, wear a longer wrap around plaited of pandanus with a similar hibiscus fringe that sways as they dance to the music. A shoulder sling of plaited, fringed pandanus may be added. Sometimes a plaited circlet, and most recently a plume, may be worn on the head. Dancers carry fighting sticks reminiscent of customary dueling clubs and keep the beat with ankle rattles and/or sounding board or idiophone percussion (*kafa*). Figures 10a and b illustrate recent costuming for the performance of traditional *tagi*. Notice the increasing elaboration of costumes over the four and a half year interval separating the performances.

But *Futuna Fatuana* also pleases audiences with today's music which they perform dressed in brightly colored store bought lavalavas. *Kastom* ankle rattles and conch shell trumpets are combined with a bottle piano, bamboo xylophone, improvised bass and guitars in the production of popular Pacific sounds. Christian hymns are an additional dimension of their stock-in-trade. This diverse repertoire reflects the pluralism of present circumstances intertwining Western, Oceanic and Pacific rim influences with local *kastoms*.

A deep pleasure in musical practice seems to be pervasive among islanders. People sing on every occasion: walking to school, preparing for a young girl's coming-up ceremony, in formal and informal choirs, at inauguration events for new buildings and businesses, in competitive performances at feasts and festivals, and at home with friends and family on the porch or around the hearth (see also Moyle n.d.). Lyrics today may be in West Futuna, Bislama, French or English. Translating foreign

Figure 9: *Moega* or woven *lavalava* for male dance performances, 1974.

Figure 10a: Performing in Port Vila, *Futuna Fatuana*.
Janet Dixon Keller 1999.

compositions constitutes a pleasant pastime. Groups practice at will and jam sessions are so common, at least in the city, as to compete as nightly or afternoon entertainment with the ubiquitous TV, radio and homework or rarer video and books.

This present proliferation and popularity of musical styles is informed by the genres known from the recent past. *Tagi* are the most frequently remembered and performed of these earlier styles. One of the principal purposes of these compositions was

> to remember and record events and people. Songs document history, especially the activities of individuals. Though called '*tagi*,' a word with associations of weeping or lamenting over death, the songs are not predominantly [literally] mournful, but are factual accounts of events in a person's life. [Thomas and Kuautoga 1992:13]

The word *tagi* also captures feelings of exasperation, desperation and frustration. Many *tagi* focus on problematic moments

Figure 10b: Performing in Port Vila, *Futuna Fatuana*. Kirk Huffman 2003.

in island history or personal biography. The songs may ridicule someone mired in difficulties or propose a resolution or outcome to problematic events. Such motivations account for the verses of musical productions throughout the Pacific (Donner 1987).

'Although *tagi* recount events of the life of a specific individual that person is not usually namcd [cxplictly] in thc song' (Thomas and Kuautoga 1992:13, cf., Monberg 1974). In addition, the use of *furi fesao* creates a challenge to translation and to the maintenance of a shared sense of meaning among contemporary community members. (See also Capell 1958:54; Thomas 1992, 1998. For comparative Pacific material see Bonnemaison 1994:114; Donner 1987, 1992; Feinberg 1998b:857; Feld 1990;

Firth and McLean 1990, especially pages 38-9, 137-38, 195, 201; Gauguin 1977 [1921]:44; Love 1998:836; and Monberg 1974.) As we mentioned earlier *furi fesao* is a way to convey spoken messages with private import in public contexts. This figurative use of language is an aesthetic hallmark of the *tagi*. Such verbal artistry enriched the pleasures of interpretation, and perhaps created a safety net for the composer whose politics, plight or self-aggrandizement might be partially disguised in the tropes.[2] For the listener or translator generations removed from the moment of composition, the metaphoric connections obscure reference to past events. We have revisited the translations of *Najeji* and *Tiata* numerous times over many years. In the process members of the West Futuna community have been extremely patient and helpful as we unraveled identities and metaphors eventually arriving at our present versions.

Thomas argues that 'these songs recreate history, not primarily by preserving historical data, but by allowing the experiences of the past to be re-lived' (1992:236) as shared experience in the present. In their choreography and spectacular presentational forms, *tagi,* he suggests, 'undeniably "verify" for the present day community the events of their history' (Thomas 1992:236; see also Rossen 1998:852) without preserving details. He may be right, but only partly we believe. Close examination of the texts and patient contextualization by islanders themselves reveal details of encounters memorialized in the lyrical metaphors (Tedlock 1983:109-13). The *tagi* clearly involve performers and audience in exhilarating emotions associated with formative experiences. But the events recorded by *tagi* are also actively preserved and interpreted in local discourses. The richness of the metaphorical lyrics creates vast opportunities for sense making. Local practice values the processes of reflection and interpretation, the prying of *hkano* from the spoken *ata*. In line with the ancient value placed on private knowing, there is a general reticence to revealing hard won insights regarding hidden meanings too quickly and an even greater reticence to share interpretations with outsiders. However, as we focused on *tagi* in discussions, hand written verses were recovered from safe havens, debates regarding significance ensued, and substantive details of island history emerged. Gradually it became clear that these musical compositions serve not only to recreate an ethos or collective emotional experience associated with a common past, but also offer themselves as resources too little used, but nonetheless available, to illuminate details of community roots and to interpret, influence and anticipate activities in the present.

Tagi, when originally composed, were a significant part of ongoing social commentary and negotiations (see Donner 1992; Lindstrom 1998:211). They are heteroglossic, combining disparate voices impinging on issues at stake. These secular songs were frowned upon by missionaries of the nineteenth and early twentieth centuries who found the raucous celebrations that accompanied performance violated Christian norms. In the 1970s the then influential Presbyterian Church preserved the ban imposed by their predecessors and *tagi* were rarely performed. The recent effort among Christian congregations to embrace traditional customs, to find God's Word revealed in local forms, has reversed this trend (see Orta 2004 for related discussions). In combination with the tourist trade, this Christian acceptance has allowed performers to return to their traditional musical arts to reinvigorate older styles even as they experiment with the new.

Currently opportunities in Vanuatu abound for shaping identities, registering political objectives and advocating for causes through neo-traditional venues (cf., Eisenman 1997:156; Kenzo and Associates 1992). The local populace has seized upon these conditions to explore their musical arts, reinventing performances as visual/aural experimentations in emergent causes. Celebrations of Independence, building dedications, religious holidays, even the Sabbath, are marked by the staging of customary songs. Interest in and development of indigenous arts serve to infuse local communities with pride and to distinguish indigenous peoples from outsiders (Lindstrom 1998:211; Rossen 1998:852).

For the people of West Futuna this re-emphasis gained particular credence during the 1990s as national priorities were expanded to include the recording of 'aspects of traditional cultures now known only by the oldest generation, to foster an interest in learning these customs in the younger generation, and to raise awareness at all levels of the importance and value of *kastom*' (Reganvanu 1999:98). As a result we have been able to record particular *tagi* compositions repeatedly since the seventies in diverse performance contexts.[3]

Hkai

Hkai, also known as *fesaoga*, are traditional tales, myths or allegories. *Hkai* are told as entertaining stories. They are narratives recounted in standard prose and thus subject to infinite variations and expansions. These stories may include episodes referred to as *tagihkai,* that are fixed forms set to music and sung in the process of story telling typically to depict a character's lament, but the prose of the major part of each tale unfolds in a personal rhetorical style. (For comparison see Facey 1988:22; Feinberg 1998a; Feld 1990; Firth and McLean 1990; Gifford 1924; Luomala 1955; Māhina 1992; McLean 1999; Moyle 2003.)

Multiple, perhaps unlimited, versions of these spoken narratives exist. The processes of telling and the practices of communication by which oral literature is transmitted are typically more variable than are performances of musical pieces (Bauman 1986; Lord 1982:254). Narrated versions of a tale tend to preserve characters, and primary events with their sequencing and moral import, but may vary in phrasing and details of episodes according to the style and expertise of the raconteur, the intended audience, and the setting of the narrative speech event (Brewer and Nakamura 1984; Neisser 1976, 1998). Sometimes stories are the grounds for innovations such as in adaptations to church programs, tourist performances or other events, in which case the transformed tales may grow quite significantly beyond an inspiring form (Capell 1960; Rakau pers. comm.). Sometimes, as with most stories, alternatives reflect a process of drift from one teller to another, one era to another, one moment to the next. Who learned from whom, in what setting, with what interests at stake, as well as strengths and weaknesses of memory are all reflected in contemporary tellings.

By contrast with *tagi, hkai,* recount supernatural events[4] relevant to understanding history and contemporary life. The five *hkai* printed here relate incidents associated with the genesis of the landscape, cultural knowledge and practice. As myths these narratives embody less internal dialogism than is apparent in the intertwining of voices through which events of *tagi* are staged. They recount from supernatural perspective the origins and values of customary life and remark connections among diverse Pacific peoples. A supernatural genealogy can be recovered from inter-textual comparisons. These imagined kin ties not only provide relational links for characters within a story, but connect the allegories one to another through family histories of the members of the mythical pantheon.

Hkai seem in less danger of becoming semantically opaque than *tagi*. Perhaps this is because of the inclusion of characters' names in these stories, and the familiar genealogies of the super-human beings from which the characters are drawn. Then too, *furi fesao* is an uncommon feature of these stories. The texts were not originally composed to articulate a thorny matter of the moment, but received as gifts of enduring wisdom from the super-natural. As a result direct translation is less difficult than for *tagi* even though the interpretive process is open ended and multiple versions are in circulation.

The place of *hkai* in everyday West Futuna life was summarized in a remark from Thomas and Kuautoga as 'a lively story tradition, not frequently performed today as family evening entertainment, but well remembered nonetheless' (1992:17). Indeed memories of *hkai* are strong and in recent years the genre has been pulled into the service of public as well as family arenas. Church services incorporate local narratives that convey communal values. Paji and Tamalua, the story of a fisherman who returns home to find his wife heavy with child is one example. Sermons also comment on the risks of misbehaving as evidenced in the chicanery of the ever-conniving rat of West Futuna animal tales, a popular genre we are unable to explore in this volume. Even national interests might be entertained by versions of stories like several of those to follow in which community and alliance are intertwined. Outsider interest such as my own has suggested the stories can serve to communicate local ways to foreigners. Despite or perhaps because of the supernatural authority conveyed by *hkai,* these tales are subject to dialog with external discourses, past and present. The principles they embody may serve as standards by which to judge an emerging and uncertain present (Geertz 1980:18). And yet there is more, for these compositions are readily subject to processes of (re-)accentuation in shifting contexts and for changing purposes (Goody 2000). Creative and situated transformation of the prose is part of the art of telling. As *ata* are reinvented the *hkano* implied may be reconstructed and contemporary circumstances may thus be incorporated into the texts of the genre over time.[5] We explore some of this potential in what follows.

Notes

1 Goody argues cogently against verbatim memory and yet finds reason to make exceptions for ‘short events such as proverbs and songs’ (2000:41). Rossen offers some evidence for a kind of rote memory for Bellonese songs by indicating that ‘omission of a stanza [in Bellonese musical performances] is unacceptable, as are incorrect rhythms in clapping and incorrect numbers of sequential repetitions’ (1998:830). Cognitive psychologists have effectively established schematic/thematic memory processes in human cognition. However, musical and poetic forms are often exceptional in that rote memory is made possible by virtue of a convergence of constraints enabling strict continuity in these arts over generations (Neisser 1998). The consistency in West Futuna song lyrics over almost thirty years of recorded performances constitutes a striking example.

2 Compare Luomala on Hawaiian chanting (1955:35), ‘Characters often communicate with each other through chants which outwardly describe

the rain or the sun or the ocean but inwardly convey a personal message, usually intelligible only to the composer and to the object of his devotion'.

3 Thomas and Kuautoga offer further discussion of musical genres in their published work contextualing and interpreting West Futuna recordings collected during a UNESCO sponsored Territorial Survey of Oceanic Music undertaken in 1990 (Thomas 1992; Thomas and Kuautoga 1992). They (1992:17) note that most of the stories [*tagi*] they recorded originated in the Matagi and Herald Bay [Mouga] districts of the island. However, the significance of this is unclear. In 1973, it was primarily residents of the Mouga district who organized and performed *tagi* in a late night gathering where I recorded Najeji and Tiata for the first time. However, in the narrative corpus of this volume we find each district is featured in the stories or songs we have collected at least once and islanders from Pau and Matagi figure commonly among storytellers and interpreters. Ties among raconteurs, performers, stories, songs and places of origin and enactment draw on history, biography and geography but much remains to be explained of these connections.

4 See Bonnemaison (1994), Firth (1961), Herzfeld (1982), Hill (1988), Kapferer (1988), Kuschel and Monberg (1977), LeRoy (1985); Māhina (1992); Salmond (1991); Sutton (1998) among many others for useful discussions of myth and history.

5 Firth (1961) presents a useful argument for the influence of differential interests on the part of raconteurs in the construction of different versions of Tikopia stories. And Donner notes musical genres in transformation in the performances of Sikaiana in the Solomon Islands (1992). As English language versions of several *hkai* have been recorded (Capell 1960; Gunn 1903, 1914, 1924; Ray 1901), comparative analysis of these with more current translations derived from recordings made between 1970 and 2001 by us may be a place to start to investigate patterns of change. Documentation of the ongoing use of traditional tales as inspiration for novel forms is the next step.

5

Ta Pasiesi ma Majihjiki[1] / The Monster and Majihjiki

This story develops from a threat to the landed identity and very existence of the people of West Futuna. This threat takes the form of a wicked monster, *ta pasiesi*, who sets out to devour the human inhabitants of the island in order to have the land for himself. As the monster goes from village to village, destroying homes and eating people, he saves two children from each original community, a boy and a girl. These youngsters he takes home where he secludes and feeds them in anticipation of future meals. While *ta pasiesi* continues his destruction, the children come to forget the trauma of their capture and ignore their present confinement. They receive new children as playmates and appear content in their fine abode to play together and be fed. The children even come to respect and honor their captor, who provides for them and they come to believe that he is their grandfather.

Majihjiki, a culture hero much loved by the people of West Futuna, observes the evil doings and takes action to return the island to a place teeming with people and social interchange. He outwits the monster by appearing as a child himself and *ta pasiesi* sends him to join the others. Majihjiki convinces the imprisoned youngsters of their true plight and leads them in an escape. A lengthy chase ensues involving a series of escapades during which the monster and hero display their magical prowess competitively. The children cannot hide from their evil pursuer for he has a supernatural ability to find them anywhere. By doubling over, he exposes his buttocks and uses this part of his body as a compass to point him unerringly in the direction of his fleeing prey. So Majihjiki encourages the children to work as a team[2] to keep the evil one at bay. Typically they use mounds of food as a distraction. At one point they disguise themselves as the seeds of a breadfruit. Majihjiki joins the children as the fruit's central core. *Ta pasiesi* attracted by the enormous size of the fruit decides to cook and eat it only to be frustrated by the hidden children urinating in unison on the fire to extinguish it (see similar elements in Elbert and Monberg 1965:132; Monberg 1991:105). Forced to seek dry firewood the monster disappears and everyone escapes. In this and other episodes it is the monster's greedy and gluttonous nature, repeatedly displayed, that allows Majihjiki and the children to prevail.[3]

In the end the monster falls to his death, tricked as he attempts to reach his intended victims high in the branches of a tree. Afraid their pursuer may be faking, the children send various animals to disturb the corpse until, after seeing no response time and again, they come to accept his death. The young ones descend from the branches and Majihjiki sends them two by two back to their original villages to resettle in their proper places around the island of West Futuna.

Background and Connections

I initially recorded this story as told by Popoina Magau in 1973. Popoina and I transcribed and translated that version together. Subsequently I heard the story several times and in 1999 formally recorded another version recounted by Takaronga. Takaronga and I transcribed and translated his telling collaboratively. These two primary recorded versions of *Ta Pasiesi ma Majihjiki* are similar thematically although particulars of narrative episodes vary. The final published version is based upon Takaronga's oral performance as expanded by him in subsequent editing. The most noticeable differences among the versions are their relative lengths and variation in the way one theme, the evils of gluttony, is made apparent.

Capell published a version of this allegory as told to him by Charlie Nimoho of West Futuna. (1960:19-36). The Reverend William Gunn, medical missionary of the United Free Church of Scotland in West Futuna from 1883 to 1917, published a version in 1903. A letter, written on 24 December 1891, to Gunn from the Reverend William Gray, resident missionary on Tanna, refers to a version of this story that must have been relayed earlier to him by Gunn. Gray indicates in his letter that a similar story was being told on Tanna in the late nineteenth century. In 1901, Sidney Ray published both Gunn's version as it later appeared in the *New Hebrides Magazine* (Gunn 1903) and Gray's story from Tanna.[4] These dates and references to *Ta Pasiesi ma Majihjiki* indicate that the story has been popular in southern Vanuatu at least since the late nineteenth century.

Majihjiki is a hero well known in Pacific, most especially Polynesian, lore (e.g., Anderson 1995 [1928]; Bonnemaison 1994; Capell 1960; Elbert and Monberg 1965; Gifford 1924; Gunn 1914; Luomala 1955; Feinberg 1998a; Firth 1961; Monberg 1991; Moyle 2003; Rice 1971 [1923]). Typically, Majihjiki, known elsewhere as Maui, Mauitikitiki and by cognate constructions, is 'an ugly misbirth cast away by his' parents, but survives to become a hero, perhaps half-man half-god, with the supernatural powers of a changling (Luomala 1955:85, Feinberg 1998a:19, 30). He is often, although not always, the youngest of several brothers (Feinberg 1998a:19, 30)[5] and usually has one sister, Sina or Hina. I have not heard Majihjiki's birth recounted on West Futuna, but his sister, Sina, is a familiar member of the supernatural pantheon here as elsewhere.

The people of West Futuna tell at least one Majihjiki story that is commonly told throughout Polynesia. The theme is the origin of the island and its relationship to other places. There are many versions, but all involve Majihjiki using a rope or fishing line to pull islands into position. Sometimes his object is to bring

West Futuna up from the ocean's depths. In related tales he aims to pull neighboring islands, including Fiji, closer to West Futuna. In this latter tale the rope snaps leaving evidence of his attempt in a row of stones representing the broken cord (Capell 1960:25; Gunn 1914:217). This tale of Majihjiki's fishing exploits are not the only West Futuna origin myth but part of an array of familiar creation stories.[6]

Like the origin stories *Ta Pasiesi ma Majihjiki* is a great myth (Bonnemaison 1994) encompassing the entire island and its populace. It is a story we find seldom documented in repertoires of other Pacific lore. Beyond the versions from southern Vanuatu the only tale we identified with similar thematic developments is told on the Polynesian outlier of Bellona.[7] Among West Futuna residents, people of Pau seem most inclined to tell the story and Takaronga, who is from that village, considers this allegory to be a rightful part of his family heritage. It is one that was told to him by his great-grandfather, Breisa, a skillful narrator who would entertain the family in evenings with the tale. Takaronga worked in polishing this myth to retain the structure of episodes as he recalled they were related to him and to convey the humor, terror and vitality of characters and events. We translated the story together and I later presented Takaronga with written versions that he edited meticulously, each time adding details and rephrasing to craft the final product.

Several problematic issues that arose during translation are noted in the second chapter. Not mentioned there was the difficulty we encountered in translating the monster's bizarre method of searching for the runaway children. One of *pasiesi's* signature traits is the ability to turn into a compass. The monster doubles over (*fakatulele*), achieving a position that allows him to circle with his rear-end upward. As he slowly turns around the monster opens his buttocks (*farakohi*), points his bottom either toward the horizon, or straight up, and waits for his rectum to turn red and project outward like an arrow designating precisely the location of the escaping children. This bizarre magical feat insures that no one can long avoid detection.

In a version of this same tale from Tanna the monster is said to run, head down, in various directions until 'he feels it hot' (Ray 1901:149) at which point he knows he's going the right way. In the early published versions from West Futuna no explicit mention of the monster's method of seeking others appears (Ray 1901, Capell 1960). In the version I collected in 1973, Popoina speaks somewhat euphemistically, ... *neisara ta hne uai raro. Pe roura, rohmea kaie aia koiroa* ..., '... he searches with that place down below. If it turns red, if it reddens then he knows ...' Takaronga is more direct, ... *kofakatulele nohfarakohi nofori nanoa i ta mrae*. '... (he) bent over, opened his buttocks and circled round within the village.'

The passages in which the monster employs this outlandish behavior create shared mirth for audience and narrator alike. The behavior itself is humorous as is the implied comparison with western compasses. Translation of this practice for foreign readers, however, posed a challenge. While the monster's behavior in local eyes is quite outlandish it is not obscene. We found it difficult to recreate the proper ambiance associated with this act. Ultimately we resorted to a parenthetical description. This inevitably falls short of the original prose where brief mention is sufficient for listeners to imagine a ludicrous scene tinged with overtones of fear.

Cultural Geography and Direction

Figure 11 locates the places entailed in *Ta Pasiesi ma Majihjiki* and illustrates the directions in which primary actions develop. *Ta pasiesi* initially surveys the land deciding to destroy the villagers. He starts his decimation in Pau and moves to the left as one faces the central plateau, going around the island village by village to carry out his misdeeds. This directional progress portends the dire consequences fulfilled by his destructive acts. Later in the story as the children escape, they travel in the opposing, and more auspicious, counterclockwise direction as described

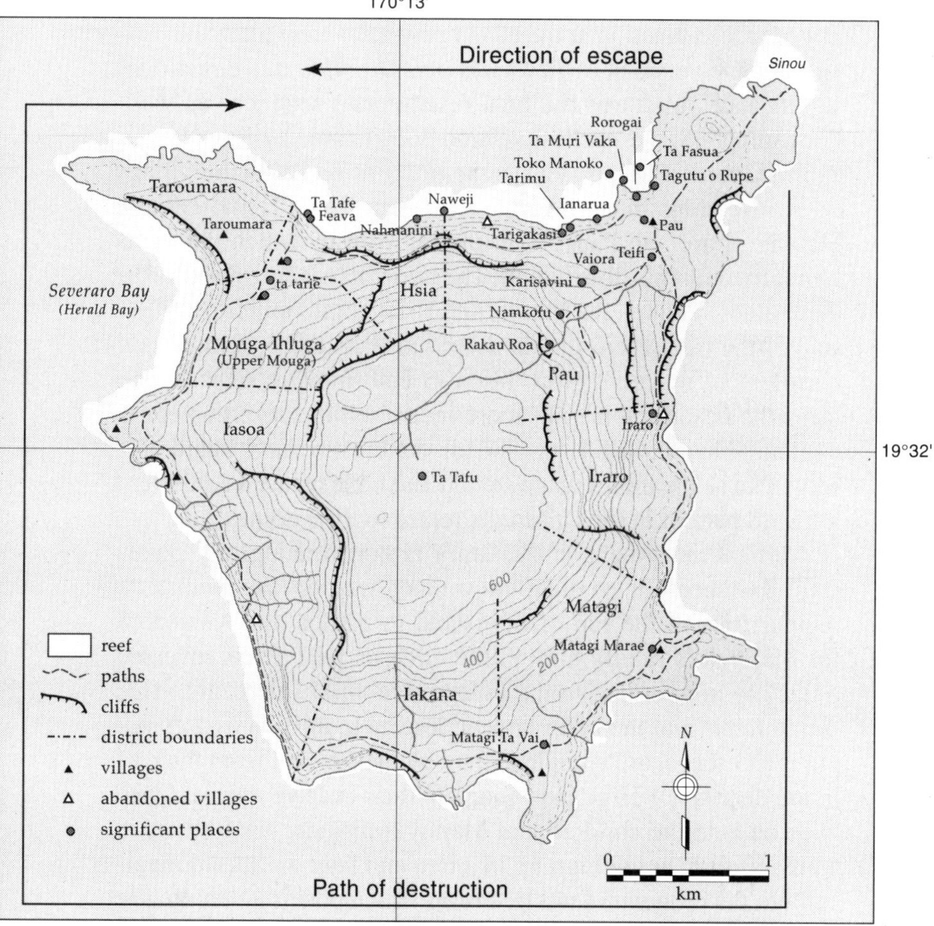

Figure 11: The cultural geography and significance of direction in *Ta Pasiesi ma Majihjiki*.

from a bird's-eye view with north at the top, or rightward determined from a position at the island perimeter and facing the center. In some versions of *Ta Pasiesi ma Majihjiki* this directional significance structures the final resettlement sequence as well. For example, in the earliest version documented by Ray (1901), and in Gunn's version (1903), the order of return to the villages is auspicious in its trajectory (Mouga, Hsia, Iasoa, Iakana, Matangi, Iraro and Pau), inverting the path by which the monster carried out his destruction. The two villages first resettled in these older versions are Mouga and Hsia, communities on either side of the tree where the monster was dispatched. Subsequent resettlement proceeds from Iasoa to Pau, moving right as one faces the island interior. In more recent tellings resettlement is a bit more haphazard. However, all versions we have heard preserve Pau as the final village settled and none create a consistent leftward pattern in the children's return to their homes.

Vertical movement in this story is not meaningfully polarized. Instances of vertical movement include the monster's regular trips to the top of the island to garden and his search for Majihjiki's family high in the cliffs as well as his reversed trajectory in returning to the village. Majihjiki's descent to free the children, and their subsequent descent to the reef as they begin their escape, are complemented by their ascent from the reef to the districts of Hsia and Mouga in their evasive moves. Once back on land the children and Majihjiki disguise themselves in a breadfruit hanging high up in a tree and later are raised magically to the crown of a nut tree from which position they finally defeat the monster, pulling him up and letting him fall to his death.[8] Neither ascent nor descent seems to have uniformly valued consequences. This lack of consistent symbolic associations with vertical orientations is discussed in the final chapter.

Ta Pasiesi ma Majihjiki evokes throughout a circular or spherical geography. The primary verb for referring to travel along the island coast or on the paths connecting villages is *fori* 'to go around', a verb which is used repeatedly in this tale.

The monster moves serially to each village going around the volcanic cone as he progresses in his path of destruction. He frequently describes his forays to the children using the verb, *fori*. In addition when the monster seeks the fleeing children he circles (*fori*) about until he identifies the direction they have taken. Resettlement resulting in the proper placement of people in villages around the island circumference is the overt object of the narrative and the story in this regard involves the entire populace and a complete circuit of the island.

This geometry is reinforced metaphorically in several episodes. Initially the children are confined to a chiefly residence that is most likely hemispherical in its shape reflecting traditional architectural design perhaps as depicted in Figure 12 (see also Capell 1958). The monster secures the children in the house by removing his diaphragm and stretching it over the arched house posts.[9] The image evoked here is of a half circle tightly wrapped in the membranous material. The subsequent breadfruit episode relies on the imagery of the spherical fruit shown in Figure 13 in which the children are directed to disguise themselves as seeds, while Majihjiki becomes the inner core. The imagery of this episode is transparent if one cuts a breadfruit in half. For the distribution of seeds around the central core can be seen to recreate the circular distribution of island villages and their districts surrounding the central plateau as shown in Figures 4 and 11.

Cultural Geography and the Body

The monster's outlandish transformation of his buttocks into a compass is another metaphor that may take the island's geography as its source. If so, the symbolism here is complex. In doubling over the monster shapes his body into a form reminiscent of the outlines of the hemispherical island. As he circles, the vectors radiating from his center recall district boundaries radiating from the island's tableland. It is as though the monster's body in this posture alludes to the potential for inverting the physical and social order of the land. His postural inversion grotesquely transforms

Figure 12: Hemispherical house frame, Matagi. Janet Dixon Keller 1987.

male sexuality as though proposing a subversive alternative oriented to destruction of life rather than procreation. The ultimate transformation envisioned by *ta pasiesi* would establish his own pre-eminence as an isolated, controlling being, whose destiny is achieved by capturing and destroying children. Such acts stand diametrically opposed to human valuing of procreation and social interdependence. As long as the monster reigns, his bizarre habit persists as a symbol of the risks of individualism and nonconformity to human social formations and the very continuity of life. With his demise the land and its populace can return to original order, youths are resettled in gendered pairs, domesticity and procreation re-emerge and the reproduction of society and the populace can proceed.

Cultural Geography and Place

The circular geography is punctuated by places identified in the narrative. Events are situated at well-known sites providing a framework for the unfolding tale. Simultaneously the places themselves are imbued with mythical significance. Narrator and audience envision landmarks and emplaced actions as a tale is told. In turn, during daily life as people pass one locale or another named in the story they may recall events and connect their experience with aspects of the tale. These links between narrative and place provide a deep sense of belonging, a sense of connection with a landscape in which past and present are interlocked.

For example, Majihjiki is associated in the present story with the village and district of Pau, with a specific place in the cliffs above Pau, Karisavini, and with Ta Faga Majihjiki, a boulder on a pathway leading to the central plateau from Pau. *Ta pasiesi* is associated with Kamkaveni at the edge of the Pau *marae*

Figure 13: Breadfruits roasting on a fire. William R. Dougherty 1973

where the *fare ariki* was located, and with his gardening place in Namkofu high on the plateau. Eventful happenings are memorialized in the many places such as Ta Fasua, the point of origin for the children's escape route photographed in Figure 14, and Tagutu o Rupe, the cliff from which the monster first spies his escaped prey and where people today often stand to watch ships approach. The *tarie* tree, too, where *ta pasiesi* met his demise still stands where the districts of Hsia and Mouga join marking the children's victory. Such associations have become part of the many significances enriching local senses of ancestry for which places on West Futuna are constant mnemonics.

Ta Pasiesi ma Majihjiki also recounts the genesis of numerous landmarks. One of the obstacles created to foil the evil ogre

Figure 14: Ta Fasua. Janet Dixon Keller 1998.

Figure 15: Ianarua located on the northeastern shore of West Futuna.
William R. Dougherty 1973.

is the fringing reef along the island's northern shore. After rounding Rorogai to approach Ianarua, photographed in Figure 15, the children's path ahead was sandy beach. 'There was no reef.' Majihjiki, by his supernatural powers, called forth corals and rocks to cover the sand in the wake of the children's escape route impeding the monster's pursuit. Reciprocally as the children progressed in their flight, *ta pasiesi* conjured up blockades: a series of rock and cliff formations jutting out into the sea. Ta Muri Vaka (Stern of the Canoe), and promontories at Tarimu and Naweji, are among these. Majihjiki inevitably split these cliffs apart to allow the children to pass. The hero's actions transformed the monster's obstacles into pathways and left permanent traces of the story's adventures in reef and rock formations on land and at sea. In this way the episodes of escape create the physical manifestation of the reef along the north shore and appoint it with reminders of the supernatural mythology embodied in this tale.

Confinement and Freedom

A tension between confinement and freedom is noted by Kirtley (1971) as prominent in Polynesian oral literature. In *Ta Pasiesi and Majihjiki* confinement and freedom are juxtaposed in a constant dynamic out of which the story's episodes develop. As the monster proceeds in his destruction he captures children and sequesters them. The children, unaware of designs to fatten and consume them, appreciate the monster's nurturing care. Well-fed while confined the children appear content. But Majihjiki rebels at their confinement. He has witnessed the slaughter at the hands of *ta pasiesi* and determines to free the children to fill the land again with the joys, responsibilities and richness of everyday interactions.

Once the children have been freed from their prison, the tale recounts the dynamics of their escape. Again and again the monster creates obstacles intended to stop the children's flight in order that he may consume them. Majihjiki foils the ogre's evil designs repeatedly, eliminating barricades and advising the children against dallying to feast on tempting foods put in their path. Ultimately, it becomes clear that the children's goal must be to recreate the conditions under which their customary life-ways can flourish. Toward this end the monster must be dispatched. His demise allows the children to resettle the island and regain control over their circumstances. The population can multiply, sharing and exchanging with one another around the perimeter in the customary manner that creates fulfillment.

Gluttony and Conservation as Narrative Motifs

Ta pasiesi is a monster or ogre described as enormous and often strikingly colored green or red. His name is said to mean, 'a strong god with a big mouth' (Nimoho cited in Capell 1960:26). His size, appearance and bizarre behaviors are intimidating and give him powers to be feared. His desire to live alone and have the land to himself is unnatural and reprehensible, but perhaps his most anti-social trait is gluttony.

Ta pasiesi is always hungry. He destroys people to satisfy his hunger. He imprisons children in anticipation of later feasting. As this story progresses and the children escape, the monster tries to distract them by conjuring up desirable foods: mackerel, red snapper, garfish and sprouted coconuts. He hopes the children will feast and become sluggish, giving him time to catch up to them. But this is not to be, for Majihjiki repeatedly convinces the children to take just a small portion, just one item and proceed on their way. They leave piles of food behind them which, in turn, local commentators suggest, distract the monster himself as he approaches, giving the children time to get farther away and providing time for them to plan with Majihjiki for the monster's demise. In Popoina's version of this tale it is Majihjiki who creates the primary diversions by conjuring heaps of fish or coconuts to distract the monster into wasting time gobbling the food. In that version Majihjiki, having magically created piles of food, again allows the children to take just one each of the delectables before continuing their flight.

Whichever way the episodes develop, gluttony is negatively contrasted with moderation. In both Popoina's and Takaronga's versions of *Ta Pasiesi ma Majihjiki*, it is the monster's insatiable appetite that leads him to attempt to cook the enormous breadfruit in which the children are hidden and drives him to seek a way subsequently to reach the treetop where the children await him. This insatiable hunger, exploited by Majihjiki's ingenuity and social sensibility, is responsible for the monster's demise. The children's victory is a triumph of customary restraint over self-indulgence, a value that will serve them well in rebuilding society.

Ta Pasiesi ma Majihjiki

Tasi a nopogi i tuai nonofo ta pasiesi i Pau i a Kamkaveni. Nopoginei notukua pe ta nohnea nipura niu i a Situ ma Meiri Matua i Pau. Nonofo i ta nohnea tenei, ta foi pasiesi, neipena ta foi fare sore i kora, ta fare ariki.

Kai eia ninofo nofo komanatunea sohkoia pe kaitaia tagata kapuni kai sohkoia kainofo i ta fanua. Tasi a nopogi eia kofakea taia fakai i Pau. Neitaia. Neitaia neikaina, kaina, kaina, kaina kopuni a fakai i ta pito fanua i Pau. Kai eia kainagkea tasi a tama ta tane ma ta fine. Eia koiamoa kiraua neinage tiona mrae, i ta fareriki. Eia nofiji norovere i Namkofu. Ta nia fanua novere i ta foi pasiesi i Namkofu.

The Monster and Majihjiki

One day long ago there lived a monster in Pau at Kamkaveni. Today it is said that this is the place where Situ and Meiri Matua planted coconuts in Pau. He lived in this place, the horrid monster did, and built a big house there, a chiefly residence.

He lived here for some time when he thought to himself that he should kill everyone so he alone would occupy the land. One day he set out to kill the people of Pau. He killed them. He killed them and ate them, eating and eating and eating until he had consumed everyone in the district of Pau. But he put aside one boy and one girl. He took them and put them in his home, the chiefly house. Then

Tasi a nopogi kai aia kofakea i Pau ma fano ki Iraro. Eia nifano ki Iraro neitaia koikaina fakai Iraro. Neitaia koikaina kaina kohpuni.

Kai eia kainagkea tasi a tama ta tane ma ta fine. Neiamoa kiraua komeinage ma rutama erua nimeinage oji i Pau i tiona mrae. Akirea nohnofo nofo kai eia nifano norovere i Namkofu. Novere noamo-kai nomeifojia i a gatamanei.

5. Tasi a nopogi eia kafano foki ki Matagi. Eia nifano ki Matagi koipen ta penaganea tasi ana. Neitaia a fakai i ai. Neikaina kopuni. Kai aia koiamkea te tasi a tama ta tane ma ta fine koiarafia koromai ki Pau komeinagkage i a gatama ta mrae.

A gatama nigkonalupai i tiona mrae. Ta kanieni e sorekage i akirea. Eia nonofo nokovere i Namkofu noamo-kai nomeitanoa neifojia agatamanei.

he ascended to garden at Namkofu. The bit of land where this monster gardened is Namkofu.

One day he set out from Pau to go to Iraro (Place Below). He went to Iraro where he killed and consumed everyone of Iraro. He killed the people of Iraro, eating and eating until they were all gone.

However, he put aside one boy and one girl. He took them to put them with the two children, the two he had already put in his house at Pau. They all stayed together just living while he would go to garden at Namkofu. He gardened and harvested food to bring to feed these children.

5. One day he decided to go to the Matagi area. He went to Matagi (Windy Place) to do the same thing. He killed the people there. He ate them all. Except, he took out one boy and one girl child to take back to Pau to sequester with the children in the village.

The children were now many in his home. Their love for him was great. He lived by gardening at Namkofu to harvest food and busy himself feeding the children.

Tasi a nopogi kai eia kotu pe, 'Avau kefano foki manara uai ta tafa fanua.'

U aia kofakea kofano ki Matagi – Ta Koga Fanua ma i Marae ma i Ta Vai ma. Neitaia a fakai i ai. Neikaina, kaina, kaina kopuni. Kotoekea ana tasi a tama ta tane ma tasi ta hfine kaiamoa kiraua koafemai ki Pau. Kirea nohnofo kai ta foi pasiesi nopena kai noifojia gatamanei.

A gatamanei nikokanieni hmafi i a tupunorea. E rufie tapu iana penaganea. Neifojia kirea segapu i a nopogi ma nopogi. A gatama nikonalupai ta mrae ta kanieni i a kirea nikosorekage. Nikomari pe eia ta fakausore i ta mrae. Nikotapa kirea pe a tupunorea i ta foi pasiesi. Kirea nokanieni pe a tupunaorea e rufie iana penaganea i taimatakina fakarufie kirea.

10. Ta foi pasiesi nonofo ma gafatumupuna noitataria kotuaikea. Kai aia keitu pe, 'E rufie pe avau kaforikage uai Matagi ma

One day he (the monster) said, 'I'm going out again before all else to the other side of the island.'

And so he set out to go to Matagi – to Ta Koga Fanua (The Strip of Land) between Marae (The Center) and Ta Vai (The Water) this time. He killed the people there. He devoured them, eating and eating until everyone was gone. There remained only a young boy and a girl for him to bring back to Pau. They all lived together and the monster prepared food and fed the children.

The children came to love their grandfather very much. His ways were exceptionally kindly. He fed them without fail day after day. The children in the village had become numerous and their affection for him was considerable. Truly this man was the grandfather of the place. They called him their grandfather, that horrid monster. They were all happy that their grandfather's ways were kind in caring for them so well.

10. The evil monster lived with his grandchildren, biding his time for a long while. Then he said, 'Its time for me to go

i Iakana ma.'

Tasi anopogi kai ta foi pasiesi keitukage i a gatama pe, 'Gafatumupuku, akoua kahnofo pera i ta mrae, kai avau kaforikage mana uai Matagi ma i Iakana ma karoasikea mana kaisaafemai.'

'E rufie pua, kimea kahnofo pera i ta mrae kapena kai kakaina nohtari i a takoe.'

Tasi anopogi ta foi pasiesi kofano ki Matagi ma i Iakana. Neitautaria a mrae oji i ai neitaia a tagata neikaina. Neitaia tagata i ai neikaina. Kaina, kaina, kaina, kaina, kaina kopuni. Kai aia koamo tasi a tama ta tane kai tasi ta fine koafe-mai ki Pau kaminagkage ma a gatama nei i tano mrae.

Ta kanieni akirea nigkosore hmafi pe anofajaga oji kaie a tupunorea neiarafiamai a gatama jiki rua ki ta mrae orea kameinofo kirea. Kirea nohnofo kai ta foi pasiesi nofiji norovere i Namkofu. Eia rovere vere roafiafi kai aia koamo-kai, a taro ma fuji toga ma kairei ma rei ma a kai oji neipura i a vere iana i ai. Neifakina kaminage i tamrae

around through Matagi to Iakana and surrounds.'

That day the monster said to his grandchildren, 'Grandchildren, all of you should stay like this in the house, while I go round past Matagi to Iakana and its surrounds to work the gardens there before I return.'

'Okay, grandparent, we'll stay here in the house and prepare meals to eat while we wait for you.'

That day the monster set out for Matagi and Iakana. He destroyed every home in the area and killed the people and devoured them. He killed people there and he ate them. He ate and ate and ate and ate and ate until everyone was gone. Then he took a boy and a girl and returned to Pau to put them away with the other children in his house.

The affection of the children increased because all the time their grandfather would lead children two at a time to their place to live with them. They all just passed the time while the one and only monster ascended to garden at Namkofu. He would garden until evening and then he would collect food, taro and bananas and roots and kamipena kai i a gatamanei.

sweet potatoes and every kind of food he had planted in his gardens there. He harvested it all to store at home to prepare meals for the children.

15. Eia konofo nofo kohtuai htuaikea. Tasi a nopogi kai aia kofakea i Pau koforikage uai Iasoa. Eia nifano neitautaria oji a fare, jiki tasi o fakai Iasoa nihpuni. Neitaia koikaina oji kohpuni kai aia koamkea tasi a tane ma ta fine. Kiratou koafemai ki Pau pe kameisireia a gatama i ta mrae. Ta pasiesi noimatakina ano gafatumupuna. Nopena kai, nokai, nohnofo.

15. The monster kept on like that for a long, long time. One day he set out from Pau to go round to Iasoa. He went and destroyed all the homes – every house of the people of Iasoa was gone. He killed everyone and ate them all until no one was left but one boy and one girl he had reserved. The three of them returned to Pau to see the children in the village. The monster took care of his grandchildren. They prepared food, ate and so they lived.

Akirea pe hnofo hnofokage kai eia koitukage i ano gafatumupuna pe, ‘Akoua nei kunei gafatumupuku. Avau kafenagemana uai Mouga ma karoasikea mana kai saafe mai.’

They all lived on and on and on like that until he said to his grandchildren, ‘You all stay here my grandchildren. I will go over to Mouga where I will garden awhile before I return.’

‘E rufie pua, akimea kahnofo pera i ta mrae kahtari i atakoe.’

‘Okay grandfather, we’ll stay like this in our place and wait for you.’

Ta pasiesi kafakea kofano ki Mouga karoitaia a fakai i ai. Eia neitautaria oji nihpuni a fare i Mouga. Neitaia neikaina a tagata nihpuni kai aia koiamkea ji tama tane ma ji fine. Kiratou

The monster set off going to Mouga to slaughter the people there. He destroyed everything wiping out every house in Mouga. He killed everyone and ate them all but he kept one boy koafemai ki Pau. Kiratou nimeirako i Tanagi koragona a gatama nohkulihkuli nokavau i ta mrae.

‘Akaima ena?’ rutama nifakauia ta foi pasiesi.

20. ‘A gafatumupuku ena kitatou karosireia kirea.’

Kiraua nikanieni mafi. Akiratou nirako ta mrae ta kanieni i a gatama nisorekage. Nohvaro noturituri ta mare.

Kirea nihnofo hnofokage kohtuai htuaikea kai ta foi pasiesi koitukage iano gafatumupuna pe, ‘Akoua neikunei kai avau koforikagemana uai Hsia ma karoasikea mana.’

Akirea kotukage pe, ‘Pua, e rufie. Akimea kafetakaro kahtari pera i atakoe ta mrae.’

Ta foi pasiesi kofakea kofano ki i Hsia ma i Taroumara. Korofasi i Hsia. Taia fakai i ai. Nifano ki Taroumara nitaia fakai i ai. Neikaina nihpuni sa, nitoekeana tasi a tama tane ma ta hfine i Hsia ma i Taroumara. Eia neiarafia kirea koafemai ki Pau, tiona mrae. A gatama noinage i ai.

and one girl. The three of them returned to Pau. When they reached Tanagi they could hear the children playing and making noise in the village.

‘Who are they?’ the two children asked the ogre.

20. ‘Those are my grandchildren who we will go to visit.’

The two children were excited. When the three reached the house the others were really pleased. They shouted and ran around the place.

They all remained, dwelling there for a long, long time until the ogre said to his grandchildren, ‘You all stay here while I circle round first to Hsia and garden a bit there.’

They all replied, ‘Grandfather, Okay. We’ll play around here in the house and wait like this for you at home.’

The ogre departed to go to Hsia and Taroumara. He destroyed Hsia. He killed the people there. He went to Taroumara and killed the people there. He ate every single one, until there remained only one boy and one girl from Hsia and also from Taroumara. He led them back to Pau, his place. He

25. Romai ta retu noragona ta hvaro ma ta vakuli i a gatama ta mrae. Kirea foki nikanieni hmafi pe kirea karofapa ma gatama ta mrae. Nirako kirea ta mrae gatama oji niromai nomeihtau i a tupunorea. Notapa ekirea pe, 'Pua, pua, akoe nikomeirako?'

'Ho, nankarafiamai foki enei pe akoua kameihnofo i ta mrae. Kamatakina ta marae otea.'

Pasiesi ma gatama nohnofo. Kai eia nofiji norovere i Namkofu. Eia novere vere roafiafi kai eia koamo-kai kotomai. Neifakainamai marea kai ma toro ma a ne papura i ai. Neiamoa kameiavage a toro ki a gatama nonoua kirea kai eia nopena kai marea kakaina ti afiafi. Kirea nohnofo sohkirea ana i ta fanua. A tagata oji nipuni. Neikaina nifori ta fanua nipuni sa. Jikai foki tasi. Ninofo soko gatama rihriki ana ma tupunorea ta foi pasiesi.

put the children there.

25. Approaching by the path they could hear the shouts and sounds of the children playing in the house. They also (the children from Hsia and Taroumara) wanted very much to be with the others in the village. They reached the house and all the children crowded close round their grandfather. They called to him, 'Grandpa, Grandpa, you've arrived?'

'Yes, and I brought these (children) so you all can stay in the house. We'll take care of our place.'

The monster and the children stayed together. The ogre would ascend to garden at Namkofu. He gardened hard until evening and then he collected the food and descended. He fed them the food including sugarcane and the things he planted there. He brought sugarcane to give to the children to chew on while he fixed food for them to eat in the evening. They lived thusly by themselves on the island. Everyone else was gone. He had eaten the people all around the island, everyone, everywhere. No one remained. There were only the little children and their

Nopogi ma nopogi kirea nohnofo, kai ta foi pasiesi tiana fijikauga ta fiji norovere i Namkofu. Afiafi eia koamo-kai kofemai nomeimatakina iano gafatumupuna.

Tasi a nopogi eia niviri ta pohpo pena kai koinage ma gafatupuna. Kai eia koitukage i a kirea pe, 'Akai aua e nohtau i farena. Avau konofenake mana uai Namkofu ma karovere matea. Koua kafetakaro pera ta mrae otea kahtari.'

30. 'Ho, e rufie pua, kimea kafetakaro pera i ta mrae.' A gatama nioriage pera i ateia.

Ta foi pasiesi kofakea kofano ki ta vere. Fenake ki Teifi ma karofenake foki Karisavini kai katea tasi a tama sisi nopuku neitara ta toki ona i ta faga i ta retu sore. Ta faganei ta fatu notukua ta noigoa ta Faga Majihjiki. Ta tamanei eia Majihjiki. Eia notara toki kai ta Pasiesi komeifenake seifarigoina ma pe eia akai.

Eia neitukage pe, 'Tumupuku, e gaugau ki ta fanua. Kai akoe nifakei?'

grandfather, the evil monster.

Day after day they stayed together, and the monster's work was to ascend to garden at Namkofu. Evenings he gathered the food to return to care for his grandchildren.

One day he awoke very early to make food to leave for his grandchildren. He said to them, 'Your food is hanging here in the house. I am going first to Namkofu to garden for us. You all play about as you do in our place and wait.'

30. 'Okay, that's fine Grandpa, we'll play around here.' The children answered him thus.

The monster left and went to the garden. He went up to Teifi and from there up to Karisavini where he saw a small child sitting and sharpening his ax at a sharpening stone in the main path. This stone was a boulder known as Ta Faga Majihjiki (The Sharpening Stone of Majihjiki). This child was Majihjiki. Hc was sharpening his ax and the monster came upon him having no idea who he might be.

The monster said to him, 'My grandchild, the island is empty. Where did you come from?'

Majihjiki koitukange pe, 'Akimea ma pua ma nohnofo i a Foropaki kake uai Rakau Roana ma.'

Ta pasiesi neifakauia eia pe, 'Koe nofenage uafe?'

35. 'Vau nohsara gatama pe kimea ka fetakaro,' Majihjiki neitukage ta Pasiesi.

Ta pasiesi neioria, neitukage penei, 'Sefanifo akoe uai marae. Kafanifo akoe karofakea Tagafunamea kourogona a gatama nokulihkuli, novakina i marae. A gatama e fonu. Pe akoe nokanieni toifo kofano ki marae korousireia kirea.'

Majihjiki neitukage pe, 'Pua, e rufie. Avau nokanieni i a gatama pe kimea karofetakaro. Avau nofetakaro sohkovaukage ana.'

Ta pasiesi kofiji ki Namkofu karovere kaia a Majihjiki kotoifo kofano ki marae. Nifanifo i Tagafunamea. A gatamara nohvaro i ta mrae. A gatamanei nohvaro i tamrae. E sorekage ta kanieni i a kirea.

Ta foi pasiesi neitaoa ta fare. Neinage a gatamanei i ai. Anofajaga eia rokea i ta mrae kaie neiamkea tano maskaro neiputogi ta farenei te pe

Majihjiki replied, 'We all including my elder kin and everyone live at Foropaki up by Rakau Roa and that area.'

Then the monster asked him, 'Where are you going?'

35. 'I'm looking for children to play with,' Majihjiki said to the ogre.

The ogre replied, speaking like this, 'Go down to the big clearing. You'll go down and emerge at Tagafunamea to hear children playing, calling out from the sacred clearing. There are plenty of children. If you want to go down and go to the clearing you'll find them all.'

Majihjiki said, 'Grandfather, that's great. I do yearn for other children so that we can play. I'm always playing all by myself.'

So the monster ascended to Namkofu to garden while Majihjiki went down to the clearing. He went to Tagafunamea. The children were yelling from the house. These children were hollering inside the house. Their joy was great.

The incredible monster had built the house. He put these children there. At those times when he would go out of the house he would grasp his own kataruia a gatamanei serorukea. Ta lok tera.

diaphragm to stretch over the house making it impossible for the children to leave. It was a lock.

40. Majihjiki kotoifo. Kofanifo korofori ta mrae. Nirofori ta fare. Norofori ta fare nofori fakarua fakatoru.

40. Majihjiki began to descend. He went down going to circle the area. He circled the house. He went around the house, circling twice, three times.

Majihjiki neitapana a gatama pe, 'A gatamanei, aha nopena akoua i farena?'

A gatamanei nioria kotukage pe, 'Akoe, akai te nofesao fafona? Akimea nohtari i a tupunomea. Nifano karovere kaiahmai mamea a kai ma toro ma … Kai akoe akai tena notapa fafona? Fakea akoe.'

Majihjiki called to the children, 'Children here, what are you doing in that house?'

Those children responded to him, 'You, who is it who speaks outside there? We are waiting for our grandparent. He went to garden and will bring food for us including sugar cane and other things. So who are you to call us from outside? Go away you.'

Majihjiki neioria neitukage pe, 'Akoua notahri tupunaoua niroamoa kai ma toro ma kaifojia koua pe kahsore saikaina!'

Majihjiki answered, 'You all await your elder kinsman who has gone to fetch food and sugar cane to feed you so you will grow big enough for him to eat!'

'Kaikaina koua feipe i a vehtamanoua ma vehjinanoua neikaina oji kopuni. Neiahmai akoua kamenage kunei koimatakina koua kahsore. Kai seikaina foki akoua.'

'He will eat all of you just like he ate your fathers and mothers who are now gone. He brought you all to house here where he could care for you all so you would grow to be big. Then he'll devour you all too.'

45. A gatamanei kotataruana. Ta mataku ma htagi akirea nisore. Nohtagi. Nohgege ta hmate. Akirea kanieni pe kamauri. Akirea nohtagi.

Notu pe, 'akimea karukea pekua? E hpono ta fare.'

Majihjiki neioriage, 'Pe akoua nokanieni ta mauri kai akoua kaisohtagi kaie hnofo fakaparapari i fare. Avau kanfasia ta fare kai akitea kafura.'

'Ho, kausitokina kimea. Akimea koromari nohnofo sohkimea i omea fakausore nipuni oji.' Kirea nioriage i a teia pera.

Majihjiki neiamkea ta toki ona neijikijia ki hluga kofesaokage i ai pe, 'Avau a Majihjiki nokanieni pe kanfakapopoiage ta farena kamavaekea karukea agatama uai ta farena.'

50. Neiakona taisaua ta fare, kai ta fare komavaekea kai a gatamanei konorukea.

'Auei, akoe tane nifakea uafe uakoe kohmai komisitokina kimea?'

Majihjiki saitukage i a kirea pe, 'Au nonofo i a Vaiora e kakera. Kai kankateamai koua kankarafaina pe nigkopuni oji a tagata i ta fanuanei. Nokanieni

45. The children became confused. Fear and desperation overcame them. They wept. They didn't want to die. They wanted to live. So they wept.

They spoke thus, 'How can we leave? The house is sealed.'

Majihjiki replied, 'If you all want to stay alive then quit crying and wait quietly inside. I will break apart the house and we will all flee.'

'Okay, you must help us. Truly we've been living here alone and our elders are all gone.' They all answered him thus.

Majihjiki took up his ax and lifted it high speaking out to it saying, 'I, Majihjiki, want this house to divide when I strike it so the children inside can come out.'

50. He made an attempt to chop down the house, and the place split apart so the children could come out.

'Wow, you just appeared from nowhere and you came to help us?'

Majihjiki said to them, 'I live at Veora up there. I have watched what happened to you all and wanted to help before everyone disappeared from pe a tagata kamaraga foki pe kahnofo i ta fanuanei. Vau nihmai pe kankarafiakea koua kunei. Akitea kafura.'

A gatama kofakauiage pe, 'Akitea karoro ki?'

Majihjiki saitukage pe, 'Akitea karoifo uai taina karohmuni mana i ai.'

55. A Majihjiki koiarafia akirea kohtoifo ki Ta Fasua. Nirokaukau kirea Ta Fasua. Nokaukau nifetakaro. Nopena tapalia noturituri i tai ma ta kanieni.

Namkofu nohvere ta foi pasiesi. Novere vere vere vere kaie neiragona eia nikotaru ta fijikau.

Nigkotata hmafi ano ivi. Ta tereva i a teia nikosorekage. U aia nopuku notavenaga mana sohkoia pe, 'A nopogi oji na avau nohmai kamivere sentereva mana penei kai tane taha te nankauna fakamokagea ki ta mraera? Taha i ta mrae? Sanea i tamrae. Avau kaafe mana karosireia taria pe taha i tamrae.'

Neikoina ta vere kai eia konotomai ki ta mrae. Eia nifano

this island. I want the people to multiply plentifully again and live on this land. I have come to lead you all from here. We must flee.'

The children asked, 'Where shall we go?'

Majihjiki replied, 'We will go down by the sea and hide first there.'

55. Majihjiki led them all down to Ta Fasua. They went to swim and splash about at Ta Fasua. They played in the water at Ta Fasua. They played tag playing in the sea with pleasure.

At Namkofu the monster was still gardening. He kept on gardening and gardening, until he felt that he couldn't continue working.

His bones ached with tiredness. Exhaustion was overpowering him. So he sat and said to himself, 'These days I come to garden and never tire like this but what have I sent to precede me to the village there? What is going on in the village? Something is happening in the village. I will return right away to find out exactly what is going on there.'

He left the garden and came down toward the village. He

fano fano fano nirotuhkea i Tagafunamea. I Teifi neifakarogonaifo ta mrae pe kairogona sa tama ma pe hkuli i tamrae, kai sehva ta mrae.

Eia nomanatunea, 'Anopogi ojina sefeipenei mana kai nikua i ranei? A gatama nijikaikageana nikua?'

60. Eia neiragona e sa tiona roto i ai. Eia nifano nimeifakea ta mrae kai ta fare fakamama kai a gatama e jikai. Eia neiragona e sa hmafi tiona roto. Neiragona i a teia pe nikosa hmafi pe nikaroji i akirea kotamotua kai kofura i a teia.

Tiona mentua pe kaikatea kirea kaikaina oji kapuni. Kai aia nigkopuhpusikageana pe a gatama nirokage uafe.

'E rufie, tane taruana, kansara.'

Eia kofakea kofakatulele nohfarakohi nofori nanoa i ta mrae. Kai farakake uai ta fanua, kaie jikai tasi a nera pe kaitusia.

walked and walked and walked and walked until he could stand and look out from Tagafunamea. At Teifi he listened straining down toward the village to discover whether he could hear that child and the rest playing in the house, but they weren't hollering from the house.

He wondered, 'I have never had a day like this so what is happening today? How have the children disappeared?'

60. He felt terrible. He went on to arrive at the village to find the house open and the children gone. His heart ached. It occurred to him everything had gone very wrong, because he cared for those children while they grew strong yet they fled from him.

He decided when he discovered them he would eat them all. But he didn't know where they had gone.

'Okay, It doesn't matter, I'll search for them.' (He had a special way of searching.)

He went out and bent over at the waist and he opened his bottom and circled all around within the village (pointing himself in this upside down posture everywhere. He made himself into a compass this way). He directed his bottom all about the land, but his search didn't point out any place. (Sensing the presence of people the monster's bottom would redden and his rectum would actually extrude like an arrow to indicate the direction in which people could be found.)

Uaia koifarakea uai Sinou ma i Tekau ma kaie jikai. Neifarage uai Ianarua ma i Uana ma. Eia no manatunea, 'Akirea nirokage uafe na? Jikai saha.'

He pointed himself upside down toward Sinou and Tekau, but nothing. He directed his buttocks toward Ianarua and toward the other side of the island. Then he wondered, 'Where have they all gone? There's nothing.'

65. Eia nigapu fakahpotoana kai safakatulele kohfara kai kourukea tanopuku kohi kohmeakea Uaia koitu pe, 'Akirea mari ena.'

65. He rested a short while and then turned himself upside down again opening his bottom and his rectum extruded and turned bright red. So he said, 'That's where they are.'

Eia nitukake kofano nirotukea Tagutu o Rupe neikateaifo a gatama nokaukau. Kaie e faru nopena tapalia kaie faru nohturituri nohvaro i Ta Fasua. Nokanieni nofetakaro. Eia kotu i Tagutu o Rupe nofesaoifo, 'Akoua mari nei kunei, gafatumupuku, kai avau nigokomate rufie tansara koua. Avau kafenatu foki. Akoua kahtari avau kafenatu akitea kafetakaro.'

He stood just at the lookout, Tagutu o Rupe (Cliff of Doves), and looked down at the children who were swimming. A few were playing tag and some were running about and hollering on the beach at Ta Fasua (Giant Clam Beach). They were happy just playing. So he stood at Tagutu o Rupe and called down, 'All of you are really here, my grandchildren, and I've

Kai a gatama kotukage pe, 'Akimea hgehgae i atakoe. Kai pe akoe kahmai kimea ka fura i a takoe.'

Kai ta pasiesi koitukage penei, 'Avau komate i ta karoji i akoua kai akoua nihgegae i atavau pe nikua?'

'Ah! Akimea pupusi i atakoe,' kirea nitukage i ateia.

70. Ta foi pasiesi neioria neitu pe, 'E rufie. Akoua hgehgae i atavau kaie avau kofenatu akitea karofetakaro.'

Eia neikavajia ti eture i ta namo Ta Fasua. Neikavajia ti eture pe a gatamanei kamatanoa i ai. Kai eia kafanifo karoirikofia kirea kaitaia kaikaina.

Majihjiki koitukage ki a gatamara pe, 'Gatama, ti eture tena kai pe akoua nokanieni i ai jiki tasi ana koua i ai. Kosoamoa ekoua kanalupai su. Pena kamatanoa a koua i ai kahmai ta foi pasiesi kai rikofia kitea kaitaia kai kaina kahpuni. Romai. Kitea keroro.'

exhausted myself in searching for you. I'll join you. Wait for me to join you and we'll play together.'

The children responded to him, 'We despise you. If you approach us we'll run away from you.'

And so the monster said, 'I exhaust myself in caring for all of you and you all despise me, why?'

'Ah! We don't know you,' they all replied to him.

70. That incredible monster said, 'Okay. You all despise me but I am going to join you and be with you.'

He conjured up a school of mackerel in the pool at Ta Fasua. He conjured up the fish so the children would preoccupy themselves with (eating) them. Meanwhile he would descend and come upon them (the children) to slaughter and eat them.

Majihjiki said to those children, 'Children, there is a school of mackerel close by and if you like them, take just one each. Don't take lots. If you dawdle over the fish the monster will catch up to us and kill and eat us all. Come on. Let's get going.'

A gatama kotukage pe, 'E rufie.'

Kirea nijikitasikageana i a foi eture. Kai kirea koforikage uai Rorogai ma. Kirea nororona i a hgaone. Tano fajaganei a hgaone ana ninofo kofori ta fanua. Jikai a kasifa.

75. Majihjiki neitu pe, 'E rufie pera pe avau kaikavajia a kasifa pe kataru ta pasiesi tairikofia kimea weiwaha.'

Nei tu pe, 'Avau Majihjiki. Au nokanieni pe akimeanei karoro i a hgaone nomokage, kaia kasifa ma pahtoka kahsomo nomuri pe eia kahmai kameitaru i ta fano i ai. Kai kitea nofura.'

Eia neitukua ta fesaonei nirava kaia kasifa kamata ta hsomo. Majihjiki ma gatama nomokage nororo i a hgaone kai ta foi pasiesi kotaru i ta fano. A kasifa emtakaikage nikopojina tiona retu.

Kaie ta foi pasiesi nomate rufie tahtoro. Nohmae ano vae i ta htu i a kasifa. Eia nitamoto tairikofia kirea waiwaha. Eia neisireiage a gatama kai nigkororo kotatana ta forikake uai Ianarua ma uaia konotaru. Neikavajia ta turinca, ta turinea

The children said, 'Fine.'

The children took one magical mackerel each. Then they went round about Rorogai. They could travel along the sand. At this time only sand encircled the island. There was no reef.

75. Majihjiki said, 'It would be good if I conjured up a reef so the ogre won't be able to reach us quickly.'

He said, 'I am Majihjiki. I want us to go along a sand beach first, and then have corals and rock crop up behind us so that if he approaches his progress will be impeded. Then we'll escape.'

As soon as he finished saying these words coral began to grow. Majihjiki and the children went first along the sand but (behind them) the monster was prevented from walking. The sharpest coral obstructed his path.

The monster hurt badly from crawling. His legs and feet hurt from being pierced by the reef. He was too weak to reach them quickly. He saw the children were getting close to circling round up by Ianarua but he couldn't get there. So tanoeigoa Ta Muri Vaka te notukea i tai Ta Fasua. Kai nosafeage uai Ianarua ma.

he conjured up a cliff, the cliff known as Ta Muri Vaka (The Stern of the Canoe), that projects into the sea near Ta Fasua. He looked toward Ianarua and beyond.

Eia neitukua penei, 'Avau, ta foi pasiesi, nokanieni sa turinea katerekea kaipojinamai a gatama uanei pe akirea kataru ta roro uai tantafa pe kamaru i atavau tan rikofia kirea kantaia oji kapuni kankaina.'

He said this, 'I, the special monster, want a cliff to extend outward to keep the children blockaded in here so they can't escape to the other side and so it will be easy for me to reach them to kill every last one of them and eat them.'

80. Ta turinea nimiterekea neipojinamai agatama uai Ta Fasua. Kirea kotaru ta fura. Majihjiki neiamkea ta toki ona, neijikijia neitu pe, 'Avau, Majihjiki, kanfakapopoiage ta turineana ta tokinei. Kantumusiakea ta turineana.'

80. The cliff extended out and barricaded the children within Ta Fasua. They couldn't escape. So Majihjiki picked up his ax, raising it he said, 'I, Majihjiki, will bash apart the cliff with this ax. I will divide that cliff.'

Neifakapopoiage. Eia neifakpopoiage neisaua kai ta turinea kamotukea. Ta pito turinea te i tai i ta moana taneigoa, Tokomanoko. Kai tano pito te i gauta, Ta Muri Vaka, kai akirea koforikage i ai. Kofori kororokake uai Ianarua ma. Akirea norofetakaro nokaukau Ianarua kaia ta foi pasiesi nohtoro i a kasifa ma pahtoka nomuri. Tuhtu ruano rima ma ruano vae i a kasifa. Eia nifano fano ni-

He struck at it. He hit and chopped it until the cliff broke apart. The piece of the cliff in the sea in the deep water is named, Tokomanoko. And the remnant near shore, Ta Muri Vaka, the children all went around it. They went round and continued up to Ianarua and that area. They all played and swam at Ianarua while the unbelieveable monster crawled on the corals and rocks behind.

meiforikea ta turinea neikatea a gatama nokaukau Ianarua.

His hands and legs were pierced by the reef, yet he kept coming round the cliff until he could see the children swimming near Ianarua.

A gatama nisafea eia nohmai kotata. Akirea nitukua pe, 'A pua kohmai! A pua kohmai! Akitea kafura.'

The children spied him coming close. They called out, 'Our grandparent is coming. Our grandparent is coming. Let's run away.'

Ta foi pasiesi neiragona kirea nofesao pe kirea kafura, uaia konofo i ta turinea kavajia ta paua, ta paua ta ika. Ta foi pasiesi neitu pe, 'Avau nokanieni pe sa paua kafenake Ianarua kamatanoa i a gatama kafano avau kanrikofia kirea kantaia kankaina oji kapuni.'

The evil monster heard them saying they would flee, and so he stayed at the cliff and conjured up red snapper, red snapper the fish. The evil one said, 'I want some red snapper to come ashore at Ianarua to preoccupy the children so I can go and overtake them to kill them and eat them all until not one is left.'

Neikavajia ta paua, kai a Majihjiki koitukage ki a gatama pe, 'Akoua kajiki tasi ana i a foi paua. Akitea konororoifo uai Tarigakasi ma. Pe makamatanoa kitea i a paua kai ta foi pasiesi kameirikofia kitea kameitaia akitea.'

He (the monster) conjured up the red snapper, and then Majihjiki said to the children, 'You all can each have one of the magical snappers. We will go down to the Tarigakasi area. If we dawdle with the red snapper the monster will catch up with us and arrive to kill us all.'

85. A gatama nijiki tasi ana i a ika kai kirea konororoifo uai Tarigakasi ma. Ta pasiesi neikatea kirea kororo. Eia koikavajia ta turinea Tarimu.

85. The children each took one from among all the fish and then they went down to the area of Tarigakasi. The Monster saw them go. He cast a spell

Eia neitukua penei, 'Avau, ta foi pasiesi, nokanieni pe katerekea sa turinea i Tarimu kaipojinamai a gatamana kankaina.'

Ta turinea koterekea nirorako i ta moana. A Majihjiki neijikijia tano toki kofesaokage i ai neitukua penei, 'Avau, Majihjiki, kanfakapopoiageana ta turinea, tioku toki kamotukea tano pito.'

A Majihjiki neiamoa ta toki. Neifakapopoiage kai komotukea ta turineara. Tanopito kokero. A matoka i ai no i teriari. Eia neiarafia a gatama akirea kororo ki Tarigakasi norokaukau i ai. Akirea nororo i ta rufie nomokage kai a kasifa nomuri. Ta foi pasiesi nomate i ta hkava i a pahtoka ma kasifa ma. Notuhtu ano vae ma anorima.

Kirea nei Tarigakasi kai eia komeiforikea neisafea kirea nofetakaro i ai. Eia neikavajia ta mutukau niroro i ta namo Tarigakasi. Eia neitukua penei, 'Avau, ta foi pasiesi, nokanieni pe sa mutukau kafenake i ta namo Tarigakasi kamatanoa i a gatamana. Au kafano kanrikofi

conjuring a cliff at Tarimu.

He said this, 'I, the special monster, want a promontory to extend out from Tarimu to barricade the children so I can eat them.'

The promontory extended out to the ocean depths. Majihjiki lifted his ax and spoke out like this, 'I, Majihjiki, will just bash the promontory, my ax will split off one end.'

Majihjiki picked up the ax. He bashed away until that promontory broke apart. One end submerged. There is a reef there way outside. Then Majihjiki led the children and they all went to Tarigakasi and swam there. They traveled on a good surface first and the reef came up behind them. The monster was exhausted from climbing over rock and coral formations. His legs and arms were pierced.

All the children were at Tarigakasi and the monster came round to see them playing there. He conjured up a school of garfish in the pool at Tarigikasi. He spoke like this, 'I, the incomparable monster, wish for garfish to come up into the pool at Tarigakasi and preoccupy the akirea kantaia kankaina oji kapuni.'

90. Kaia Majihjiki neitukage i a gatama pe, 'A mutukau jiki tasi ana koua i ai kai kitea kororo.'

Kirea nijikitasikageana i ai kai konororoifo uai Naweji. Ta pasiesi neimojikeage kirea kai nigkororo. Neiragona e sa hmafi tiona roto. Kirea nororo kai ta foi pasiesi koikavajia ta turinea i Naweji. Eia neitukua penei, 'Au nokanieni sa turinea katerekea Naweji kaipojinamai a gatama kataru ta roro. Avau kafano karikofia akirea kantaia kankaina oji kapuni.'

Mehlouana ta turinea Naweji nihpalokea nirako ta moana. Kai a Majihjiki neiamoa ta toki ona neitu pe, 'Avau, Majihjiki, kanfakapopoiage ta turineana makamotukea tano pito karoro akimea ma gatama karoforikea uai tan tafa.'

Ta turinea nimotukea. Nikero tano pito i tai kai akirea konororo i a hgaone koroforikake uai tan tafa. Akirea niroro nirorako Naweji. Kirea nigapu nofetakaro i ai.

Ta foi pasiesi nohtoro fariki

children. I will go there and when I reach them I will kill them and eat them all, everyone.'

90. But Majihjiki warned the children, 'You can each have one garfish only then we'll go.'

They all took one each and then fled down to Naweji. The monster watched them as they went. He was terribly upset. They were getting away so the special monster wished for a cliff at Naweji. He spoke like this, 'I wish for a cliff to extend out from Naweji to keep the children from going on. I will catch up with them and kill and devour them all, every one.'

At that moment the cliff at Naweji grew extending out to reach the deepest part of the sea. But Majihjiki took up his ax and said, 'I, Majihjiki, will bash apart the cliff to split off a piece so the children and I can go around the end.'

The cliff broke apart. One piece submerged in the sea so they all continued on the sand going around the newly exposed face. They kept going until they reached Naweji. There they stopped to rest.

The monster persisted in

ana nomuri akirea. Nisagasaga eia neirikofia kirea Naweji, neitukage kirea pe, 'Gafatumupuku, akoua mari noikunei. Avau komate rufie tankatagia koua, kai koua nofura i atavau i aha? Koua kafetakaro kahtari, avau kofenatu foki.'

95. A gatama nitukage pe, 'Akimea hgehgae i a takoe. Akimea e hgehgae i a takoe ta muri i akimea.'

Gatama nifura i ta Pasiesi i Naweji kororo ki Nahmanini nirogapu i ai. Nofetakaro i Nahmanini kaie ta foi pasiesi komate rufie ta htoro i a pahtoka ma kasifa ma. Ta pasiesi nifano fano nimeirako Nahmanini kaie kirea jikai. Kirea kofura i Nahmanini kororo ki Feava. Kirea niroro ki Feava nofetakaro i ai. Kai ta foi pasiesi nohtoro nomuri.

Akirea nei Feava kai akirea nigkohmate ta oge pe ta nopogi pakeni se kai ma i akirea. Ta pasiesi neifarigoiakea pe kirea nikohmate i ta oge. 'E rufie pera pe avau kankavajia a niu somo i Feava kamatanoa a gatama i ai kafano avau kanrikofia kantaia kankaina.'

slowly crawling along after them. He was determined to catch up with them at Naweji and he called out to them, 'My grandchildren, truly you are all here. I have exhausted myself following you all, but you run from me, why? Stay and rest where you are, I'll come to you again.'

95. The children said, 'We despise you. We don't want you to follow us.'

The children fled from the monster leaving Naweji to go to Nahmanini to rest there. They rested at Nahmanini while the monster exhausted himself thoroughly, crawling along the coral reef. The monster kept on going and arrived at Nahmanini but there was no one there. They had all fled from Nahmanini to go on to Feava. They went to Feava to relax there. So the monster crawled on after them.

While they were all at Feava they became hungry because for a full day they had eaten little. The monster realized that they were really hungry. 'I should conjure up some sprouted coconuts at Feava to hold the children's attention while I go to catch up with them so I can

Eia kofakea kofesao neitu pe, 'Avau ta foi pasiesi, au nokanieni pe nofo sa hnani i a hgaone i Feava kamatanoa a gatama i ai vau kafenage kantaia akirea kankaina.'

Ta hnani i a niu somo nohtakape i Feava. A gatama nigkohmate hmafi ta oge. Nirokake kirea nohtu nofori ta toma niu somo. Akirea pe nikanieni hmafi kakokoia e faru katafoia kakaina weiwaha. Kirea nikoroifo nomatanoa i ai.

100. Kai a Majihjiki nofenake neitukage i akirea pe, 'Gatama, kosomatanoa akoua i a niu somo, ta tomaniuna. Koua kajikitasiana i ai kai kitea konororo. Kahfiji ki ta mrae. Pena. Kahmai ta foi pasiesi kairikofiamai kitea kunei kaitaia kitea kaikaina. Kai akitea kafura.'

Kirea nihtukake nijikitasiana i a foi niu somo. Konoamoa konororo ki hluga i ta mrae i Hsia. Kirea niroro roro nirorako i ta mrae i Hsia kaia Majihjiki saitukage i akirea. 'Kitea kagapu kakainakea e koua mana a niusomo aua kai kitea sa fura kahmuni.'

kill them and devour them all.'

So he went on saying, 'I, the special monster, wish for sprouted coconuts to lie on the sand at Feava to occupy the children while I come after them to kill them all and eat them.'

The sprouted coconuts appeared at Feava. The children were very hungry. They went up and stood all around the heap of sprouted coconuts. They wanted very much to husk some and gobble them up. They all focused and busied themselves at this.

100. But Majihjiki approached saying to them, 'Children, don't you be diverted by the sprouted coconuts, the heap of coconuts here. You can each pick out one and then we must go. We'll go up to the village. Do it. The monster is coming and if he reaches us here he will kill us all and eat us. So we must flee.'

So they each took just one magical sprouted coconut. They took them and went up to the village of Hsia. They went on and on until they reached Hsia where Majihjiki said to them, 'Let's all rest and you all eat up your sprouted coconuts first and then we'll run and hide.'

Kirea nikainakea oji a niusomo kai Majihjiki koitukage pe, 'Gatama, avau, Majihjiki, kantukatu i akoua. A fijikauga nipena oji kitea ta fura ta foi pasiesi. Nigkotoeana tantasiana. Akitea kamuri foki i ai. Pe eia seroisafea ma akitea uakitea komauri.'

A gatama nigkomataku fakasore. Kopupusi pe aha pena foki. Majihjiki koitukage i akirea pe, 'Avau kankavajia sa foi kuru notau i hluga kai akitea karukage i ta kuru.'

Ta kurunei ta noeigoa ta makopu.

105. 'Kitea kaurukage, avau tano funa kaia koua anofatu. Akoua kafakarogona ekoua vau. No i ai tano fajaga katuna ta foi kurunei ti afi kai avau kantukua pe, "Tawianiso". Kai koua kaoria pe, "HO!" Akitea oji kahmimi. Kahmia ti afi kamate.'

'E rufie ta matau atea, aia oji tera,' a gatama nioriage i a Majihjiki.

Ta pasiesi nifano fano fano fano fano nirako i ta mrae kai kopupusikage ana pe a

They ate up all their sprouted coconuts while Majihjiki spoke to them saying, 'Children, I, Majihjiki, will speak to you. We have accomplished our escape from the monster. There remains just one thing to do. We must follow through with this too. If he doesn't see us we will all stay alive.'

The children were very frightened. They didn't know what to do next. Majihjiki spoke to them thus, 'I will conjure up a magical breadfruit to hang above and we will all enter this breadfruit.'

This breadfruit is the makopu variety.

105. 'We will go inside, I will be the core while you will become its seeds. You all will listen all of you for me. The time will come when this magical breadfruit will be cooking in fire and then I will call, "Tawianiso". You all answer "YES!" We all will pee. We'll all pee on the fire to extinguish it.'

'We understand, so that will be it,' the children responded to Majihjiki.

The monster went on and on and on and on and on until he reached the village but he didn't gatamara nikorokage uafe? Eia neitereva hmafi kaie ta kanieni pe kaikatea ana a gatama. Uaia konofakatulele nohfarakohi neisara a gatama. Eia noifakatulele nohfara kohi neisara a gatama nofori nanoa raro. Nofori a hne oji seikatea ma.

Eia nomanatunea nofesao mana sohkoiana, 'A gatamara nirokage uafe?'

Eia kogapu gapukage kai eia koukamata foki ta fakatulele nohfara kohi nofori. Neisaraifo raro seikatea ma. Eia neifarakake i hluga kai kohmeakea ta hne waimuri. Eia nitukake neisireia a rakau oji i hluga seikitea ma sa tama noeke i a sa rakau. 'Akirea no i uafe?' eia nomanatunea.

110. Eia nigapu gapukage kai eia kohsara foki. Nohfara kohi nofori fori fori fori fori kaie jikai saha nifakea. Eia neifarakake kaie kohmeakea tano kohi foki. Eia nitukake neisireia i hluga e jikai sa tama. Ta foi kuru ana notau.

know where the children had gone. He was really tired but all he wanted was to locate those children. So he bent over and opened his buttocks to search for the children. He bent over and opened his bottom to search for the children all around below. He made a complete circuit without sign of them.

He was puzzled and said to himself, 'Where have those children gone?'

He rested and rested some more and then he began his search again bending to open his buttocks and turn in a circle. He searched low and saw no one. He searched high and his bottom reddened. So the evil monster stood and looked up in all the trees above but he couldn't see a single child perched in the branches. 'Where are they?" the monster wondered.

110. He rested and rested awhile longer then he searched again. He opened his buttocks and circled, circling and circling and circling and circling but nothing was revealed. When he searched high his bottom reddened. The monster stood and stared up high but there was not a single child. Only an

Uaia koitu pe, 'Morefuma ta foi kuruna. Kantoria, kantuna, kankaina.'

Uaia konotoriaifo ta foi kurunei. Amoa konofano. Niroinage kai eia kofano koro hta fie. Neisaramai a hfie. Neitafuna ti afi nihka fakarufie kai eia koinagaifo ta foi kurura tiafi.

Uai ta koro Majihjiki tano funa, gatama ano fatu. Majihjiki nifesao ki a gatama, 'Koua kananaki.'

Neinagaifo ti afi, Majihjiki nei tu pe, 'Tawianiso'.

115. Kaia gatama ko 'Uh: wu uh.'

Kirea oji nihmimi, komate ti afi. Se moa ma ta foi kuru.

Ta pasiesi neiamoa ta foi kurunei laoa i ta porapora neitnuria ta mrae. Eia kofano korohta hfie, hfie mahtua neipena. A rakau teitai mo notu pe hfie mahtua. Neiamoa koafemai ki ta mrae. Nei tafuna foki teke afi nihka fakarufie. Neiamoa ta foi kuru neipagiaifo ti afi. Majihjiki ma

exceptionally large breadfruit dangled above.

So he said, 'That must be a very special breadfruit. I will pluck it, cook it and eat it.'

So he picked that particular breadfruit. He took it away. He put it down while he went to chop firewod. He sought firewood to bring back. He made and tended a fire until it burned hot and then he placed the special breadfruit down in the flames.

Inside Majihjiki was the core and the children were the seeds. Majihjiki said to the children, 'Get yourselves ready.'

When the monster placed the breadfruit in the fire, Majihjiki called, 'Tawianiso.'

115. And the children responded, 'Uh: wu uh.'

Everyone peed and the fire died. The fine breadfruit was not cooked.

The monster took that special breadfruit, stuffed it in a coconut sack and hung it at the hearth. Then he went to cut firewood, mature wood he sought. Standing dead hardwood is referred to as mature firewood. He took some and returned to his fire site. He made and tended ana gatamtane kopena ta penaganea tasiana feipei mokage.

'E sa!'

Nihmia kirea ti afi komate. Ta kuru e mata. Nitaru ta moa.

120. Ta pasiesi neiamoakea ta foi kuru neifaoa i ta porapora nage kai aia kofano karosara hfie fou. Teke a tapu e hpaikea i a tapu oji nirohsara fie i ai eia.

Majihjiki neifarigoinakea oji pe jikai foki tasi a nea nitoe kapena kirea uaimuri. 'Akitea roitaia oji. Tanofajaga mehlou eia noipapai nohsara hfie, kitea kafura.'

Ta pasiesi norohsarahfie, Majihjiki neifasia ta foi kuru a gatama kourukea. Akirea konororo ki Mouga. Nirako i Mouga a Majihjiki neikavajia ta tarie. Ta tarienei nisomo. E sisi, eraro, kaia eia kaitukage i a gatama pe, 'Akoua kahkavakake ta tarie. Akoua oji.'

another fire until it burned hot. Then he took out the special breadfruit and threw it down on the fire. Majihjiki and all his children did the same thing they had done the first time.

'This is bad!' muttered the monster.

They all peed and the fire died. The breadfruit was still hard. It's impossible to cook it.

120. The monster took up that special breadfruit and stuffed it in a coconut sack to store while he went to seek out other firewood. He would go to a different restricted area far from the sacred spots where he had already gathered wood.

Majihjiki decided there was nothing more that remained for them to do. 'He will kill us. Now while he is far away gathering firewood, we must flee.'

While the monster searched for firewood, Majihjiki broke open the magic breadfruit and the children ran out. They set off for Mouga. When they got to Mouga Majihjiki conjured up a nut tree. The nut tree sprouted. It was small, close to the ground, and Majihjijki said to the children, 'You all should

Akirea nikavakea ta tarie. Kai a Majihjiki tukage i a gatama pe, 'Kankavajia ta tarie pe kasore.'

Eia nifesao neitu pe, 'Avau Majihjiki. Au nokanieni pe ta tarie nei kasore, kagaro kaiamoa kimea oji karohmuni i ai i hluga. Pe ta foi pasiesi kamai kai serorikofia ma. Kai sara. Akimea kohmuni.'

125. Kirea kohkavakake kai ta tarie konofenake. Fenake fenake fenake fenake kohgaro. Neiamoaifo a rakau oji. A gatamara nei hlugakake. Ta tarie nei tanoeigoa, Ta Toko Marino.

Akirea nei hluga kai ta pasiesi koafemai ki ta mrae ma hfie. Niafemai neisara ta nera, foi kuru te neifaoa i ta porapora. Kai ta kuru nipusakina. Kojikai ano fatu. Jikai tano funa. Uaia kokoli. Ta pasiesi kokali. Neitu pe, 'Avau nohsara hfie koforimai komeifijikake kai ta foi kuru nipusakina? Nikokuara i ai, kirea nirokage uafe? Kokua? Avau kasara foki.'

climb up the nut tree. Every one of you.'

They all climbed up the nut tree. Then Majihjiki told the children, 'I'm going to wish for the tree to grow big.'

He spoke, saying, 'I am Majihjiki. I wish this nut tree to be big and tall, to rise up and take us all to hide in it high above. If the horrible monster should come he won't reach us. He'll search. We'll be hidden.'

125. So they all climbed up and the nut tree rose up. It went up and up and up and up to an enormous height. They went up highest of all the trees. Those children were very high. This nut tree is named, Ta Toko Marino (The Peaceful Staff).

They were all up high when the monster returned with firewood. He returned and looked for that thing, the special breadfruit that he'd stuffed in the coconut sack. But the breadfruit had burst open. Its seeds had disappeared. Its core had disappeared. And so he got angry. The monster was upset. He said, 'I look for firewood and circle back to come up here and meanwhile the special breadfruit bursts open? What happened

Eia nifakatulele, neifara tano kohi noforinanoa i a nohnea oji i raro. Kofori jikai sa farigoi pe kaikatea kirea. 'Nikokuara, kasarakakera uai hluga?'

Eia nomanatunea i ai. Eia nifakatulele fakatauraga nifara kohi kake uai hluga kai kohmea. 'Akirea mari ena.'

Eia nihsirekake kai akirea noeke i hluga ta tarie. Uaia konofesaokage i akirea pe, 'A gafatumupuku, akoua nirokea pe pekua? Avau kokanieni pe kafenatu foki.'

130. A gatama niresia eia kooriakage pe, 'Pua, akimea nihtaukake ta vavanei komeirako i hluga nei. Kai pe akoe nokanieni, akoe kataukage foki kai akimea kafujiakake akoe.'

Ta pasiesi neitu pe, 'Ho, e rufie. Avau kafenatu foki. Fujia ekoua avau. Kajiriifo ta vavanei.'

Gatama nifujiaifo ta vava kai ta foi pasiesi kotaukage i ai kai a gatama kofujiakake kirea eia. Tena notau nofujia kirea.

here? Where did they go? What is this? I have to search again?'

He searched in his special way opening his buttocks and circling every place in the landscape. Round he went but there was no sign that he would find them. 'What's happening, shall I search for them up high?'

He puzzled over this. Then in his upside-down posture he opened his buttocks to point up high and it turned red. 'Sure enough they must be there.'

He looked up and there they perched high in the tarie tree. So he said to them, 'Grandchildren of mine, why did you leave? I want to come with you too.'

130. The children replied deceitfully, 'Grandfather, we hung from this rope to reach these heights. So if you want, you can hang on too and we'll pull you up.'

The monster said, 'Yes, okay. I'll follow you too. Pull me up you all. Throw down the rope.'

The children threw down the rope and the evil monster grabbed on so the children could pull him up. That one hung on and they all pulled.

Kai a Majihjiki koitu pe, 'Avau Majihjiki. Avau nokanieni pe kahnofo a kapau ma punpuninea emtakai raro pe katakaifo ta pasiesi korohtu i ai kamate.'

Kirea nofujia kai a Majihjiki neikavajia a punpuninea emtakai ma fatu uai raro. Kai a gatama kofujiakake. Kirea nofujia fujia fujia fujia nirotata ta taukake kai akirea koveteakea ta vava. Ta foi pasiesi nitakakea nihtu i a punpuninea ma fatu uai raro.

135. Nihmae ano kaulegi. Eia neigorosia kirea. 'Gafatumupuku, nigkopena pekua koua vau? Kantaia koua kankainana ma paku oua.'

A gatama kooria pe, 'Pua, pua, akoe hmafa su pe akoe e hmaru hmafi. Nifujia fujia fujia kimea koe kai kohmae omea rima kohnusikea ta vava uakoe kotakakoe. Kokua akoe kotaukage foki? Akimea kafujiakake mehlou akoe kamirako i hluga.'

Eia kotaukage foki ta vava kai kirea kofujia. Pena ta penaganea tasianara. Kirea kofujia fujia eia nirorako ihluga kai koveteakea.

Then Majihjiki said, 'I am Majihjiki. I appeal for angular, cornered things, sharp stakes to appear down below so if the monster falls he'll be pierced by them and he'll die.'

So they were all pulling while Majihjiki conjured up sharp stakes and stones down below. The children kept pulling him up. They pulled, pulled, pulled and pulled until he was close to the top and then they let go of the rope. The monster fell landing on the pointed posts and rocks below.

135. He was really shaken up. He scolded them all, 'My grandchildren, what have you done to me? I'm going to kill you all and eat you and your excrement.'

The children replied, 'Grandfather, grandfather, you are really heavy, really huge. We pulled and pulled and pulled but our hands hurt so the rope slipped and you fell down. What will happen if you hang on again? We'll pull you up this time until you reach the top.'

So he hung on to the rope again and they all pulled. They did just as before. They pulled and pulled until he was very high

Nitakakea ta foi pasiesi nitekaifo i a punpuninea ma fatu i raro. Nimate fakatasiana. Kai a gatama nikomataku ta htoifo. Kirea nikohlika pena kahtoifo kai eia komasike kai taia kirea kai kaina. 'Kafarigoina ekitea pekua eia pe mate mo e mouri?'

Kirea noeke i hluga notavenaga i ai. 'E rufie pe kitea kakauna ta roata kafano karoipapaia eia kaviri. Pe eia seroviri ma kaie nimate.'

Kirea kokauna ta roata, te uri e hmagu. Eia kofano fano fano norohtoro i a teia. Neipapaia eia. Tano hkano i ai pe noimagujia. Neimagujia pe eia kahkini kahlika i ai kaviri. Magujia ano vae ma ano rima ma ano foimata kaie ta pasiesi segarue. Notakape.

140. Ta roata koafemai nimeitukage i a kirea pe, 'Nanpapaia kaie notakape. Morefuma nimate.'

Kai akirea komataku. Kauna foki ta rago. Eia nifano, norere nofori ruano tariga. Neimumuia ruan tariga kaie notakape segarue, se viri ma. Nimate.

and then they let go. The monster fell down and landed on the stakes and stones below. He died at once. But the children were afraid to climb down. They feared if they descended he would rise up to kill and devour them all. 'How can we tell whether he is really dead or alive?'

They sat perched up high and discussed this. 'It will be best if we send the large black ant to bite him until he quivers. If he doesn't jerk then he must be dead.'

They sent an ant, the black one that bites. He went down, down, down to crawl all over him. He chewed on him. The meaning of this is that he bit him. He bit him to see if he would react with a jerk or quiver. He bothered his legs and his arms and his eyes but the monster didn't move. He just lay there.

140. The black ant returned and said to everyone, 'I have chewed on him but he lies still. It is likely he is dead.'

But they all were still frightened. They next sent a fly. He went to flit around his two ears. He buzzed his two ears but the monster just lay there without moving, without shaking. He

A gatama sefakarogo ma pe nimate. Kokauna foki a nemauri nalupai. Niroro koropena ekirea faru a fijikauga pe a gatama kafakarogo i ai pe mate mo e mouri. A gatama sefakarogo ma i a nera nipena kirea. Kirea komataku ana ta htoifo.

Anemauri oji niroro nikopuni nitoekeana ta manu mea. Tano fakarava. Ta manu mea koitu pe, 'Avau kafano karofarigoina mana foki pe mouri mo nimate oji.'

Eia korere kourukage tano fafa nofano uaitakoro i ano gavava komeiurukea ta kohi o ta pasiesi. Ta hne te hmea i tano kohi neitusia ta uru o ta manumea. Ta manumea e hmea tano uru, uri tano hkano. Kirea nisafea ta manumea nimeirukea kohmea tanouru. Kirea safakarogo pe nimate. 'Aia seroikaina ma kitea. Kitea kahtoifo karoro ki marae.'

145. Kirea nihtoifo niroro ki marae. Majihjiki neifatakina kirea oji neifakauia jikitasi, 'Akoe ta tama i?'

Ta tama neioriage pe, 'Avau

was surely dead.

The children couldn't believe he was dead. They sent lots of animals. They all went to do something that would let the children know whether he was dead or alive. But the children didn't believe in anything they did. They were just afraid to descend.

All the living things went until there remained only the red bird. The last one. The red bird (who was all black at this time) said, 'I'll go and see for sure whether he is alive or completely dead.'

He flew into the monster's mouth and around his insides until he emerged from the bottom of the monster. The place that is red at the monster's bottom colored the head of the red bird. The red bird is red on his head, black on his body. The children saw the red bird come out with a red head. They believed the monster was dead. 'He won't devour us. Let's go down and go to the sacred clearing.'

145. They all descended and went to the clearing. Majihjiki gathered the children all together and asked each one, 'You are a child from where?'

One child replied, 'I am a

ta tama i Iakana.'

Majihjiki neifakauiage foki pe, 'No i ai tasi foki i Iakana mo jikai?'

Eia neioriage pe, 'Ho, no i ai.'

Majihjiki neitukage i akiraua pe, 'E rufie akorua karoro.'

150. Eia neifakauia foki pe no i ai sa tama i Iasoa mo jikai? Kirea notu pe, 'Ho no i ai.'

Majihjiki neitukage pe, 'E rufie. Akorua komurikage i a kiraua. Koua kororo.'

Ta penaganea tasiana nei, neifakauiage i Hsia ma i Mouga ma i Taroumara ma i Matagi, ta Koga Fanua ma Iraro. Neikauna fafekina kirea oji nipuni. Notoeana ru tama i Pau. Kai a Majihjiki koitukage pe, 'Romai akorua. Akitatau konororo korohnofo i Pau.'

Kiratou niafemai ki Pau. Ru tamanei nirohnofo i ta mrae kai eia nironofo i Sinou.

Aia oji tera.

child of Iakana.'

Majihjiki asked of everyone then, 'Is there someone else from Iakana or not?'

And one would answer, 'Yes, there is.'

Majihjiki said to those two, 'Okay, you two should go (back to Iakana).'

150. Then he asked again whether there were some children from Iasoa or not? They said, 'Yes there are.'

Majihjiki said, 'Good. You two shall follow those two (to go back to your village). You all go.'

He went on like this asking about Hsia and Mouga and Taroumara and Matagi, ta Koga Fanua and Iraro. He sent them all back together until they were all gone. There remained only two children from Pau. And Majihjiki said to them, 'Come here you two. The three of us will go to live in Pau.'

The three of them returned to Pau.These two children went to live in the village while he went to stay at Sinou.

That's all there is.

Notes

1 Luomala translates the Maui character of Polynesian mythology, clearly cognate with Majihjiki, as the South Sea Superman (1955:85). This is an apt translation capturing the superhuman powers of this culture hero, his proclivity for transforming his physical shape (Capell 1960; Kirtley 1971; LeRoy 1985; Ray 1901), and his clever trickster-like character (Feinberg 1998a; Luomala 1955:88). Capell (1960) suggests the name Majihjiki likely spread throughout southern Vanuatu from the island of Aniwa.

2 Teamwork is a common theme throughout Oceanic mythology (Kirtley and Elbert 1973; Kirtley 1955, 1971:k11.1).

3 Greed and gluttony are traits often punished in Polynesian lore (Kirtley 1971:432).

4 Capell (1960) suggests that the version collected on Tanna is likely a borrowing from West Futuna. A comparative analysis would be interesting as the story is significantly transformed in the Tannese version. Many aspects of the myth as told on West Futuna are not replicated. The contest between monster and culture hero drives both stories, and the issues of capture, confinement and escape are common to both. In addition, the monster falls from a tree and dies at the hands of the children and their leader through trickery in both versions. Various animals are sent to insure the monster is dead in both as well. But the Tannese tale culminates in rebirth of a murdered populace rather than resettlement by those who escaped confinement. Gluttony plays a role in both tales, but is less important in the short Tannese version available to us. Details are not sufficient to allow a comparison of cultural geography, directional significance and place. We note also a story of Semo-Semo reported by Bonnemaison (1994:131-37). The tale shares some of the themes of Ta Pasiesi ma Majihjiki. Similarities are evident in the terror of destruction and consumption of people by a giant, the chase scenes, the final confirmation of death by a small bird who flies through the monster's body, and the partitioning of the land for settlement. The Tannese suggest Semo-Semo's home is in Aneityum, but that he would travel to neighboring islands and exterminate inhabitants at each place.

5 In Tonga Gifford notes the brothers, Maui Kisikisi, Maui Atalanga, Maui Motua and the culture hero, Maui (Gifford 1924:21-3 also see Gifford's references to others). Capell (1960) names the Maui brothers in New Zealand stories as Maui-taha, Maui-roto, Maui-pae and Maui-waho. Luomala cites the names of the Maui brothers as known on Tahiti from the eighteenth century as Maui-mua, Maui-muri, Maui-roto, Maui-taha, and Maui-potii. The youngest brother is known as Maui-the-abortion or Maui-of-the-hair-headdress (Luomala 1955:88). Feinberg (1998a) recorded a

story entitled, Motikitiki the Trickster and the Creation of Anuta, in which Motikitiki is the eldest of three. The brothers' names are noted as Poematua and Poerangomia. Elbert and Monberg (1965:116-17) note three brothers, the eldest of whom is Mautikitiki, Bellonese culture hero. The younger brothers are named 'Agotokitehoe or 'Anabeka and Maui.

6 One story attributes the origin of West Futuna to the uplifting of a huge brain coral that appeared to give Majihjiki's wife a resting place after she had been thrown out of his canoe by a pasiesi. While Majihjiki was diving his wife awaited him in their canoe. The monster took the opportunity to dispatch the wife and disguise herself as the hero's mate, a trick Majihjiki failed to uncover for many years.

7 A brief story from Bellona, entitled 'Eating People', shares the initial emphasis of Ta Pasiesi ma Majihjiki on a monster's gluttonous and destructive acts. The denouement of both tales involves the monster tricked into falling to his death from a rope (Elbert and Monberg 1965:167-68).

8 Destruction of a wicked god or monster who falls from a tree to his death (often because he is tricked into trusting a dead branch, a development that is not the case here) is a common motif of Polynesian lore and the cutting of a rope to drop a victim to his death similarly recurs throughout the oral literature of the region (Kirtley and Elbert 1973:261-62; Kirtley 1971:K895.1 page 393 and K963 page 397). A Samoan story, Tuivalea and Tuiatamai, involves a conclusion similar to that in Ta Pasiesi ma Majihjiki. In the Samoan tale an ogre is tricked into putting a loop of rope around his ankle so that two boys can pull him up toward the mountain top. As he gets near to the top Tuiatamai singes the rope and the ogre falls to his death (Moyle 1981:91-100; see also Elbert and Monberg 1965:167-68).

9 Kirtley (1971:3050) documents removable organs in other Polynesian tales including narratives from the outliers, Nukumanu and Ontong Java.

6
Majihjiki ma Fafine Toga / Majihjiki and the Women of Tonga

This narrative begins where *Ta Pasiesi ma Majihjiki* ends. West Futuna is settled. Majihjiki is living in the district of Pau. He falls in love with a beautiful, winged woman who, with a group of young female friends, regularly flies to West Futuna from afar, probably from Tonga, to play in the sea at Sinou. Sinou, depicted in Figure 16, is a magnificent area of reef and beach at land's end on the northeast corner of the island where the currents flow in ripples over the coral and sand. The site is located on the map in Figure 11 in the previous chapter. After watching the women on several occasions as they arrive, play in the sea, sunbathe and then depart, Majihjiki surreptitiously hides the wings of the woman he considers most beautiful. He transforms himself into a handsome youth and befriends this woman in a fruitless search for her wings. By this deception he is able to convince the lovely Tongan to stay with him and takes her home to his two-room abode where he will provide for her through his daily gardening.

The young wife is allowed to occupy only one of the two rooms of Majihjiki's home. The second is forbidden to her. She obeys this interdiction and while cohabiting the couple have a child together. They seem to live contentedly until the woman finally discovers Majihjiki's original deception. With her young son she ventures into the forbidden room and uncovers her wings buried there. After this, the wife makes preparations to return to

Figure 16: Sinou. William R. Dougherty 1973.

Tonga. In her turn, deceiving her son and husband, she deserts them to fly to her homeland. Here this telling ends.

I was told in subsequent discussions that Majihjiki is reputed to have left West Futuna after the events of this story to be re-united with his Tongan wife. When Majihjiki departed, it is said he took his first son, Jikimanu, with him. Other children were later born in Tonga to Majihjiki and his Tongan wife including, from older to younger, Jikisa, Jikitavaega, then the twins, Jiki and Jiki, and finally, Jiverau, the last one.[1] It is Jiverau, whose name means Rays of the Dawn, who returns to West Futuna in the next story to find his wife, Sina Fine Ariki.

Background and Connections

I recorded this story in 1973. Teikona of Matagi was the narrator and assisted in transcription and translation at the time. The tale and translation were later lightly edited as Takaronga and I collaborated on this book project. *Majihjiki ma Fafine Tonga* is set primarily in the district of Pau at Sinou, at Majihjiki's home and in associated gardens, enriching the local significance of these places. Yet the narrator, Teikona, makes his home in Matagi when he is residing on West Futuna. The choice of the tales Teikona would relate to me on the occasion of this recording was entirely his own. I was too new to the community and its discourses to have made a specific request. I am left to wonder how Majihjiki is associated with the Matagi district and whether Teikona feels a special connection with this particular tale as a result of his biography, family, or ties to places of West Futuna. In light of Teikona's selection it is interesting to note that high on the cliffs near Matagi, Majihjiki's mustache is ensconced in the landscape as illustrated in Figure 17.

This story as presented here begins with an introduction documenting my arrival on West Futuna and summarizing details of my trip from the United States. I had been living on the island only two months at the time of the recording. Teikona points out that I had asked for an opportunity to record some stories so that I might work with them to improve my language competence and understanding of local culture. Then the story begins.

We have no previous documentation of other versions of this story from West Futuna. However, similar tales are common throughout Vanuatu and some elements of the story are documented more widely in Oceania. For example, a similar story is recorded from Aurora (Maewo, Vanuatu) by Codrington (1891:397-98). In that tale the protagonist, Qatu, hides the wings of a beautiful woman from the heavens who has come to bathe in the sea. As with Majihjiki, Qat or Qatu, deceives the woman and eventually marries her. When she discovers the deception, she returns to the heavens. Qat follows hoping to retrieve her. The search ends, however, with his death and her commitment to stay in the heavens.

Jack Taylor (pers. comm. September 18, 2001) notes a

Figure 17: Majihjiki's mustache on cliffs between Matagi and Iraro.
Janet Dixon Keller 1998.

number of stories from northern Pentecost Island featuring female winged spirits. He indicates that such stories are pervasive throughout northern Vanuatu. In this connection, Jolly (1999) records a southern Pentecost tale similar to the one published here. Related tales from southern Vanuatu have surfaced as well. Nick Thieberger (2000) recorded a similar story in Erakor Village, Efate. This version was set in Erromango. Bonnemaison (1994:124-27) records from Tanna a myth that tells of the origins of women and human food. In this tale the first woman is transformed from a pigeon to a woman of flesh. She introduces a rich array of human foods to the original stone people. With a male of the first stone people she begets the first woman of the land. Women and pigeons are also linked in Samoan cultural and narrative history (Herdrich 1991), while Richard Feinberg notes a Polynesian practice of referring to anyone from overseas as a bird (pers. comm.). As discussed below the theme linking women and mobility unites these diverse examples with the West Futuna narrative.

Majijhjiki ma Fafine Tonga is also linked to the preceding and following stories in this book. The connection with Sina Fine Ariki through her marriage to Jiverau, the youngest of the children of Majihjiki and his Tongan wife, allows us to give a specific location to the home of the winged woman. Our translation here of *toga* builds on the specific application of the word, *toga,* in reference to Tonga in the next story, *Sina Fine Ariki*. In the language of West Futuna, *toga* may also mean 'south, foreign, distant, afar' and so the translation of *fafine toga* as 'women from some distant place' or 'women from afar' is a possible one. Historically it may be that the meaning of *toga* in this tale and the next conveyed a sense of a place far away, but that the expression has developed a more specific reference to Tonga over time.[2]

This connection with Tonga, however, has reverberations in other literatures beyond Vanuatu. Tongan traditional lore places the origins of their supernatural ancestors on an island named *Touia-o'-Futuna*, 'the first rock' (Gifford 1924; Māhina 1992).

Māhina identifies this rock as 'Futuna, meaning "rock all around," an extinct volcanic cone, [which] is the most eastern island of the Vanuatu archipelago' (1992:69, note 71). In addition the oral histories of Tikopia and Anuta remark invasions and immigrations from Tonga (Firth 1961; Feinberg 1998a, 1989).

Residence and Gender

Majihjiki ma Fafine Toga develops a gendered contrast between being rooted in place and flight or movement. This is a theme common to other ni-Vanuatu tales referenced just above. The figurative contrast evokes customary practices of patrilocal residence (Bonnemaison 1984, 1994; Jolly 1999:282; Lindstrom 1990) in which women move from the places of their birth to join the families of their husbands.

In the West Futuna story, Majihjiki is rooted in his place, Pau, as the story begins. The young women, by contrast, are constructed as bird-like in their ability to fly from one locale to another (Jolly 1999:284). Majihjiki captures a woman from afar. He literally roots her in his place by burying her wings in the ground. This is an allegorical tale mimicking normative West Futuna residential patterns at marriage. Family life and procreation, in myth and in social fact, are enabled by the conjunction of women's freedom to move, men's deeply rooted associations with place, and the power of a supernatural hero or social convention to channel and constrain women's movements through marriage.

Yet the West Futuna story is more nuanced than this mirroring of social conventions might suggest. In the tale, the young woman's escape from her husband's place constitutes a rejection of the residential norm. If we add information provided in the addendum, then Majihjiki's move to follow his wife may suggest an alternative residential pattern for married couples. Bold as this suggestion may be, the story becomes one that might be read as reflecting indigenous resistance to or flexibility regarding strict residential prescription. Today, in times of shifting resources and frequent migration, women are optionally accepted into their natal villages with their spouses and children as families strive to create opportune living conditions. This alternative pattern for post-marital residence, reinforced by the narrative, was most likely implemented in the past as well when conditions made life in a woman's natal village more advantageous than residence with a husband's family. The tale of Majihjiki and his Tongan bride, kept alive today in story-telling traditions, may be read as an illustration of socially authorized flexibility for residential decision-making. Nonetheless the flexibility comes with a price. Marital strife and at least temporary disruption of the household indexes the conflicts and compromises involved in real life as a couple reckons with ideals and exigencies of experience.

Cultural Geography: Movement and Direction

Movement in this tale is primarily along the east-west axis as shown in Figure 18. Reflecting an emphasis on conflict in decision-making, associations with direction in the myth are likewise discordant. Tongan women arrive from the east. A marriage union is enabled by this travel, but at the cost of a woman's freedom. A wife's return in the opposite direction to Tonga portends the expansion of residential possibilities yet entails the immediate dissolution of her family. When Majihjiki follows his wife, moving from west to east, family life is restored and an enduring connection between West Futuna and Tonga is established, but West Futuna loses a rooted culture hero. These positive and negative associations counterbalance one another and participate in a dissonance that drives the narrative. By contrast in oral literature elsewhere in Oceania, east and west are more often respectively valued as positive and negative (see Bonnemaison 1994:237; Goldman, Duffield and Ballard 1998:7-8; Senft 1997).[3]

Confinement and Freedom

A tension between confinement and freedom is developed in *Majihjiki ma Fafine Toga*. The hero's marriage, itself a situation of imprisonment for his wife, entails further confinement resulting

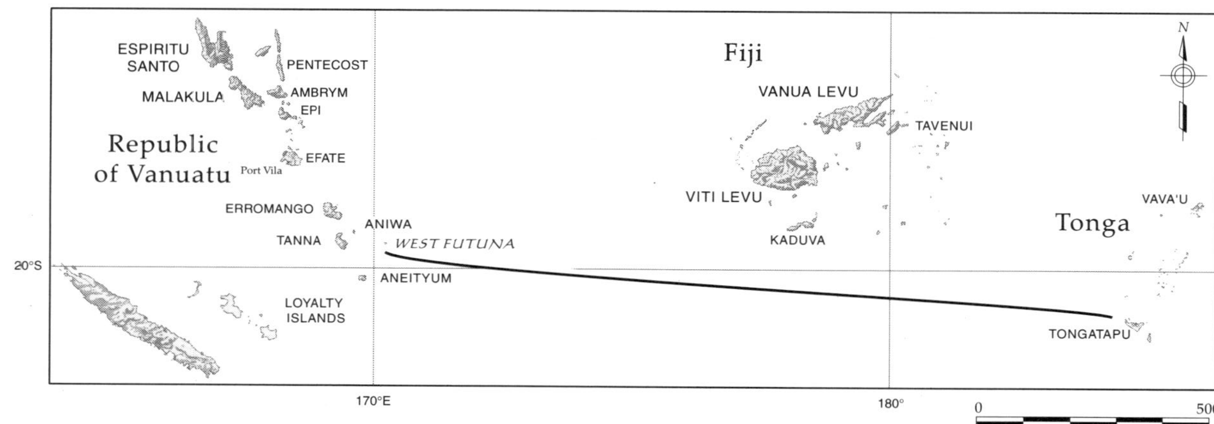

Figure 18: The journey from West Futuna to Tonga.

from the interdiction that she not enter the second room of their house. Such selective prohibitions have been noted commonly in Polynesian lore (Kirtley 1971:154; Gifford 1924:187-90; Lessa 1980:8-11). It is only through violation of her husband's word proscribing entry into the forbidden room that escape becomes possible and a woman's freedom to move is restored.

As in *Ta Pasiesi ma Majihjiki*, escape from confinement creates difficulties as well as benefits. In this case, a woman must leave her family of marriage to regain ties with her family by birth and her female cohort. A man and his young son must survive on their own separated from their wife and mother. A life free of subsistence responsibilities for the Tongan wife is also lost. Ultimately, however, residential choice emerges as flexible by virtue of events that create possibilities of movement for individuals of both genders. The tale as expanded thus challenges binary gendered associations opposing emplacement to flight. By extension the narrative capitalizes on the importance of rich social involvements and flexibility in maintaining such connections through travel. Such an emphasis takes the listener/reader to the everyday world of diverse residential arrangements flexibly connecting kin within and among West Futuna communities at home and abroad.

It is interesting that in the previous tale, Majihjiki assists those confined in their escape whereas in this tale it is he who initially confines another. Perhaps Majihjiki is operating less as an agent in this myth and more as one encompassed by the limiting conventions for movement associated by tradition with marriage. In contrast to usual practice, this tale questions the potential consequences associated with rigid residential requirements of domesticity. Between the lines we read that movement and emplacement must be jointly and conditionally reckoned with to facilitate fulfillment of individual responsibilities as well as construction of new households. Perhaps I have read too much into this myth. Takaronga, himself, is skeptical of the conclusions reached here. Still the reading seems especially relevant in light of contemporary migration patterns and diverse living arrangements. Reflection on this ancient allegory might well prove both liberating and provocative in today's communities.

Majihjiki ma Fafine Toga

Ta hfinenei, tano eigoa Janet, nifakea i Niu Kalifornia. Neirikofia Fiji kai aia kofakea i Fiji koirikofia Fila. Fakea i Fila koirikofia Gauta. Nifakea i Gauta koirikofia Futuna. I mahlonei aia nopuku i tasi a mrae i Tagutu kai nokanieni e faru a fijikauga kaipena. Aia nokanieni pe kanfesaoa mana enei, faru a fijikauga kaipena i ai. Nokanieni pe kanfesaoa mana faru a fesaoga, a hkai i a Majihjiki.

I mahlonei au kanfesaoa mana ta hkai i a Majihjiki, tahi a fakau sore o fakai Futuna i tuai. Ta tagata tenei nonofo i mrae i Pau, kai i ta tagutu i Karisavini. Ta tagata tenei nonofo i ai.

I a nopogi oji ai rofakea karoitara tano toki. Kaie aia koisisireiakea mana htoragi pe e rufie ta nora mo e sa ta nora.

I tera nopogi eia rofakea karoitara tano toki. Kai eia

Majihjiki and the Women of Tonga

This woman, named Janet, departed from New California. She reached Fiji and then she departed from Fiji and arrived at Vila. She departed from Vila and reached Tanna. She left Tanna and arrived at Futuna. And now she sits in one residence at Tagutu and she wants some work to do. She wants me to tell her these, a bit of work she'll do with them. She wants me to tell her some stories, tales about Majihjiki.

So now I will tell her the story of Majihjiki, a respected ancestor of the people of West Futuna from times past. This individual lived in an area of Pau, among the cliffs at Karisavini. This individual lived there.

Everyday he would go out to sharpen his ax. But first he would peer out at the horizon (to see) whether the weather was good or bad.

On one particular day he went out to sharpen his ax. He

koisisireia mana htoragi kai saitara tano toki.

5. Tasi a nopogi eia nirohsirakea foki i a htoragi. Eia neisireiakea foki kaie fafine toga konohlele konoromai.

Romai, romai, romai. Nihlele koromai komeihtakaifo i Sinou. Htakaifo i Sinou, kaie akirea konororo karokaukauia i ta mahmiji. Noroifo i ta tafera kai tafea, tafea, tafea koro ko uai teriari kai kirea kohkaukake. Tiarea tera.

Nokaukau pera rofano, fano, fano romakahligi. Kai akirea korokake ki a hgaone karofakara. Kirea rofakara, fakara, fakara, fakara romatu, pe akirea rokanieni kai korokaukau foki.

Kirea rotanoa tanoa pera. Roafiafi kai kirea kokanieni ta afe kai kirea koafe.

A nopogi ma nopogi kai kirea nopena kirea ta fijikaugara.

assessed the horizon first and then sharpened his ax.

5. One day he looked out at the horizon again. He scanned the horizon once more and women from Tonga were flying, coming (toward West Futuna).

They kept coming and coming and coming. They flew coming (toward West Futuna) until they alighted at Sinou. They came down at Sinou, and then they all bathed themselves in the current. They went down into the flowing water there and it took them, carried them, carried them away and they swam back to shore. That was their way.

They swam like that and kept on and on and on until they felt chilly. Then they would all go up to the beach to sunbathe. They would sunbathe, soaking up the sun, soaking up the sun and soaking up the sun until they were dry, and if they so desired then they would all go swimming again.

They would amuse themselves for a while like that. Come evening they would want to return and so they all would return (to Tonga).

Day in and day out they would all repeat this activity.

Noromai nomeikaukau. Eia pe hsirakea.

10. Tasi a nopogi kai kirea koromai foki. Kirea koromai foki kameikaukau. Nirokaukau korava kai kirea koafe. Eia neisafea kirea niafe ti afiafi.

I ta nopoginei eia neitu pe, 'Aratu tioku a nopogi. Au roaratu kafano karomoetaoa. Kankitea taria pe a ne aha ena.'

Eia nivirikake i ta nopogi tenimurikage i ta pohpoana. I ta nopogira eia konofano ki Sinou norohmuni, norohmuni i ta hpoana. Kai kohmai ta nofajaga pe kahlelemai a fafine toga, eia nihsirakea. Kai kirea nohlele noromai. Noromai kai eia nomatahtu i ai.

U akirea nimeihtakaifo. Kai eia nikomahtatukea i te rufiekea ano mahmata. Eia nimatahtu i te rufiekea ano mahmata ma. Neisireia fakarufie pe eia nokaukau kai ano pahkau kainagaifo uafe. Eia neinage ruano pahkau Majihjiki nikomatahtukea i ai.

Kirea nihsopoifo i a ta mahmiji nokaukau kai a Majihjiki

They would come to swim. He would watch them.

10. One day they all came again. They all came again to swim. They all swam until they had enough and then they all returned. He watched them until they left in the evening.

On this day he said, 'Tomorrow (will be) my day. Tomorrow I will go to select one. I will watch closely to see just who they are.'

He awoke on the morning that followed at dawn. On that day he went off very early to Sinou to hide, to conceal himself. When the time came to expect the women of Tonga to fly in, he watched carefully. They arrived flying. They all flew in while he stared at them.

Then they all alighted. He looked carefully (to find) the one whose appearance was most beautiful. He looked for the one loveliest in appearance. He looked closely to discover where her wings were placed while she was swimming. While she put down her two wings Majihjiki watched her carefully.

They all jumped into the current and swam while Majihjiki

kofano koroijiroa jiroa a pahkau orea. Neijiroa jiroa a pahkau orea, koiamkea tariana te rufiekea ano mahmata. Koiamoa. Koifuna, funa no pekau. Kai aia koafe korohmuni.

went to peruse and examine their wings. He searched and searched through their wings and selected those of the most beautiful one. He took them. He concealed them, concealed her wings. Then Majihjiki went back to hide.

15. U akirea nikaukau, kaukau, kaukau nirava ta kaukau. Kirea nirokake nofakara. Kirea nifakara, fakara nimatu kai konopo. Konopo u akirea konomentua pe konoafe ki tiorea fanua. U akirea nirokea ninagkage kirea pahkau orea.

15. Meanwhile all the women were swimming, swimming, swimming, until they had enough swimming. They came to shore to sunbathe. They all sunbathed and sunbathed until they were dry and by then it was getting dark. It began to get dark and they began to think that they should return to their home. And so they all went about putting on their wings.

Nihlele kororo. Kirea niroro roro roro nipapai. U akirea kotaua kirea. Nitaua akirea kai tasi e jikaikea. U akirea kotakavini foki koromai.

They flew away. They all flew on and on quite a distance. Then they counted themselves. They were all counted but one was definitely not there. And so they turned about again to come back.

Kirea niromai kameihtakaifo i a hgaone. Kateaifo tera no i a hgaone noisara tano pahkau. Kirea kohtakaifo kasitokina eia. Nosara sara sara ekirea, kai kirea sesafea ma kai konopo.

They all returned to land on the beach. They spied her on the sand searching for her wings. They all landed to assist her. Searched and searched and searched they did, but they couldn't find (her wings) and darkness was approaching.

Kirea konomentua pena kataru kirea i ta rikofia ta fanua orea. Makarorako i ta po kapupusi. Katouaki ekirea ta fanua orea. U akirea konohlehle. Kirea konohlehle. Niroro.

They feared that if they stayed longer they might not be able to reach their island. They might arrive in the dark and not know where they were. They all might by-pass their homeland. And so they get ready to fly. They all take off. They departed.

Kai kirea kohkoina ekirea tera. Sohkoiana noisara. Konopourikage eia nihisana kai a Majihjiki konofakea. Kopena tasi a tamtane rufie. E rufiekage ano mahmata komeifakea korositu foki i ta hsara. Majihjiki koifakuiage ta finera pe, 'Aha nousara?'

They all left that one behind. All alone she goes on searching. As it began to get very dark she was surprised by Majihjiki who showed himself. He had made himself into one handsome man. He looked very attractive as he appeared to help too in the search. Majihjiki asked that woman, 'For what are you searching?'

20. Ta tama hfinera neitukage pe, 'Nansara ruoku pahkau.'

20. The young woman said to him, 'I'm searching for my two wings.'

Kiraua kosara sara sara kai sekatea ma kai nikopouri ta fanua kotaru ta katea foki tasi a nea.

The two of them searched and searched and searched but they didn't discover them and as the land got dark it was impossible to see anything.

Majihjiki koitukage i ta hfinera pe, 'Ta ne pena aha i ai? Komate akitaua ta hsara i ai. Kitaua karoro hnofo.'

Majihjiki said to that woman, 'What does it matter? We're both tired of searching for them. Let's just go to live together.'

U akiraua kohfiji ki hluga ta mrae. Kiraua nihfijimai ki hluga nimihnofo tiona mrae. Majihjiki

And so the two of them ascend to the village. They came up to higher ground to koiarafia ta hfinera kapena tiana hfine pe akiraua komihnofo i tiona mrae, ta fare ona, te neit-aua neitumusia i roto.

Ano pito e rua. Tasi ano pito, kiraua nihnofo i ai. Kai tano pito te uaitakesi, eia neipojinakea tiana hfine koisofano ki ai. Ta hfinera koisofano ki ai. Kaie ki-raua kohnofoana i tano pito tei uai ta veihtoka.

25. Kiraua nohnofo, hnofo, hnofo koamoa ta tama. Tiaraua tama ta tane.

Majihjiki neifakataria kiraua feijinana ta mrae kai eia nofano norovere. Eia norovere vere vere roafiafi kai eia koamoa era kai koafemai.

Ahmai komeinage i ta mrae. Akiratou kopena kokaina. I ta hpo tera nopogi eia roviri, kai-kea, kai konofano korovere. Tiana fijikauga tera i anopogi ma nopogi.

Ta tamara konosore, sore fakasisiana. Eia konotavenaga kiraua ma jinana. Jinana ko-noitukage i tan tama pe, 'Tasi a

live together at his residence. Majihjiki brought that woman to make her his wife so the two of them could live in his place, his house, the one he built and divided in the middle.

Its rooms were two. In the first room, they both lived (together) there. But the room on the other side, he prohibited his woman from entering. That woman wasn't to enter there. So the two of them lived exclusively in the room near the door.

25. The two of them lived together for a long time and begat a child. Their child was a boy.

Majihjiki made the two of them, mother and son, wait in the house while he would go to garden. He gardened and gardened and gardened until evening when he would gather their food and return.

He brought it to store at their place. The three of them prepared the food and ate it. In the early morning those days he got up, ate well, and left to go to garden. That was his daily work.

The child kept getting bigger and bigger, bit by bit. And he began to converse with his mother. And his mother said nopogi aia rofano foki karovere kaie akitaua kaurukage foki ta pito fare. Te feipe tei ta veihtoka, te uaitakesi gatatasi ana. Ta ne tano hkano i ai taha uaia koipojinakea kitaua pe kasorokage i ta hnena? Taha i ai?'

to her child, 'One day he'll go again to garden and we'll enter into the other room of the house. That one is just like the one by the door, the one on the other side is just the same. What is the meaning of his preventing the two of us from going there, from entering that place? What is in there?'

Tasi a nopogi Majihjiki nifano foki ki ta vere.

One day Majihjiki left again to go to the garden.

30. 'Akitaua kororora karosireia taria, eia no i ta vere.'

30. 'The two of us will go there to see it clearly while he is in the garden.'

Kiraua notavenaga i ai. Kiraua kororo ki ta pito fare uaitakesi. Kiraua kororo korosara sara e kiraua pe saha kasafea e kiraua i ai. Kai sesafea ma saha i fare.

The two of them discuss it. They go to the other room of the house. The two of them go and look all around to see what they might see there. But they find nothing in the house.

E hkira rufie ana ta fare kai notakape ana ta foiniu furi sore i ta roto ta fare. Kiraua kojikijiake e kiraua ta niu furira pe ta ne taha notakape i ai?

The room is perfectly clear, open space except one special big round stone lies in the center of the room. So the two of them lift up they two that special round stone (to discover) what kind of thing lies under it?

Kiraua nijikijiake ta niu furi, kaie ano pahkau nohtakape uai raro i ai. Eia koiamoa ruano pahkau. Kourukea ki fafo koroimojikeage i ta marama. Pena kaie uriuri.

The two of them lift up the huge stone, and her wings lie under there. She takes out her two wings. She goes outside to examine them in the light. She does this and they are very dirty.

U aia koipohpokiakea ti efu. Korava kaie eia koifuruna. Furuna, furuna, furuna, kohkira fakasisiana.

So she beats them with ashes (to clean them). When she's done she rubs them. She rubs them and rubs them and rubs them until they are a little cleaner.

35. Kaie eia koitukage ki tan tama pe, 'Akiraua kororo ki Ta Fasua.'

35. Then she says to her child, 'We both should go to Ta Fasua.'

Kiraua niroro ki Ta Fasua niroitahtaroa ruano pahkau i tai. Tahtaroa, tahtaroa tahtaroa, tahtaroa kohkira.

The two of them went to Ta Fasua and she washed and scrubbed her wings in the sea. Washed and scrubbed and washed and scrubbed again and again until they were clean.

Koifaraina i ai komatu. Kai akiraua konohfijimai. Kiraua nihfijimai nimeirako ta mrae. Kai eia koitukage ki tan tama pe, "Roafiafi rohmai a tamau. Kai akoe kosoufesaoage pe akitaua niroro ki ta pito fare tapu.'

She put them in the sun until they were dry. Then the two of them went back up. They ascended until they reached their home. And then she said to her child, 'Come evening your father will return. Don't you tell him that the two of us went to the forbidden part of the house.'

Tan tamara neimentua a fesaora, mentua a fesaora. Tamana o ta tamara nihmai i te afiafi kai seifesaoge ma saha i a tamana. Seifesaoge ma. Sa nea hterefana i ateia.

Her child remembered those words, the words stayed with him. The father of that child did return in the evening but the boy didn't say anything to his father. He said nothing. It was a small thing to him.

Kiratou nipena kai ti afiafi kokaikea korava kai kohmoeroa. Kiratou kohmoe kohviri

The three of them prepared food in the evening, ate well and slept. They three slept and i ta hpo. Kai a Majihjiki koafe foki karovere.

40. Eia niafe karovere kai ta hfinera kofakea koipena a kai rufie hmafi. Neipempena a kai nirufie, rufiekea .

Kai eia koitukage ki tan tamara pe, 'Akoe kohtari kai avau konofano. Avau konofano. Kaie rohmai a tamau roifakauia pe avau nifano ki? Kai akoe koutukage pe avau nifano karohsara hfie.'

Eia kofakea konofano nirotukea Tagutu o Rupe. Nagkage ruano pahkaura koiakona korere. Koforinanoa. Forinanoa kaie e rufieana. Eia konorerekea ki hpai. Kaie rufie.

Eia komanatunea neitukua pe, 'Avau mari kofano oku pahkau e rufie ana.'

Eia korere konofano. Eia nirere nifano.

45. Kai tiana tagata konohmai. Nihmai nimeifakauiage tan tama pe, 'Akoe tena, kaie a jinau nouafe?'

Kai tan tama koitukage pe, 'Neitukuamai pe akoe rohmai

awoke in the morning. Then Majihjiki went back to garden.

40. He went back to garden while that woman emerged to make a superb meal. She busied herself preparing the foods until everything was perfect, truly perfect.

Then she said to her son, 'You wait while I am going to go. I am going to go. When your father comes, he will ask where I've gone? Then you can tell him that I have gone to look for firewood.'

She went out to stand at Tagutu o Rupe (The Cliff of Doves). She put on her two wings and practiced flying. She went circling all about. She circled about and everything was just right. So she flew out farther. Everything was right.

She considered all this and said, 'I can fly perfectly with my wings.'

She was flying about to depart. She flew away.

45. Meanwhile her husband was returning. He arrived and questioned his son, 'You are here, but where is your mother?'

And his son said, 'She told me that when you came I should

kantukatu pe akimaua niroro ki ta pito fare tapu. Neitukuamai pe aia karohsara hfie.'

U tamana kofano koroisirea ta niufuri i ta pito fare tapu. Pena kai nijikijiake ta niufuri. E jikai ano pahkau.

Eia koafemai komeitukage tantama pe, 'Neiresia kitaua. Nikofano.'

Eia koitu pe, 'Neiresia kitaua. Nikofano. Kaie ta ne taruana. Kitaua nohnofo ana pera.'

50. Ta fesaoganei nigoravage ana.

tell you that the two of us went into the prohibited room of the house. She told me that she had gone to look for firewood.'

So his father went to check on the round stone in the restricted room of the house. He did that and (found) the round stone had been moved. Her wings were not there.

He came back to say to his son, 'She tricked both of us. She has gone.'

He said, 'She lied to both of us. She has gone. Well, its nothing. We will go on living like we did.'

50. This story has now ended.

Notes

1 Notice the prevalence of *jiki* in these names as well as in the final syllables of *Majihjiki*. *Jiki* serves to single out something. It may be translated 'each' or to emphasize some entity or process. As a transitive verb *jikijia*(*ke*) means 'lift up or exalt' (Dougherty 1983). Perhaps in these names *jiki* carries with it the connotation of 'exalted ones'.

2 Goodenough (1986:559) refers to personal communication with Mathew Spriggs indicating that, 'In Aneityum in southern Vanuatu, for example, Tonga has become the generalized place of origin of all strangers from overseas'. He goes on to note that, 'The presence of Polynesian speaking enclaves in the area suggests the historical background for this attribution; but it would now be an error to interpret a statement that certain people there came originally from Tonga as having any necessary reference to the actual groups of islands of that name'. The West Futuna wind compass illustrated in Figure 6 illustrates the more general directional reference to south in association with *toga* for these islanders. The explicit connection with Tongatapu and Queen Salote in *Sina Fine Ariki* may well be recent but given those identifications and the indication that *Jiverau* arrives from and departs toward the east, translation of *toga* in these West Futuna tales as the Tongan islands is warranted.

3 Assigning value to directions in the landscape is common in Oceanic cosmology. Senft's (1997) volume on space includes several examples. Goldman, Duffield and Ballard (1998:7-8) cite Wagner's (1972:113) demonstration that Daribi cardinality models the human life course, where the eastern headwaters and rising sun offer the promise of life and the downward, western horizon represents death, 'so that sunset and the inexorable movement of water take on the significance of human mortality. The landscape is thus temporalized, etched in terms of a moral continuum, and contains within itself the seeds of its own destruction, the portent of its own end'.

7

Sina Fine Ariki / The Princess Sina

This story introduces the Princess Sina, daughter of Sina, Lightness and Beauty, and Puga, Brain Coral. Sina, the elder, is Majihjiki's sister. She and her husband have many children, all of whom have married except the youngest, the Princess Sina, who has been shielded by her parents from the outside world. This young woman is confined to a refuge in Mouga surrounded by six gated, concentric fences. Puga and Sina go out of the sanctuary grounds everyday to garden in order to provide for themselves and their daughter, but Sina Fine Ariki remains cloistered within.

One day, Majihjiki's youngest son, Jiverau, Dawning Rays of the Sun, arrives in a canoe from Tonga. He anchors at Severaro Bay and ascends the cliffs. While the elder Sina and Puga are gardening, he opens the gates to the sanctuary and approaches the Princess. Jiverau, a strappingly handsome youth, announces his desire to marry Sina Fine Ariki and she agrees, departing willingly with him. Meanwhile her parents have a foreboding sense of something gone awry in the village and they return to find the gates open, their daughter gone.

Sina and Puga run to a lookout from where they can see the strange canoe. They recognize their daughter, Sina Fine Ariki, on board. Sina, the elder, weeps, lamenting her child's departure. The sad melody is represented in Figure 19. Her song is a plea to the Princess asking the name of the man she has chosen. But the boat is too far away for the Princess to understand her

Figure 19: *Tagihkai* 'lament' in *Sina Fine Ariki* with lyrics and musical notation.

mother's words. As the young couple rounds the northwestern most point of the island heading east for Tonga, Sina and Puga follow from one lookout to another on land watching and mourning their daughter's departure. Each time they stop, Sina entreats her daughter to tell her who the young man can be. Sina Fine Ariki hears her mother's voice but the message is repeatedly lost in the wind. She pleads with Jiverau to sail shoreward so she might understand her mother's words. Jiverau sails toward the coast time and again even as he presses constantly on in an eastward course.

Finally the canoe passes beyond the shores of West Futuna and out into the open ocean. Sina and Puga are grief-stricken. Puga jumps to his death. As his body impacts the fringing reef he is transformed into a magnificent, spherical protrusion of brain coral. From this mooring he will forever keep a vigil to the east watching for outsiders who dare to approach. Sina, frozen in her grief, is incorporated into the landscape above. She takes the shape of an enormous stone formation depicted in Figure 20. She too will stand watch forever more from her post atop the island cliffs.

Figure 20: Takaronga stands at Tapesani atop the rock representing the elder Sina who was frozen into stone as a result of her grief.
Janet Dixon Keller 1998.

And there the story ends but doesn't end. The marriage of the Princess Sina and Jiverau is said by the narrator to mark the loss of royalty on West Futuna while initiating an exalted family line in Tonga from which the late Queen Salote and the present king, Taufa'ahau Tupou IV, are descended. This addendum continues the theme of Tongan connections established in *Majihjiki ma Fafine Tonga*. The inter-island marriage is further said to have broad implications for Pacific history resulting in connections among the various languages of Polynesia.[1]

Background and Connections

This tale was recounted by Liji Sore, of *Pau*, in 1973. Liji, now deceased, was elderly at the time he offered to tell this story to me. His family and community responsibilities and his age precluded our working together intensively on transcription and interpretation. As a result the initial transcription and translation were developed primarily by me but in consultation with Liji as his time permitted. Unaware, when I first recorded this tale, to expect a family connection between a narrative text and authorized raconteurs, I never learned from Liji himself of his perceived responsibility for the episodes he conveyed to me. Yet in retrospect I imagine that as a respected elder he may have been concerned with issues of authority and connection represented here.

It is interesting that a senior resident of Pau recounted a tale of entrenched elites in Mouga. Perhaps Liji's interest in the tale rested equally with transnational linkages as with local details. As the son of a woman of West Futuna and a European beachcomber father, whom he never met, Liji may have been particularly concerned with West Futuna's ties to other worlds. I also assume that by way of this narrative Liji was indirectly accounting for an absence of pronounced social hierarchy on the island at present and directing me to look for subtle indicators of status, respect and prestige differentiating villagers. However this may be, it is Liji's version that appears here, edited with a light touch by Takaronga and augmented by a mapping of the landscape, Figure 21, undertaken by Takaronga and me long after Liji's original oral performance.

This story is connected to the other *hkai* in this volume most significantly through characters' genealogies. Sina and Majihjiki are siblings placing the current tale with the two preceding narratives in the realm of earliest mythological time. Other children of Sina and Puga appear subsequently in this book. Sina Fine Ariki's sister is said to have been the wife of Kaveiki Tan Moega, the protagonist in *Rufei Soa*. Samaine, the main character in the story that takes his name, is said to be the abandoned brother of Sina Fine Ariki. So the final three *hkai* are linked through sibling ties of a second supernatural generation. As the youngest son of Majihjiki, Jiverau is of this second generation as well. His identity links this tale back again with *Majihjiki ma Fafine Tonga*. In addition both of these narratives posit an historical connection between the communities of West Futuna and Tonga, and both develop a thematic concern with marital residence patterns.

The current story features characters well known in Polynesian lore (see Andersen 1995 [1928]; Elbert 1949; Elbert and Monberg 1965:137-54; Flood, Strong and Flood 1999; Moyle 2003; Monberg 1991:103). The name Sina, for example, occurs throughout the central and eastern Pacific. Its meanings, 'white, light, dazzling', are associated with the moon who, when personified as a lovely goddess, is often called Sina or Hina (Beckwith 1970 [1940]; Grey 1855; Luomala 1955:107-8; see also Gifford 1929:298; Moyle 1981, 2003).[2] Jiverau, also known as Tinirau, Sinilau or by related designations, is likewise familiar in Oceanic literature (Luomala 1955:104; Moyle 2003).

> Polynesians tell a multitude of stories about the romance of Tinirau and Hina. The hero is irresistibly fascinating to the opposite sex, particularly to pretty, adolescent girls like Hina. They run away from their parents to travel across the sea by any available transportation – reef fish, shellfish, sharks and

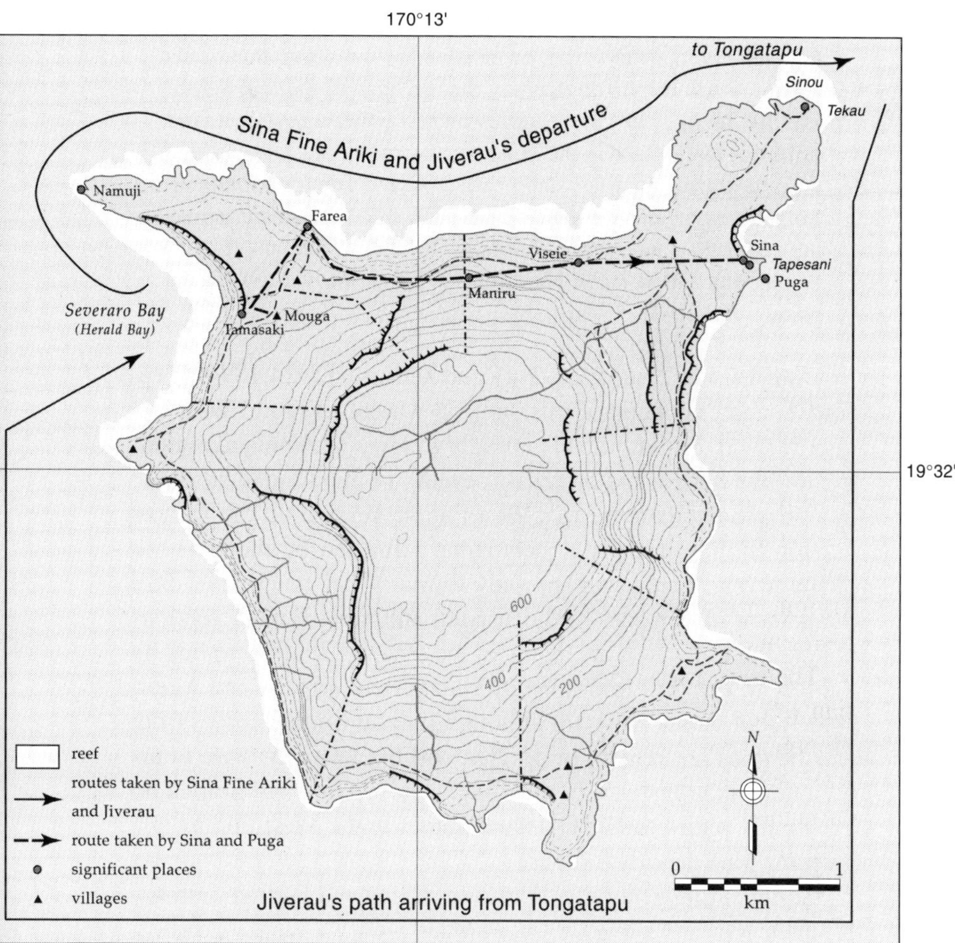

Figure 21: The landscape of the story of *Sina Fine Ariki*.

> turtles – or by swimming in order to reach Tinirau's home. The magnetic hero always lives on an island remote from that of his feminine admirers. Tongans say that he lives in Samoa; Samoans that he lives in Vavau [sic], which is either a mythical land or Vavau [sic] Island in the Tongas; eastern Polynesians put him on a beautiful, floating island called Sacred Isle, or Motutapu. Sometimes, ... it is Tinirau and not Hina who first travels across the sea for a rendezvous. [Luomala 1955:104. See also Flood, Strong and Flood 1999; Herdrich 1991:412; Moyle 1981; Poignant 1967:50-1]

Both Luomala (1955:102-4) and Gifford (1924:187-90) record Tongan versions of this story in which, as in the West Futuna version, Sinilau travels initially to Hina's homeland intending to take her for his bride. But events in the Tongan story are more extended than in Liji's West Futuna version. In the Tongan version Sinilau initially rejects Hina, affronted by the behavior of the lovely young woman, only to marry her much later. Still the pattern of episodes in the Tongan and West Futuna versions both recall aspects of the theme of the stranger-king identified by Sahlins in the oral traditions of Hawai'ians, Fijians and Maori (1985), but with a twist, for although Jiverau/Sinilau comes from afar he does not remain on foreign soil but takes his wife to his own homeland instead. In the Tongan story Hina and Sinilau do eventually return to Hina's island home. In the West Futuna tale it seems Sina departs forever.

Commenting generally on stories of Sina and Tinirau, Luomala states:

> Elsewhere in Polynesia the old stories about the couple continue to be told; and new stories are still being invented, particularly in the western islands in and around Samoa and Tonga. [1955:107]

Herein lies a suggestion of the potential we envision for continued relevance and productive transformation of customary narratives in present contexts.

Cultural Geography and Place

The present story creates significant landmarks on land and reef at the sites of the narrative denouement where Sina is frozen into rock (Figure 20) and where Puga leaps to his death to become a huge brain coral formation in the reef. Genesis of stone and reef formations is typical of folklore throughout Vanuatu (Bonnemaison 1994; Facey 1988; Lindstrom 1997; Sherkin 1999). These sites are often associated with supernatural forbearers and enduring cultural values. In *Sina Fine Ariki* the materialization of parental grief in the landscape opposes male to female as sea to land. This opposition is both familiar and contested elsewhere in Oceania. But in the simple juxtaposition of Puga and Sina the gendered contrast reflects conventional West Futuna practices associating deep-sea fishing and navigation with men by contrast with women's primary responsibilities for everyday gardening and select tree crops on land. Jiverau's journey from beyond the horizon to West Futuna reinforces these oppositional values while at the same time drawing women into trans-oceanic travel that contradicts gendered associations with land and sea.

The tale also infuses established places of land, reef and sea with mythic memories remarked as people traverse their pathways. A stop at Maniru, overlooking the north coast, spawns reflections on the voyage of Sina and Jiverau. A visit to Mouga elicits mention of this place as home of the island elite recalling not only Sina Fine Ariki but also Koitiama, the island chief who played a significant role in earliest mission encounters.

It is said, further, that Sina and Puga lived at the south edge of what is now Ravaru, a *marae* that stands at the conjuncture of two villages, Hsia and Mouga i Hluga. The area indicated as the location of Sina and Puga's refuge is a stone's throw from the *tarie* tree introduced in *Majihjiki ma Fafine Tonga,* site of an evil monster's demise. Walking in this space, as landmarks are pointed out one after another, one begins to feel the weight of the past. Once sacred *marae*s of Kaviameta and Namruke are within sight and a Presbyterian church stands on hallowed ground on the northern edge of Ravaru. Contemporary sites of worship recreate the sanctity once associated with ancestral grounds and the present landscape is imbued with the power of the ancients in the present. The significance of this region of West Futuna only grows as we encounter the next two tales.

The Significance of Direction

The primary actions of this narrative entail an inauspicious circuit of the island. Jiverau's course out of the east takes a turn to the south as West Futuna comes into view. Takaronga, in elaborating the tale, indicated that Jiverau makes a leftward circuit of the island to reach Severaro Bay, creating a directional portent of the disastrous consequences of his voyage. As is evident from Figure 21 this circuit is neither unavoidable nor the shortest path to his destination. Sina and Jiverau continue this directional circuit of the island on their return voyage.

As in the previous tale, no consistent symbolic opposition is evident for the east west contrast. Jiverau approaches West Futuna from the east. This is an auspicious direction marking the arrival of the gods in other Polynesian lore (cf., Monberg 1991:27-8). Indeed Takaronga, expanding on Liji's narration, indicated that Jiverau brought with him gifts of a variety of new foods[3] to leave in exchange for his new bride. The topic of introduced plants enhancing the indigenous resources of West Futuna is often raised in conversation. The island is small, relatively isolated, and reputedly poor in native plants for subsistence. Jiverau's visit indeed would have been highly valued for gifts of food he delivered. But the purpose of his journey is to take away the last unmarried daughter of a royal couple thereby ending, so the narrator suggests, the ranked leadership hierarchy on the island. Jiverau leaves with his new wife, ultimately returning to Tonga in the opposite direction from which he has come. This return voyage is simultaneously providential and detrimental. Sina Fine Ariki is lost to West Futuna. Yet in the wake of this disaster an enduring community of islanders is implied, suggesting a potential for transoceanic linkages by virtue of which discourses, people and objects can, with care, circulate.

Consequentially, the mood of this tale is both defeatist and promising. This tension between devastation and advantage is perhaps symbolized most poignantly as Jiverau tacks toward shore and then away, in a zigzag course that results from the simultaneous ties of affection between mother and daughter facing immanent separation and the future promise of the bond just created between prospective husband and wife.

Confinement and Freedom

In *Sina Fine Ariki,* the Princess Sina is held by her parents in a refuge where she is safe but isolated. Her sanctuary is encircled by six fences. Jiverau must open all six of the gates to reach *Sina* and offer her a proposal of marriage, a feat he accomplishes with little fanfare in the version of the story recorded here. In this act *Sina* gains maturity with her freedom. She earns the right to adulthood carrying with it responsibilities for her own subsistence and for contributing to the subsistence of others. Such is the foundation of human life.

The encircling motif representing confinement has roots in everyday architectural styles. Capell (1958:22) has noted that *kastom* homes of the early twentieth century were typically surrounded by reed fences. Today a shadow of this practice may be evidenced by decorative plants placed at the margins of home sites or by the rock walls encircling some *mrae*s.

Circular motifs, common in West Futuna songs and narratives, occur elsewhere in the Pacific as well (Gray 1909a). A Sina fable quite different from that told in West Futuna comes from Samoa where it is titled *Taligamaivalu* as reported in Moyle (1981:56-89). In this narrative Sinalemalema is encircled by ten rows of visitors who arrive with Tigilau and offer protection for the couple. In addition, according to Luomala (1955:105) the Maori contend in their version of this story that 'in his human manifestation he [the Maori version of Jiverau] has eight rings of fat around his neck'.

The circular motif is introduced again in *Sina Fine Ariki* as Puga is entrenched in the fringing coral that surrounds the island. As with the gated fences protecting the sanctuary, the reef evoked is not an impermeable ring, but, in this case, a skirt around the land offering selective passage. The coral provides a site from which Puga can establish his vigil and stand watch for strangers who seek to pass through the formations.

It is easy to imagine the island of West Futuna itself, idealized locally as circular in form, serving as inspiration for the narrative's circular motif and the theme of confinement it represents. Horizon and reef concentrically bind landed tradition within the traversable world. Sina's sanctuary located in Mouga mimics this larger cultural geography confining the princess within circular restraints and excluding her from the realms of social interchange.

Marriage and Residence

It is only by breaking the barriers around her that Sina Fine Ariki gains the opportunity to assume the conditions and fulfillment marriage provides. Yet marriage recurs here as inherently fraught. Not only is Sina free to establish her own domicile with Jiverau but, in following her spouse to Tonga, the pain of separation for the generations of a bride's family is reintroduced as a condition of patrilocal residence. This norm, disrupted when Majihjiki left West Futuna to follow his wife in the previous story, is partially restored. The emplaced continuity of a man in his homeland remains conflicted here as Jiverau and Sina Fine Ariki return to Jiverau's home in Tonga but only by alienating West Futuna where both bride and father of the groom were born.

Ambiguities

Reading *Sina Fine Ariki* with *Majihjiki ma Fafine Tonga* creates an array of such interpretive ambiguities. Taken together the stories suggest equivocal senses of proper residence, gendered movement (Jolly 1999), and implanted patrilines. With respect to post-marital residence in the previous tale, a wife tethered in her husband's land ultimately escapes to return to the home of her birth. Husband and son only reluctantly follow. By contrast in the Sina tale a young bride willingly leaves her homeland to settle with her newly found spouse. Each case involves trading losses against gains for the couple, for their families and for West Futuna. Such conflicted choices are not only features of mythology. The turmoil developed in the tales indexes a variety of factors regarding residence characteristically presented to descendents of West Futuna today as they were in the past. The tensions implicated in choosing a residential site must inevitably weaken some ties in the service of strengthening others. Perhaps, the tales remind us, no solution is perfect or perhaps perfection is a matter of tuning choices to circumstances in which normative precedents are only one factor to be considered (see also Gifford 1924:187-90).

Ambiguity involving gendered oppositions associated with movement and emplacement also arise in comparing *Majihjiki ma Fafine Tonga* with *Sina Fine Ariki*. In the latter tale an association of men with the sea and women with the land is suggested in the final episode as Puga and Sina become opposing landmarks. Yet this simple opposition is contradicted by the very event – Sina's departure overseas – that is responsible for the genesis of the sites. It is the normatively prescribed movement of a daughter to her husband's place that so disturbs the parental generation.

In *Majihjiki ma Fafine Tonga* women are initially associated with flight and men are rooted to their territories in a pattern reinforced by the return to Tonga in *Sina Fine Ariki* as well as in other ni-Vanuatu lore. Yet, at least in the addendum to the tale of Tongan women, initially established patterns are contradicted when Majihjiki and his son move from their homeland to the distant locale of their wife/mother. It seems that thesc narratives offer a variety of possible linkages among gender, mobility and landed interests that destabilize simple dualisms.

Further complicating narrative associations of gender with land and sea are the examples of gardeners in each story taken up so far. In *Sina Fine Ariki* her parents, who have confined Sina, garden for her, while in *Majihjiki ma Fafine Tonga* and in *Ta Pasiesi ma Majihjiki* it is also the privilege and responsibility of the character who has imprisoned others to do the garden work required for subsistence. Gender has little influence in these discursive developments. Instead gardening appears to be associated with power. This is a theme that will continue to emerge in upcoming tales to support the importance of garden activities for normative subsistence and exchange relations in society, simultaneously qualifying binary associations of men with the sea and women with the land.

Main characters themselves in these tales are ambiguous. Jiverau figures as hero and antihero. His father, Majihjiki, is beloved yet deceptive, innovative and bound by tradition. Those who confine others also provision them. Perhaps such ambiguities offer perspective on the inherent complexity of human nature and the need for *kastom*s including narrative to provide guidance through life without determining events. Via possibilities for inter-textual comparison, narrative opens interpretive spaces in which alternatives for right living may be juxtaposed and evaluated through nuanced debate.

Sina Fine Ariki

Sina Fine Ariki, tamana Puga jinana Sina. Ta tama Puga ma Sina. Kaie a gatamaraua e nalupai. E hsore. Niavaga oji, niavaga i eke a takau.

The Princess Sina

Princess Sina, her father was Puga (Brain Coral) and her mother, Sina (Lightness and Beauty). She was the child of Puga and Sina. Her parents had many children. Many. All of whom were married, married and living with various husbands.

Kaie Sina Fine Ariki. Akiraua nipenpena ta mrae mona.

Except the Princess Sina. Puga and Sina made a home for her (in the village of Mouga).

Nipena ekiraua akoupa e ono. Tasi uai ta koro kai e faru kofori uai tafa i ai. Tasi pe. Tasi pe. Tasi pe. Tasi pe. Tasi pe. Tasi pe.

The two of them built six fences. One is inside and the others go around, each outside the ones before. One like this. One like this. One like this. One just so. Another just outside that one. And the largest just like this. (Narrator circumscribes increasingly large rings with hands to indicate the series of concentric fences.)

Afeipa e ono nouru i ai sarorako uai ta koro. Kiraua nororo ki a teia, kaie eia nonofo i ta hnera. Se fakea. Feipe a kuin uai ta nera.

There were gates in each fence through which the interior could be reached. Sina's parents would go in to see her (and bring her food), but Sina stayed within that place. She never went out. She was like a queen inside her palace.

5. Kai tasi anopogi akiraua, tamana ma jinana, nirovere.

5. Then one day her parents, her father and her mother, went off to their garden.

Kaie Jiverau nihmai i ta vaka komeihagka i Severaro. Nifakei Toga, Togatapu, nihmai ki Futuna. Jiverau nirakai nimeiamoa tasi a hfine Futuna, tano eigoa Sina Fine Ariki.

Meanwhile Jiverau arrived in a sailing canoe coming to anchor at Severaro. He came from Tonga, Tongatapu, and arrived at West Futuna. Jiverau, (Dawning Rays of the Sun) had made himself handsome for he had come to take as his wife a woman from (West) Futuna,

Eia kohmai komifiji ki hluga komifakasara afeipara. Fakasara tasi, rua, toru, hfa, rima, ono kai eia ko fano ki fare.

Koroitukage pe, 'Avau no kanieni i atakoe pe akitaua karoro.'

Kai a Sina koitu pe, 'E rufie.'

10. Eia nitukake konomuri i ateia. Akiraua konororo ki ta vaka kai a jinana ma tamana novere.

Kiraua novere kai nikotata hmafi a ivi oraua. Ta tereva kiraua kosore. U a jinana koitukage ki tiana tagata, ki a Puga, 'Anopogi oji nomivere akitaua, kai avau sen tereva, kai ranei nikua? Taha i ta mrae? Akitaua karoro, karoro ki ta mrae.'

Akiraua niroro nimeirokea kaie afeipa e fakasara oji. Aki raua notukua pe, 'Ta tamara nifano ki? Akai nimeijigofia?'

Kiraua niwaiwahana kosara. Kiraua nirohtukea i Tamasaki

named Princess Sina.

He came and climbed up to the village and he opened those gates. He opened the first, the second, the third, the fourth, the fifth and the sixth gates and then he entered her house.

He said to her, 'I want you to be my wife, and so we must go.'

And Princess Sina answered, 'That is fine.'

10. She stood up to follow him. The two of them made their way to the canoe while her mother and father gardened.

The parents gardened but their bones ached severely. The two of them felt a great uneasiness and exhaustion. So her mother said to her husband, to Puga, 'Every day the two of us come and garden, and I am never tired, so what has happened today? What is going on in the village? The two of us must go, we must go to the village.'

The two of them left and went to find the gates had all been opened. They two muttered, 'Where could that child have gone? Who has come to steal her?'

They both hurried to find her. The two of them went to stand kosireaifo foki ki Severaro. Kai ta vakana koitakina oji. Fakea konofori ta turinea i Namuji.

at Tamasaki where they could look down toward Severaro. The boat had already weighed anchor. It had left to go around the point at Namuji.

A jinana, tano eigoa Sina, kotagi i a teia, ten tama. Korotu i tasi a nohnea kohsireifo ki ta vaka. Kaie ta tama, ten tama, Sina Fine Ariki, no i ta vaka.

Her mother, whose name was Sina, cried out to her, to her child. She stood at a place from which she could peer down at the boat. And there was the child, her child, Princess Sina, in the boat.

15. Sina korotu kotagi. Eia kotagi. Neisigisia ten tama noipen ta hgoro. Kaie ta hgoro ona fei penei:

15. Sina (the mother) stood and wept. She wept. She lamented over her child so she sang a song. Her song went like this:

te-ré te-ré iá-ko fa-no ma-fu mai ma mei: htú
man tá-gi ta-pá koe

Sina, teku tama, fe-sao mai ma-na
pe a-ka-í sa tag-a-ta ta-pu i va-ká-na

Run run you go from me with him still I come to stand
(here now) crying out to you

Sina, my child, tell me before you go
Just who is the noble captain of that canoe?

Tano hkano i ai pe, aia notagi neifakauia pe, 'akai ta tagatana, pen tapu tamotua, neiamoa tiaku tama?'

The meaning of the song is this: She is crying out to ask, 'Who is the man there, powerful aristocrat, who has taken my child?'

Kaie teriki ta vaka tano eigoa Jiverau. Sina Fine Ariki koitukage teriki ta vaka pe,

The captain of the ship was named Jiverau. Princess Sina said to the Captain of the boat,

'Teriki ta vaka, terekake an ta vaka ki gauta, katagi muma kanragona.'

Ta vaka koforikea ta turinea Namuji. Akiraua koromai komihtu i Farea. Sina koipena foki ta hgoro, neisigisia ten tama.

'Oh captain of this boat, sail the canoe up toward shore, so I may hear my mother's song.'

The boat went round Point Namuji. The two parents (anticipated its path) and came to stand at Farea. Sina again sang her song, entreating her child.

20. te-ré te-ré iá-ko fa-no ma-fu mai ma mei: htú

man tá-gi ta-pá koe

Sina, teku tama, fe-sao mai ma-na

pe a-ka-í sa tag-a-ta ta-pu i va-ká-na

20. Run, run away, you go from me, still I come to stand

(here now) crying out to you

Sina, my child, tell me before you go

Just who is the noble captain of that canoe?

Sina Fine Ariki koitukage teriki ta vaka pe, 'Teriki Jiverau, terekake ta vake ki gauta fakasisiana. Katagi a muma kanragona.'

Ta vaka koterekake ki gauta hmai komeifakaseke konomeifano. Kiraua korokea Farea komeihtu Maniru, ta hne te nihpura ta niu. Akiraua nimeitukea i ta hnera kai ta vaka komeiterekea. Sina nitu i ai neisigisiakea tan tama. Neipen ta hgorora:

Princess Sina said to the ship's captain, 'Oh Captain Jiverau, sail the canoe toward shore just a little bit. My mother entreats me and I will hear her.'

The canoe sailed shoreward while still progressing toward its destination. The parents left Farea and came to stand (and look out over the sea) at Maniru, the place where a coconut palm is planted. The two of them came to stand at that place but the canoe had already sailed past. Sina stood there and entreated her child. She sang that song:

te-ré te-ré iá-ko fa-no ma-fu mai ma mei: htú
man tá-gi ta-pá koe

Run, run away, you go from me, still I come to stand
(here now) crying out to you

Sina, teku tama fe-sao mai ma-na
pe a-ka-í sa tag-a-ta ta-pu i va-ká-na

Sina, my child, tell me before you go
Just who is the noble captain of that canoe?

Sina Fine Ariki neitukage pe, 'Teriki Jiverau, terekakean ta vaka ki gauta fakasisiana. Katagi a muma kanragona'

Princess Sina said, 'Oh, Captain Jiverau, sail the canoe just up toward shore a little bit. My mother will call out and I can listen to her.'

25. Ta vaka notere. Nofano fano komeifori ta turinea Tekau. Akiraua koromai komeihtukea i Viseie, kai ta vaka koforikake ta turinea i Tekau. Kiraua niwaiwahana nifura niroro ki ta Tapesani.

Kiraua nimeihtukea i ai, kai ta vaka konomeifori, konofano ki Toga. Jinana notu notagi, neisigisia tentama noipena ta hgoro:

25. The canoe was departing. It was going to round the point at Tekau. Sina's parents came to stand at Viseie, but the canoe was already well around the point at Tekau. They hurried, running toward Tapesani.

They both came to stand there, but the canoe had already gone round and was on its way to Tonga. Her mother stood and wept, mourning her child and sang the song:

te-ré te-ré iá-ko fa-no ma-fu mai ma mei: htú
man tá-gi ta-pá koe

Run, run away, you go from me, still I come to stand
(here now) crying out to you

Sina, teku tama fe-sao mai ma-na
pe a-ka-í sa tag-a-ta ta-pu i

Sina, my child, tell me before you go
Just who is the noble captain

va-ká-na

of that canoe?

Pena, kai ta vaka kotere konofano fano korojikaikageana i a htoragi. Nirava ta safea foki.

She sang, but the canoe was going, going until it was no longer on the horizon. It could no longer be seen.

Ta vaka nifano kai kiraua nifakainina. A Puga kokali kosopokea tai kokero. Sopokea kokero kohtu i tai.

The canoe had departed and the Princess Sina's parents were overcome with grief. Puga was so distraught he jumped into the sea and drowned. He jumped off, drowned and surfaced as a projection in the sea.

30. Kaie a jinana Sina te noeke.

Ta tai neiurakea kosa, kai i tuai noeke rufie.

30. Her mother Sina remained perched above.

The sea has (by now) washed over and eroded (the coral), but long ago it protruded magnificently.

A Sina te noeke. Sesopo ma. Noekeana hluga. A Sina ta fatu i Tapesani.

Sina remains perched above. She didn't jump. Sina forever stands above. Sina is the rock (formation high on the cliffs) at Tapesani.

Ta vaka kofano, koiamoa Sina Fine Ariki koronofo i Toga.

Jiverau nifakei i Toga koiahmai ta vaka komeiamoa ta tama hfinenei, Sina Fine Ariki, neiamoa ki Toga karonofo i Toga.

The canoe departed taking the Princess Sina to live in Tonga.

Jiverau had come from Tonga in a sailing vessel in order to take that young woman, the Princess Sina, take her to Tonga to stay.

35. Aia oji tera.

Ta nofajaganei a fakai Futuna nimokage. Kaie nihmai ta

35. And that's all there is.

Today (we understand) the people of West Futuna were the

vaka komiamoa ta hfine Futuna ta kuin koronofo Toga.

Nopoginei kojikai ta kuin Futuna. Ta tagata i Toga nihmai komiamoa ta kuin, ta hfine Futuna. Niamoa kiraua ta nauji te a kuin Salote nifakea i ai i nopoginei.

Komiamoa ta hfine Futuna kopena ta fesao i Futuna ma Toga ma Niue ma Walis ma Futuna teke ma Kelpit ma … kogatahtasi.

Akirea ta fesaoarea tan tasi ana.

beginning. Then there came a canoe and took a woman from Futuna to be Queen of Tonga.

And here on West Futuna the royal line was lost. A man from Tonga came and took the Queen, the woman from West Futuna. The two of them begat the family line from which Queen Salote of more recent times descended.

He came to take a woman of West Futuna and (as a result) the languages of West Futuna and Tonga and Niue and Wallis and the other Futuna and the Gilberts and perhaps other islands come together as one.

They all, their languages, are one.

Notes

1 Perhaps this addendum reflects the narrator's desire to connect his island with Pacific history. The story-teller himself traveled beyond West Futuna during his lifetime and was fond of epic ballads recounting adventures in foreign lands. As an elder and leader in Pau he served during much of his lifetime as liaison for his community when external matters of church or state impinged on village affairs. He took responsibility for my initial visit and residence in Pau in 1973-74. In his role of culture broker he would have been exposed to Western ideas about exploration and inter-island connections. His conclusions about linguistic relatedness and Tongan royal history may well be derived from discourses in circulation among expatriates and islanders during the twentieth century. (See Beaglehole 1961; Forster 2000 and Salmond 1991 for examples of Western ideas about linguistic relatedness in the Pacific that would have circulated in the islands during the age of exploration.)

2 The physical moon is referred to as *mrama* in the language of West Futuna. Sina has the meanings 'whiteness and lightness', qualities explicitly associated with the moon, with feminine beauty, and with light or graying hair (Dougherty 1983). According to the Reverend William Gunn the people of West Futuna traditionally built altars for worship, 'the two tallest posts in the altar representing the sun and the moon. Children were the gift of the moon' (1914:218).

3 A number of tales similarly recount prestations of new fruits and vegetables delivered by voyagers from afar. Notably, a site in the reef near Iraro, named Ta Vaka, marks the arrival of a supernatural canoe laden with gifts of novel foods.

8
Rufei Soa / Two Brothers

Cooperation between men who refer reciprocally to one another as *soa*, brothers or parallel cousins, was critical to right living among members of the West Futuna community in the past as it is in the present. I use the English word 'brothers' in translation of this relationship to include the appropriate ties among cousins as well. Figure 22, taken in the 1890s, represents this enduring bond between *soa* in the persons remembered by some as Jipa and Nakaipeni, who sit facing one another prepared with tools for subsistence and weapons insuring protection against all others. The ancestral image captures two individuals united in a life-long relationship through their kinship, cooperation in the tasks of everyday living and mutual protection of each other and their respective families.

The story we have titled *Rufei Soa*, however, is a tale of brotherly woe. In a society where children of the same parents and offspring of same gender siblings of those parents should all be mutually supportive, one man, Vahkarokaro, attempts to hasten the death of his *soa*, Kaveiki Tan Moega. The aggressor imagines himself becoming husband to his 'brother's' widow. After a series of attempts on his life, Kaveiki Tan Moega warns his wife of the danger he is in and asks her to watch for something unusual in the village. Such happenings will be a sign portending his death. Fearful of what may happen, the wife prepares herself. While the men are away, she cooks a pig and sweeps her home and

Figure 22: *Rufei Soa* 'Two Brothers'.

surrounding grounds until they are spotless. And indeed while she is at work events go awry. Vahkarokaro succeeds in causing the drowning of his brother at sea by encouraging him to probe for the meat of a giant clam while its shell is open under water. Kaveiki Tan Moega's arm becomes clamped in the jaws of the shellfish. Soon, assured of his brother's death by floating blood and feces, Vahkarokaro returns to the village expecting to take his brother's wife for his own. The return of Vahkarokaro without Kaveiki Tan Moega is unprecedented. The event is recognized as the foretold sign of danger when Vahkarokaro improperly demands that his brother's wife prepare and cook food for him as if she were his own spouse. The wife, in her turn, imagines her husband already on his journey to the underworld. She becomes determined to rescue him. Refusing the overtures of her brother-in-law, Kaveiki Tan Moega's wife uproots the center post of her home, and carrying this with her to transport carefully packaged pork to exchange for information, she sets off to search for her husband.

In her travel along the reef the woman traces a well-known path to the place beneath the sea where the dead must go. Along the way she encounters spirit children, and sings to them of her spouse.[1] The melody of her lament is presented in Figure 23. The lyrics beseech the children for information about Kaveiki Tan Moega's progress toward the underworld. The children respond with the second verse of the musical text in the same figure. They acknowledge that he has passed by, naked and injured, making his way to the underworld. Hearing this she gives them food in gratitude for their help and continues on her way. After several such encounters and nearly at the end of her supply of pork, the wife meets two spirit women, Ta Kofu Kofu and Ti Auauau. They tell her they have seen her husband and instruct her in a cure requiring a particular species of large, white cowrie[2] found on the reef. (The shell of this white cowrie is incorporated into the ornamental armband shown in Figure 22.) The wife is directed to warm the cowrie and call to the spirit of Kaveiki Tan Moega. When the smoke of the warming embers hovers just above the opening of the shell, the return of her husband is signaled. The wife is instructed to lie down with the warm shell against her chest and she falls asleep. She awakens to find her partner lying there on her chest, his vitality restored. The couple returns to normal married life on the island with their newly found knowledge, which becomes a part of the heritage of West Futuna. Their ties with Vahkarokaro, however, are forever disrupted. By his actions he is permanently ostracized, doomed to a life without brotherly support.

Translation of the *tagihkai*, the wife's sorrowful questioning of the spirit children and their sung reply, was difficult. We think the result presented in the text is a fair representation of the

Figure 23: *Tagihka*i 'lament for Kaveiki Tan Moega' with lyrics and musical notation from *Rufei Soa*.

lyrical intent though the significance of the timing of the event to coincide with the season for catching flying-fish and tuna, for example, remains unclear. The literal meaning of the last line, *pume pume,* is not known. It serves to culminate the exchanges between Kaveiki Tan Moega's wife and the children. We translate it here as 'that's all, that's all'.

Translating the actions constituting the cowrie shell cure required repeated elaboration of the original text. The oral presentation was cryptic and assumed details the narrator imagined I must know. As I questioned her, she only gradually realized I lacked the background knowledge to interpret her words and, phrase-by-phrase, she offered a more explicit account. The translation here reflects this elaboration.

Background and Connections

Napausi Teifisou of Pelitamoko is the narrator. She resides in a neighborhood of Taroumara in the vicinity of the situated narrative events. Napausi is a traditional healer and this tale tells of the supernatural origins of one among many cures constituting her expertise. First told to me in 1974, she and I translated it then. Together we revisited the translations in 1998, and again in 1999, expanding narrative segments in both languages. Takaronga's prudent questioning during these periods improved the final result.

Kaveiki Tan Moega and his wife represent the second supernatural generation to play a role in the West Futuna *hkai*. The wife in *Rufei Soa* is said to be one of the sisters of Sina Fine Ariki, heroine in the preceding tale, and therefore, sister as well to Samaine, who appears in the next story.

We have identified a few stories with overlapping themes within Pacific literature. One story, translated as Sina and the Mouse, was recorded in 1958 on Bellona (Elbert and Monberg 1965:137-40). It has all the initial elements of a covetous jealousy on the part of one man for another's wife, of deception intended to destroy the original husband, of murder achieved while the men are at sea, of a wife's journey to the underworld to find her husband and of their eventual reuniting. The tale turns out differently, however, in that the couple and their parents stay in the underworld to govern it and along the way the episodes leading to the couple's reunion are quite distinctive. Within Vanuatu, a Nguna story, *Seiseinai and Aisei,* told by Thomas Tavirana, traces a similar journey along the shore and reef making a path to the underworld (Facey 1988:222-24). Moreover, episodes in which a person, animal or god is trapped in the jaws of the tridacna, or giant clam, as happens here, are, common throughout Oceania and feature in stories otherwise quite distinctive (Ashby 1989; Elbert and Monberg 1965:116-17; Kirtley and Elbert 1973:244-45; Monberg 1991:100). Capell documents a cure similar to that introduced in the story narrated by Napausi (1938:76)[3] that he indicates is shared by peoples of what is now southern Vanuatu.

Confinement and Freedom and Other Thematic Developments

Rufei Soa entails the theme of confinement and escape that has appeared in the preceding stories of this collection. After being clamped in the jaws of a giant clam until he drowns, Kaveiki Tan Moega is released to initiate his descent into the underworld (*i o tua*). Although initially his release seems to lack the associations that accompany freedom in other tales, ultimately his journey restores his life and returns him to the full responsibilities of human existence.

Three events of special significance further enrich the meaning of this narrative. The first is Vakarokaro's demand that his brother's wife prepare food so the two of them can eat together. Commensality would signal the marriage Vahkarokaro desires, but is adamantly refused by Kaveiki Tan Moega's wife whose spousal loyalty guides her.

Secondly, the uprooting by Kaveiki Tan Moega's wife of the central house post in her abode dramatizes her rejection of the overtures from her brother-in-law and initiates her journey to find her rightful spouse. As the primary architectural support, the center post of a couple's house symbolizes the enduring strength of their social as well as physical bonds. By uprooting the post the wife emphasizes her dire situation through the physical collapse of her home. At the same time she incorporates a reassuring symbol of the solidity of her marriage in this prop that becomes integral to her search. The post serves as a shoulder support for food that is essential in the series of exchanges that guides her to her spouse. This over the shoulder mode of transport is typical of men, not women. Perhaps her adoption of the practice materializes her need to temporarily embody the union of both parties to her marriage.

The third act of interest is the wife's sweeping her home grounds spotlessly clean while she anticipates a response to her peril. Sweeping is a ubiquitous practice of daily life. Its antiquity as a significant domestic chore is unclear, but nineteenth- and early twentieth-century mission records reflect a Christian concern with this task (see also Donner 1987:212). The action appears significantly in the next story as well. A clean homestead reflects a strong, well-organized family and perhaps, symbolically, a wife able to keep the detritus of disturbing events from distracting her from her purpose. Bonnemaison (1994:221) has noted that the name of the John Frum resistance movement on the neighboring island of Tanna derives from John, in reference to John the Baptist, and Frum, stemming 'from the English word *broom*, the image of a broom being used in the Tannese language to designate the act of cleansing …' John Frum was, and by many still is, perceived as a savior with the power to purify the land. Perhaps the force attributed to sweeping in naming John Frum similarly informs the wife's actions in *Rufei Soa*.

Cultural Geography: Place, Settings and Direction

Landmarks are not literally created by this narrative, but are infused with significance in the telling of the story. The status of Mouga as home of original elite families is reinforced by the narrated events involving supernatural ancestors. In addition episodes at named points along the reef give meaning to these sites. In my many visits to Mouga, Ta Toka,[4] photographed in Figure 24, was frequently pointed out as a place of significance sometimes in connection with *Rufei Soa* and other times independent of this tale. Other sites, less visible from the cliffs, were also indicated on occasion as points of interest.

The reef itself in this tale is constructed as a pathway from the surface of the sea to its depths. In this vertical dimension mortality and supernatural immortality are mediated. Ta Toka, where Kaveiki Tan Moega's journey to the underworld begins, is a place alternatively exposed and inundated by tides, not a surprising choice for a link between the world of customary practice above and the underworld below. The reef is also the source of the cowrie shell connecting people with the supernatural through the gift of knowledge regarding life and death. The coral fringe is constituted as a transitional space where mortal and ancestral beings meet.

A dichotomy between land and sea is developed in events in this story. Domesticity and brotherly cooperation set the opening scene at a village site. And even once the despicable motives of Vahkarokaro are revealed, activities on land fail to result in Kaveiki Tan Moega's death. It is only when the brothers leave the island to dive for clams in the sea that Vahkarokaro is successful. In this context the sea takes on values of risk and danger by contrast with the relative security associated with events on land.

The symbolism of leftward and rightward movement also recurs in *Rufei Soa*. Consultants pointed this out before I had an inkling of the pattern. It was remarked that Kaveiki Tan Moega's journey toward the underworld illustrated in Figure 25 was simultaneously a leftward (facing the island interior) and westward progression.[5] His wife's desperate pursuit follows the same path.

Figure 24: Ta Toka, entrance to the underworld, is centered in the reef in Severaro Bay.

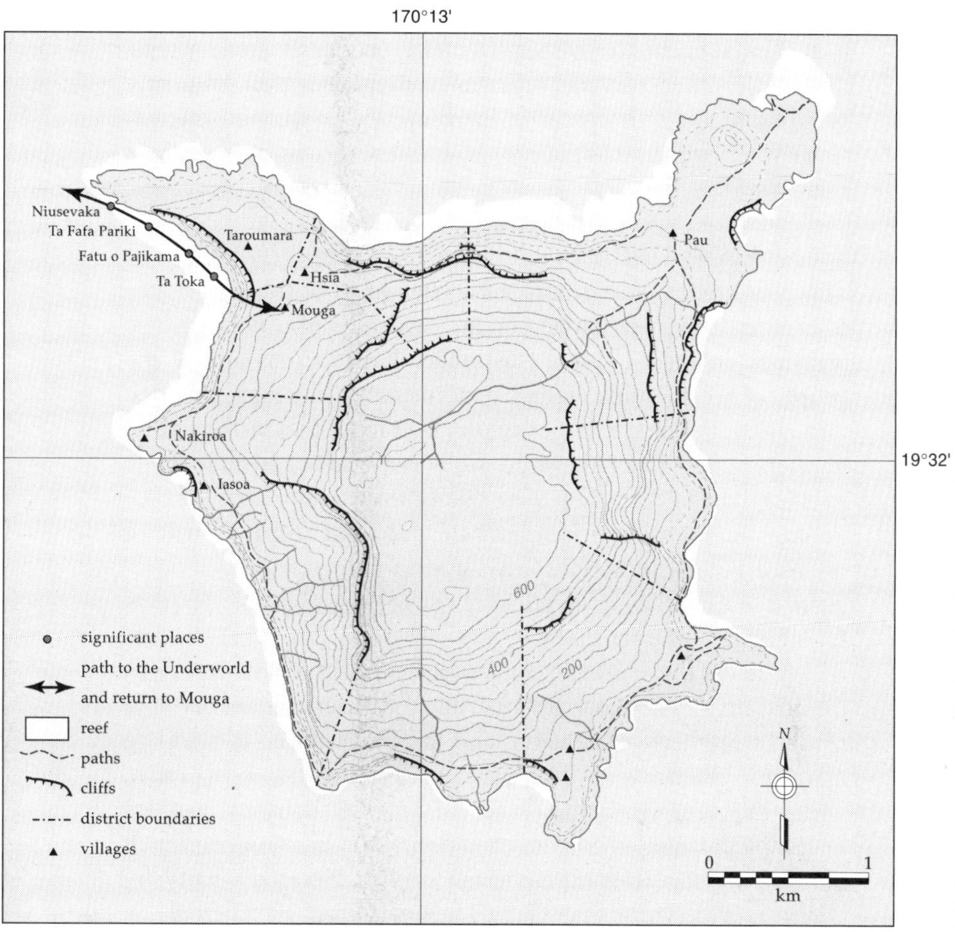

Figure 25: Landmarks and the directional orientation of the journey to the underworld in *Rufei Soa*.

These episodes carry distressing overtones until they end in a providential encounter with spirits. This encounter literally halts the couple's trajectory and reverses subsequent action. Ultimately husband and wife return in the propitious rightward orientation to climb upward to their home and renew their lives on West Futuna.

Character Traits and Social Roles in Narrative Motifs

This story relies on listeners' understandings of the importance of brotherly cooperation and on an awareness of usual marriage practices on West Futuna. Customary kin relations among the people of West Futuna include patterns much like those reported throughout Polynesia. For example, Bott notes that in Tonga, '… brothers of the same father were supposed to love and honour one another, but, in fact, they were likely to be jealous' (1982:91). Perhaps this tension arises because the ideal marriage pattern on West Futuna prescribes cross-cousin unions with the consequence of establishing identical classes of marriageable partners for siblings of the same sex.

Whatever the source, a challenge to idealized patterns drives the narrative. The story tells of near-death consequences as a result of brotherly dissension, and the threat posed to standard marriage practices by jealousy. Reinforcing the cooperative norm, the narrative consequence of hostility between brothers is complete isolation for the offender, a condition under which humans in the real world could not survive. Spousal loyalty, by contrast, is the virtue that enables recovery from such betrayal.

Rufei Soa

Tasi anofajaga nohnofo rufei soa, Kaveiki Tan Moega ma Vahkarokaro. Tioraua mrae Mouga. Rufie tapu tioraua hnofo. Kiraua nohnofo Mouga. Kaie a Kaveiki Tan Moega eia niavaga kaie a Vahkarokaro se avaga ma.

Kiraua rororo ki a vere, roafemai ki ta mrae. Kaveiki Tan Moega kogapu. Tiana hfine kopena kai maraua kakaina. Kai a Vahkarokaro eia se gapu ta fijikau i a vere ma i ta mrae. Ta pena kai mana.

Tioraua hnofo tera. Kaveiki Tan Moega nonofo rufie nokanieni segapu. Kaie a Vahkarokaro nonofo se kanieni pe eia nofijikau segapu. Jikai tasi kaisitokina eia.

Tasi a nopogi a Vahkarokaro nopuku nomanatunea. Notavenaga mana sohkoia, 'Erufie pe avau kanofo rufie feipe tuku soa. Kanpena pekua pe avau kanofo feipe eia? E rufie mari pe avau kantia tuku soa kamate kai avau kankamoa tiana hfine kahnofo kimaua.'

Two Brothers

Once upon a time there lived two brothers, Kaveiki Tan Moega and Vahkarokaro. Their village was Mouga. Their life was wonderful. The two of them lived in Mouga. Kaveiki Tan Moega was married and Vahkarokaro was not.

They would both go to garden and then return to the village. Kaveiki Tan Moega would rest. His wife would prepare a meal for the two of them (husband and wife) to eat. But Vahkarokaro couldn't stop working either in the garden or at home. Preparing food fell to him (too).

Their life was like that. Kaveiki Tan Moega lived well and was always content. However, Vahkarokaro lived unhappily because he had to work constantly. There was no one to help him.

One day Vahkarokaro was sitting and thinking. He was talking to himself. 'It would be great if I could live well like my brother. What can I do so that I can live as he does? It would work out perfectly if I attacked my brother causing his death for then I could marry his woman

5. Ta mentuanei nisorekange tiona roto. Koromai a mentua rehresia pe kaitia tanosoa. Nimokage kiraua karouofia sa vere.

Tasi anopogi Vahkarokaro koitukage i a Kaveiki Tan Moega pe, 'Kiraua karouofia sa uofaga.'

Kiraua niroro nirouofia ta uofaga. Tasi a tafito rakau sore notu roto ta uofaga.

Vahkarokaro neitukage tano soa pe, 'Avau kansauaifo ta rakau kaie akoe kausikofia ta rakau pe akoe serousikofia ma kotakaifo ta roto vere, ta vere nikosa.'

Nitakaifo ta rakau. Kaveiki Tan Moega kotere kofakasara ta rakaura. Vahkarokaro neitukage pe, 'Nigko sa tena. Koina tena.'

10. Te nimurikage akiraua kororo koropaea ta pae. Nipaea ta pae kai a Vahkarokaro kaitukage tano soa, 'Au ragfakaterekia ta fatu kai akoe kautotomia ta fatu sorenei. Pe akoe seroutotomia ma, ta pae ataua nikosa kahkoina.'

and the two of us could live together.'

5. This thought grew inside him. Gradually the vicious idea that he would kill his brother took shape. First the two of them would go to clear a garden.

One day Vahkarokaro said to Kaveiki Tan Moega, 'The two of us should go clear our garden space.'

The two of them went to clear the garden. A single tree trunk stood in the middle of the clearing.

Vahkarokaro said to his brother, 'I will chop down the tree and you must catch the trunk because if you don't, it will fall down into the middle of the garden and ruin our plot.'

Down came the tree. Kaveiki Tan Moega ran and in the nick of time dodged that tree. Vahkarokaro said: 'This isn't working. Enough of this.'

10. After that the two brothers went to build a stone fence. They worked moving and piling the stones until Vahkarokaro said to his brother, 'I'll push a boulder to make it roll and you catch it. If you fail to grab it, our fence will be spoiled and we'll have to quit.'

Eia neifakaterekia ta fatu sore. Nitere nivatatage i ateia, eia nitere ta fatu komeifano.

Vahkarokaro shoved the boulder. It rolled toward Kaveiki Tan Moega who diverted it and it kept on going.

Vahkarokaro nigkokali neitu pe, 'Nigko sa tera. Koina ta pae kiraua.'

Vahkarokaro became frustrated and said, 'That is not working. We'll just leave the fence.'

Niroro. Karohsau raga fare. Kiraua nirosaua raga fare. Vahkarokaro neitukage tano soa pe kaisikofia pe rotakaifo. Ta rakau nitakaifo kai eia kofakasarakea iai. 'Nigko sa tera. Hkoina kitaua koafemana ki ta mrae,' Vahkarokaro neitukage tano soa.

(The two brothers) went on. They were going to cut house posts. They started to cut house posts. Vahkarokaro told his brother to catch them as they fell. One tree fell but Kaveiki Tan Moega dodged it. 'That didn't work. Let's just quit and go back to the village for now,' Vahkarokaro said to his brother.

Nimeirako ta mrae Kaveiki Tan Moega kamitukage ki tiana hfine, 'Nigko puni a ne hluga, tiaku fine, kaie rororo kimaua ki tai.'

When they got home, Kaveiki Tan Moega came to say to his wife, 'We're done with our work up on land, my wife, so the two of us will go to the sea.'

15. 'Morefuma avau romate. Pe roukitea sa hkite ta mrae, tera ta farigoi pe avau nikomate oji.'

15. (Then he cautioned her,) 'Most likely I am going to die. When you notice something different in the village, that will be the sign that I am already gone.'

Tasi a nopogi kiraua niroro ki tai. Akiraua kosua i ta vaka ki ta moana. Kiraua feisoa nirohsuru fasua. Nigkoraga e kiraua a fasua nalupai. Koronage oji.

That day the two brothers went to the shore. They paddled out in their canoe to the ocean depths. The two brothers decided to dive for giant clams.

Vahkarokaro nisuruifo tai nimei ekake neikaina ta nia utu niu. Neinageifo tano pono. Eia noikaina Kaveiki Tan Moega neifakauiage tano soa pe, 'Taha tena?'

Vahkarokaro neitukage pe, 'Ta numata fasua.'

Tano soa neifakauia pe, 'Nouamkea pekua?'

20. Eia neitukage pe, 'Akoe rousafea rofakamama kai akoe kouworoifo tourima kounigijiakea tano numata. Koukaina.'

Kaveiki Tan Moega kofano korokitea tasi. Koisuruia kofano fano fano kororouia ta foromaga o ta fasua. Neirouiaifo kai ta fasua kototomia tano rima.

Eia nofusu i ta tai raro. Nofusu nofusu ma kai e mahkei, kai a Vahkarokaro nomanu i ta vaka hluga.

Neiajia kai korokake htae nomeihmanu. Kai eia nomanu ta poruku. Noimoetaoa kaie se

They harvested many. All were stowed (in the canoe).

Vahkarokaro dove beneath the sea and then surfaced eating a bit of coconut. He had had it hidden in his penis cover. While he was chewing on it, Kaveiki Tan Moega asked his brother, 'What is that?'

Vahkarokaro said, 'The meat of the clam.'

His brother asked, 'How do you get it out?'

20. Vahkarokaro replied, 'When you spy one with an open shell insert your hand down in to pinch and lift out the meat. Then eat it.'

Kaveiki Tan Moega went to look for one. He dove for it and kept going deeper and deeper and deeper in order to bring up the body of the clam. Kaveiki Tan Moega inserted his hand down (inside a giant clam), but the shellfish clamped shut on his arm.

Kaveiki Tan Moega struggled in the sea below. He struggled and struggled but was held tight, while Vahkarokaro floated in the boat above.

He kept watch and soon human feces surfaced and floated toward him. But he just drifted fenake ma. A htae ma ta toto ana nimei ekake. Eia nikomate. Eia konosua konotau. Eia nifano nirorako ki ta mrae.

in the boat. He kept watch but (his brother) didn't follow. Just feces and blood came up. Kaveiki Tan Moega's spirit had left his body. Vahkarokaro began paddling and reached the shore. He went on until he came to the village.

Kai ta hfine nigkoitia ta pakasi nigkoputoia i ta mrae. Neiputoiakea ta putoi kai eia koseri-mrae kohgamakara. Kai eia nopuku nohtari i a ta nuane, tiana tagata.

Meanwhile the wife had killed a pig and was cooking it in the village. She had wrapped the food and was cooking it while she swept the village spotlessly clean. Then she sat to wait for that man, her husband.

25. Nisehtuai ma Vahkarokaro kameifenake neitukua pe, 'ta nafune nei, koupena ti afi kotuna i a ikanei.'

Ta nafunera neifakauiage eia pe, 'Akoe tena kaie a Kaveiki Tan Moega tehe?'

Eia neioriage pe, 'No uai muri.'

Ta nafunera kopuku pukukage koifakauia foki, 'Akoe tena kai a Kaveiki Tan Moega tehe?'

Eia neioriage foki pe, 'No uai muri.'

30. Ta nafunera neitukage ki a Vahkarokaro, 'Ta nikua u avau nagfakauia kai akoe noutu pe, "No uai muri?" '

25. It wasn't long before Vahkarokaro arrived and said, 'Woman, here, make a fire and cook this seafood.'

That woman questioned him thus, 'You're here, but where is Kaveiki Tan Moega?'

He answered her, 'He's coming.'

The woman sat and sat there and she asked again, 'You're here, but where is Kaveiki Tan Moega?'

(Impatiently) Vahkarokaro replied again, 'He's coming.'

30. That woman said to Vahkarokaro, 'What has happened that I question you and you answer me that "He's coming?" '

Vahkarokaro saitukage ta nafunera, 'Ta ne penaha te noufakauiana? Seupena ti afi katuna kitaua i a ika kakaina.'

Vahkarokaro said to the woman, 'Why do you persist in asking questions? You ought to make the fire so that we can cook this seafood and eat it.'

Ta nafunera seitukua ma foki sa fesao. Eia nirukea fare neifukea ta putoi. Neifukea fukea fukea korava. Koifaoa i a porapora.

The woman said not another word. She went out of the house and uncovered the cooking pig. She removed hot stones and kept at it until she was finished. Then she stowed (the pork) in coconut frond sacks.

Koiamoa foki kourukage ki fare koitakinakea ta pou ta fare oraua ma Kaveiki Tan Moega.

She picked everything up and reentered the house to uproot the center post of the home of the two of them, hers and Kaveiki Tan Moega's.

Kaie eia koruifo kofano kororako i a Ta Toka. Nirako i a Ta Toka kai a gatama nofetakaro i a Ta Toka. Uaia koifakauia a gatamara pe:

Then she descended to go to the reef at Ta Toka. She arrived at Ta Toka and found children at play. So she asked the children there:

35. ni tama ni tama

koua nisokitea
Kaveiki Tan Moega?

35. Oh children, Oh children
Haven't you all seen
Kaveiki Tan Moega?

Kai a gatama kooriake pe:

And the children answered her:

Kaveiki Tan Moega
samei suruifona
e amo tano maro
e feinu tano rima
nei fan tarian

Kaveiki Tan Moega
He came diving down here
He came fully naked
Protecting/Cradling his arm
He went on to wait for

ta ramaga

pume pume

The season when the flying fish soar

That's all, that's all

Ta nafunera neinagaifo tasi a araga pakasi marea kai.

Kaveiki Tan Moega's wife gave a portion of the pig for the children to eat. (Then she continued following her husband's path.)

Eia kofano korotapa i Fatu O Pajikama neifakauia a gatama i ai:

She went on until she reached Fatu o Pajikama (Rock of Pajikama) where she sang out to the children asking them:

40. ni tama ni tama

koua nisokitea
Kaveiki Tan Moega?

40. Oh children, Oh children

Haven't you all seen
Kaveiki Tan Moega?

Kirea kooriakage a gatamara pe:

The children all answered her:

Kaveiki Tan Moega
samei suruifona
e amo tano maro
e feinu tano rima
nei fan tarian
ta ramaga

pume pume

Kaveiki Tan Moega
He came diving down here
He came fully naked
Protecting/Cradling his arm
He went on to wait for
The season when the flying fish soar

That's all, that's all

Ta nafunera neiragaifo tera araga pakasi marea kai eia kofano kororako Ta Fafa Pariki.

The woman handed the children a portion of meat to eat and she went on farther until she reached The Fafa Pariki.

Korofakauiaifo a gatama i ai pe: 'Nei kunei akoua, nikitea akoua Kaveiki Tan Moega mo jikai?'

45. Neifakauia foki a gatamara penei:

ni tama ni tama
koua nisokitea
Kaveiki Tan Moega?

Kaie kirea kooriage pe:

Kaveiki Tan Moega
samei suruifona
e amo tano maro
e feinu tano rima
nei fan tarian
ta ramaga

pume pume

Ta nafunera neiamkea tera araga pakasi koinagaifo marea kai. Eia kofano fano kororako i Ta Niusevaka. Kai eia kohtapaifo i ai.

50. Nirorako i Ta Niusevaka kai nikotoekeana ta ipu pakasi. Kai koitapaifo Ta Kofukofu ma Ti Auauau:

Then she called down to the children there asking them: 'All of you here, have you seen Kaveiki Tan Moega or not?'

45. She entreated those children again like this:

Oh children, Oh children
Haven't you all seen
Kaveiki Tan Moega?

And one of them answered her thus:

Kaveiki Tan Moega
He came diving down here
He came fully naked
Protecting/Cradling his arm
He went on to wait for
The season when the flying fish soar

That's all, that's all

The wife took out some of the pork and offered it for the children to eat. Then she went on until she reached Ta Niusevaka. Then she called down.

50. She arrived at Ta Niusevaka with only the head, of the pig remaining (to offer in return for assistance.) So she called down to Ta Kofukofu (Mist) and Ti Auauau (Foam) (two ancestor women of the spirit world):

ni tama ni tama
koua nisokitea
Kaveiki Tan Moega?

Oh children, Oh children
Haven't you all seen
Kaveiki Tan Moega?

Akiraua nioriage pe, 'ho'.

The two old women answer, 'yes.' (They have seen Kaveiki Tan Moega and they begin to instruct his wife in a cure that will bring him back to the living.)

Kiraua kotukage i ateia pe 'Akoe rohmai kokitea eia. Kaie kouamoa ta pure kaia ma sania vahka afi. Am sania vahka kounagkage tata ta pure. Kanomafana kaia koe kohtapa. Peroi apojiage ta nia afi kai ko iakea foki te ke tera.'

The two of them tell her, 'You have come to look for him. Pick up a large white cowrie shell and a burning stick. Take up the glowing stick and place it near the cowrie. When its warm call (to your husband). If the shell gets obscured by smoke, then pick up another for it is a different life spirit (inside).'

'Kai akoe kotapa foki.'

'So then you need to call again.'

55. 'Pe roiputoigiakage kai koinahkea, teke tera. Kai pe roputoigiage romakei, kai akoe koukumia fakamake. Koukumiage ruou rima kounahkage tou fahfata.'

55. 'If you warm it and (the smoke) dissipates (right away), then that shell has a different life spirit too. But if when you warm it all about (the smoke) just hovers (above the opening), then hold on firmly. Hold the white cowrie shell in your hand and place it on your chest.'

Ta nafunera neipena oji feipe kiraua nitukage i ateia. Tanofakarava eia neikumiage ruano rima komahkei koinagkage tano fahfata. Ta nea neifakara-

Kaveiki Tan Moega's wife did everything as she was told. The last time she holds the cowrie with both hands firmly and places it on her chest. That vegia eia nomafana i ai nomoe. Eia nomoe nomoe nivirikake.

Kaie a Kaveiki Tan Moega nomoe i tano fahfata. Nikoafemai ki ateia.

Kiraua nihnofo, nimouri.

shell makes her think of him as it warms her and she sleeps. She sleeps and sleeps and then wakes with a start.

Kaveiki Tan Moega is lying on her chest. He has returned to her.

The two of them stayed together in good health. (The couple offer the last meat to the spirits and then return to land. Vahkarokaro must live alone ever afterwards.)

Notes

1 Not uncommonly in Polynesian mythology, spirit children stay near the path to the underworld to direct the dead on their way (Poignant 1967:62).

2 In West Futuna as elsewhere in the Pacific 'knowledge of medicines and magical spells and such arts as house building, canoe building, and navigation' were gifts of the supernatural. 'Everything that was especially efficacious ... came from the spirit world' (Goodenough 1986:558). The case of the cowrie shell cure is one example. I was made aware through a treasured gift associated with my attention to this narrative, that people today may have pendants suspending a large, white cowrie shell from thongs of leather or cordage. I never saw such an ornament worn and can only surmise that they are kept hidden, protected as reminders of the powers they embody.

3 'One means of bringing an unconscious person back to consciousness was to lay a burning stick at the feet and over it a small white shell. When the stick ceased to burn, the natives said the spirit had come out of the fire and entered the shell, which they then placed on the chest, so that the spirit might re-enter the body' (Capell 1938:76).

4 *Ta toka* is an expression literally meaning reef, abbreviated from *matok*a 'reef'. *Toka* also refers to a 'stick used to pluck fruit from a tree' and in reduplicated form *toka toka* refers to a 'walking stick'. Perhaps these senses are fused in the significance of the place itself as starting point for life's final journey.

5 *Ta Toka* is centered on the reef fringing the northwestern shore of West Futuna. As entrance to the underworld this reproduces the cultural geography of many Polynesian communities for whom the entrance to the Place of the Dead faces west (Poignant 1967:62). However, we are told that paths to the underworld from West Futuna are many. Originating in each district these pathways guide the dead to the ancestral abode.

9
Samaine / Samaine

This tale recounts the adventures of an abandoned child, Samaine. He has been cast out of his home in Nakiroa on the island's west coast by his parents, Sina and Puga, to live on the fringes of their space. His parents throw their food refuse over the fence around their home. Samaine must gather their leavings for his meals. Eventually the youth plants some of the food waste and makes his own gardens, but he is continually lonesome. Then one day he is summoned by the people of Pau. Samaine travels to that village to meet with people there and finds, to his surprise, that he is respected and well treated. Indeed the villagers go deep sea fishing and return with a tuna to present to him. Samaine accepts the gift and prepares to return home. As darkness is approaching he fears losing his way, so Samaine attempts to catapult himself from the branches of a *sinu* tree in Pau over the island's plateau to reach his home village. Figures 26-7 respectively illustrate Nakiroa as it was in 1999 and an example of a *sinu* tree currently growing in Pau district. Though the *sinu* tree depicted in Figure 24 is not the actual tree Samaine would have used, it does illustrate the radiating formation and curvature of the branches of this species suggesting its utility as a catapult.

The effort to fling himself home fails, however, and instead of landing in Nakiroa, Samaine finds himself abruptly halted in the misty cloud world of the spirits above the island cliffs (see Kirtley

Figure 26: Nakiroa, West Futuna. Janet Dixon Keller 1998.

1971 for comparison with connections to a spirit world in the sky in Polynesian lore). Figure 1 of this volume illustrates the cloud formations characteristically present over the northwest quadrant of the island. It is here Samaine found himself entrapped.

Two spirits inhabit the world above the island. Ta Kofukofu greets Samaine and hides him for fear her companion, Ti Auauau, will be angry at the intrusion. Ti Auauau returns home and remarks on the noticeable smell of a human. Ta Kofukofu denies that anyone has come but Ti Auauau persists and ultimately Ta Kofukofu brings Samaine out telling Ti Auauau the youth has brought a tuna with him. The spirit women then test Samaine's mettle. Ti Auauau models a series of fantastical grass skirts meant to disturb and frighten their human visitor. But Samaine has

Figure 27: A *sinu* tree, Sele Sele *mrae*, Pau district. Janet Dixon Keller 1998.

been warned by Ta Kofukofu not to react negatively. Ultimately, Samaine satisfies the spirits that he is neither intimidated nor repulsed by their habits and attire, but, in fact, accepts their bizarre mien. His supernatural hosts agree to protect Samaine and nuture him within a fenced and gated village. Eventually the spirits create a women of human form to live with Samaine and these two have a child. Everyday the spirits go to garden. They secure the village gates and prohibit the family from going out in their absence. But after a while Samaine and his wife and child become lonely and bored. They unloose the gates and wander out discovering in the process a hole in the clouds through which they peer down to see children at play in Mouga.

The family longs to join these other humans and ultimately the three prevail upon their spirit keepers to allow them to descend to Mouga. A canoe full of food is provided and the family jumps in to be lowered down to earth. The supernatural pull the canoe back up to the sky when emptied of the supplies, but promise to lower it down again when more food is needed. For awhile Samaine and his family live among their new human companions surviving handsomely on the food sent to them from the clouds. But an ogre discovers their source of wealth and tricks the spirits into sending the canoe filled with food to him. He greedily devours it all. Subsequently the ogre cuts the rope to sever the connection to the supernatural world above. Samaine and his family must in turn learn to provision themselves and live in the world as humans do.

Background and Connections

This story was first told to me by Teikona Nuaita of Matagi Ta Vai in 1973. It was transcribed initially with Teikona. I did a literal translation shortly after this early recording. Subsequently Takaronga and I edited the tale during our collaboration.

Samaine is the youngest offspring and only son of the supernatural ancestors, Sina and Puga. He is the brother, therefore, of both Sina Fine Ariki and Kaveiki Tan Mocga's wife. The spirit women he encounters are Ta Kofukofu and Ti Auauau, the same two who appear on the reef in the story of Rufei Soa. In addition, the ogre of this tale is referred to as a pasiesi by Takaronga although Teikona did not use that expression. As expected by the pasiesi's behavior in the story of The Monster and Majihjiki, the ogre in this tale is evil, gluttonous and greedy.

Another version of this story is presented in English only by Gunn (1924). And a tale similar in many respects to Samaine is attributed to Yap. This latter story is titled Haluwai and was collected by Lessa from Taiethau who stated he had originally heard it on MogMog islet where he assumed it had entered the local repertoire from Yap (Lessa 1980:8-16). Lessa indicates that many episodes of this tale reapear throughout the lore of Polynesia and Micronesia (1980).

It is interesting to note that in similar tales told elsewhere in the Pacific the protagonist's motivation for visiting the spiritual world is often negatively charged: a suicidal impulse, a search for missing family members or an attempt to recover an ornament of someone recently deceased. Samaine's visit, however, is unintentional, an accidental stop in a journey that turns out to be a lucky diversion enabling the completion of his transformation from abandoned child to fully competent husband and father.

Translation

We encountered some difficulties in translating this story. The first hurdle was to understand how blindness might be significant. The two spirit women are named Ta Kofukofu, 'Mists and Fog,' and Ti Auauau, 'Sea Foam or Foaming Ocean Currents'. One of the spirit women is blind. (For examples of blindess in other Pacific narratives see Grey 1855:46-61; Lessa 1980.) In the version we report here the afflicted spirit is Ti Auauau. In the various translations we developed it became clear that there was some ambiguity over which spirit was sightless. The significance of the names themselves would make Ta Kofukofu the more likely one to be blind. Her name refers to fogs and mists that obscure vision. Dusty or filmy surfaces are also labeled this way in everyday parlance. It is even possible to refer to a blind person as *ta kofukofu*, 'the blind one'. In the quite different version of the story reported in English by the Reverend William Gunn (1924:170-72) indeed Ta Kofukofu is blind at the outset and Samaine cures her as the narrative develops. This is also a theme of the Micronesian stories noted by Lessa and referred to above as similar to Samaine. However, no such transformation from blind to seeing occurs explicitly in the version reported here. One wonders whether restoring sight to one of the spirit characters might not indeed have been Samaine's gift in exchange for being given a family and for enabling his life as a man. However this may have been in earlier tellings the connection was not made explicit in the versions we heard. We suspect that as the story was told time and again on West Futuna episodes changed, and characters' names per se consequently came to carry less significance. Given the lack of conviction when we questioned people as to which spirit was blind, we choose to stick with the version Teikona recounted in 1973. Gender confusions sometimes arose as well with regard to the two spirits but as they were most often considered female we retain that designation here.

We also had difficulty translating Ta Vavanea, the name of the spirit world. Literally this refers to 'space in between or empty space', but it also refers in the narrative context to a specific but 'insubstantial, airy region' inhabited by spirits. From people's descriptions, the specific place designated is quite clearly above the cliffs overlooking Mouga where cloud cover is almost always present. The connotations of 'space' for most English speakers are not the right ones here and 'Sky World', used in many other Pacific translations,[1] or even 'Cloud World' sacrifice the literal emphasis on 'emptiness' as well as the specific reference to a particular place of cloud cover just above the northwest quadrant of the island. Ta Vavanea is a distinctive name independent of colloquial West Futuna terminology such as *rangi* 'sky', and *poapoa* or *kofukofu* 'clouds or mist'. Such terms might suggest the translations mentioned above. In their absence we ultimately chose just to use the West Futuna expression, Ta Vavanea, in our texts without translation.

Conveying the episodes involving the testing of Samaine by the spirit women presented an additional challenge. Ti Auauau models a series of skirts of bizarre and potentially frightening appearance. In Figure 28 we illustrate a style of skirt commonly worn by the women of West Futuna in the nineteenth and early twentieth centuries. Often women would layer these skirts, frequently made of hibiscus, wearing two or three at one time. Takaronga indicated in our discussions that the skirts in the story were frightening. One was made of lizards, bound by their tails at the waistband. The garment would have been repulsive and terrifying to any human. These animals embody supernatural forces. They are best left alone. Binding them into a skirt would emphasize the power of the ancestors. The other skirts were apparently similarly fantastic. Samaine, warned by Ta Kofukofu not to show fear or displeasure, extols the beauty of these garments, eventually much to Ti Auauau's pleasure.

In these episodes the word *karoa* which I had previously understood to mean 'necklace' is used in reference to the skirts. *Karoa* in this context seems to refer more generally to an 'encircling item of ornamentation'. Traditional objects of ornamentation worn around the neck are illustrated in the photograph presented here as Figure 29. The first *karoa*, skirt in this context, is given to Samaine as a gift.[2] After this Ti Auauau models three more skirts each more frightening than the last. To each Samaine responds with the expression *niotatau* literally 'It belongs to or encompasses the three of us'. I take this expression to mean the three are somehow united or brought together by their shared appreciation of the skirts. Although Takaronga and I discussed these passages at some length we were unable to find a more idiomatic English expression that would serve in translation and perhaps reveal more fully an underlying significance for this series of narrative episodes.

Figure 28: Adult woman's skirt with detail of waist binding. This style of skirt was commonly worn in the nineteenth and early twentieth centuries by the women of West Futuna.

Firth and McLean (1990:37-8), in discussing the figurative language of Tikopia songs, point out that 'bond friends are represented as headbands or head circlets or necklets of leaves or flowers ...' They go on to say 'Imagery of this kind plucks out the concepts of bodily adornment and fragrance as emblematic of the human object of affection and uses them as a simile or metaphor to express a positive emotional commitment'. Perhaps the *karoa* of the West Futuna tale are such encircling adornments signaling friendship bonds. The tension and ambiguity of relationships between supernatural and mortal humans may be symbolized by the frightening appearance and outlandish raw materials for the modeled skirts.

Confinement and Freedom, Community and other Themes

Thematically this tale contrasts confinement and freedom as the others in this volume have done. Samaine and his family are secluded in their misty, supernatural village encircled by multiple gated fences. As was the case in *Ta Pasiesi ma Majihjiki*, *Majihjiki ma Fafine Tonga* and *Sina Fine Ariki* it only becomes possible for the protagonists to live normal human lives by giving up reliable provisioning by others and breaking out of protective confinement. Perhaps indicative of the demeaning state of being provisioned, the family ultimately must crawl on their knees to communicate to their supernatural benefactors when they are in need of food. It is only in the complete severing of their material link with the supernatural that the family becomes fully human, eligible to incur the risks but also the satisfactions of a mortal existence.

Escape from overprotection becomes an opportunity for rebirth of both the individuals and the principles of life in human communities. Originally abandoned Samaine seeks

Figure 29 (opposite): Photograph of a man from West Futuna wearing traditional *karoa* dating to the early twentieth century. William Gunn, photographer. © The Field Museum, CSA77942; reprinted with permission.

companionship and in the early episodes establishes a garden on his own and then initiates relations of exchange with the people of Pau in steps crucial to establishing the fundamentals of human existence. But he is still incomplete, without a wife and children. His initial attempt to return to his home village is interrupted when he lands with the supernatural in the misty world above the cliffs. Here Samaine eventually gains a family but still lacks fellowship and mutually supportive relations with other humans. The episode of his family's descent through a hole in the clouds symbolically initiates the final phase in Samaine's birth as a full human. The passage is effected in a canoe, *vaka*, lowered down to earth by a rope. In the language of West Futuna *vaka* is richly polysemous, designating the 'womb' as well as a 'community' or even 'generation of people' (*vaka tagata*). The family descends to earth and shortly thereafter the ogre severs their umbilical link with the supernatural. This ultimate act then thrusts them into a new *vaka*, the community of Mouga, and by extension, into the larger community of people encircling the island. This new *vaka* of human life will envelope, protect and provision Samaine, his wife and child as long as they engage in the customary practices essential to survival.

Minor motifs include the significance of sweeping, an act perhaps intended to symbolize the clean and orderly state of the supernatural village, and the Fee-fi-fo-fum motif so identified by Kirtley (1971:340) in which a supernatural being returning home, often a cannibal in other Pacific lore, smells a human presence and exclaims about the stench.[3]

Cultural Geography

A number of landmarks are symbolically enriched by events of this tale. Ta Vavanea, Mouga, Ravaru, Pau and Kamkaveni are all mentioned and acquire enduring significance as a result. The species of tree, *sinu*, noted as Samaine's catapult, retains its narrative import today.

A circular island geometry underlies this narrative as it has

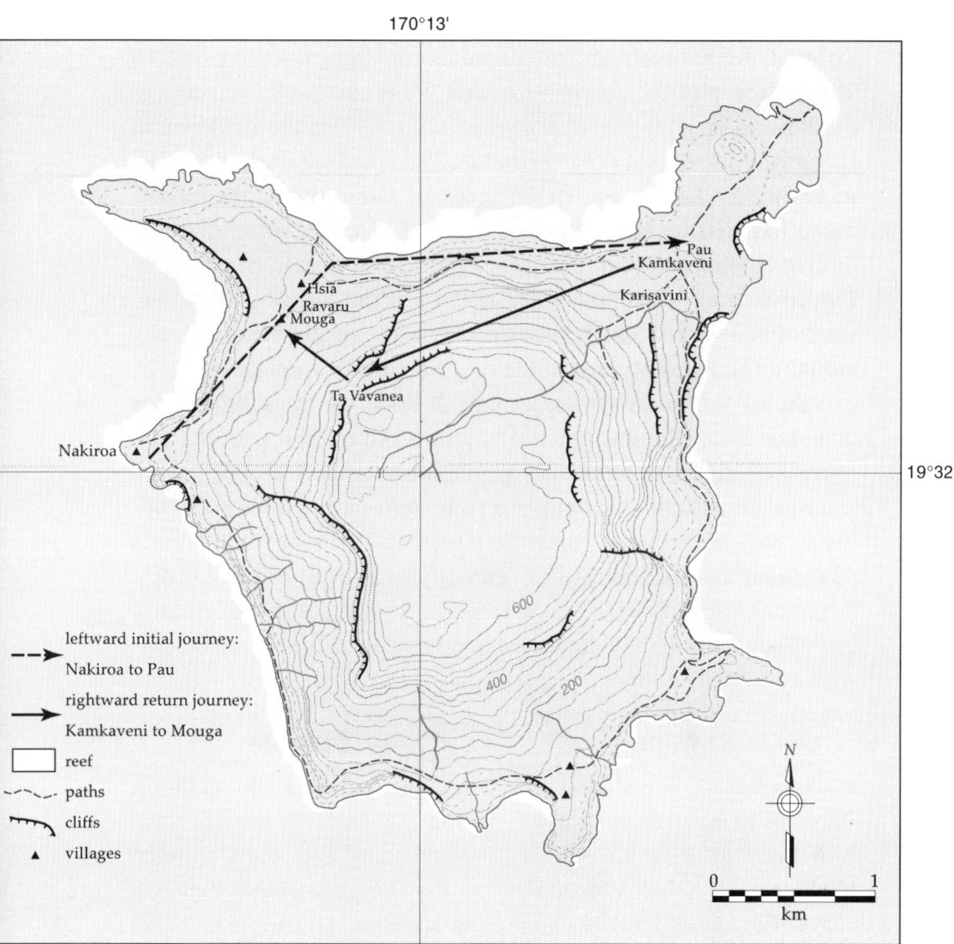

Figure 30: Location and directions for episodes of *Samaine*.

others. Unmentioned but taken-for-granted, this imagery is reinforced by several metaphors including the protective fences which surround the spirit *mrae* and grass skirts which encircle their wearers. The use of *karoa* in reference to the ornamental skirts emphasizes this spatial theme. The *sinu* tree itself as shown in Figure 27 has a circular base out of which branches radiate much like district boundaries emerging from the central plateau.

The directionality of events are traced on the map constituting Figure 30 and follow the usual pattern at the outset with movement out of the west (Nakiroa) in a leftward direction thereby signaling uncertainty and reflecting Samaine's trepidation as he travels to Pau with only a glimmer of hope for transcending his abandonment. The journey to Pau, turns out to be rewarding and Samaine intends to return home in a new status. This homeward journey would take him along a rightward path. However, landing in the spirit world above the island cliffs disrupts the simple directional opposition. Still, eventually as a result of his journey, Samaine descends with a new family into Ravaru, a *marae* joining Mouga and Hsia where he becomes part of the human community.

Samaine

Samaine ta tama Sina ma Puga. Kiraua niamoa kaie kiraua kohgege i ai. Kiraua kohkoina eia i Nakiroa. Nonofo sokia. Eia nonofo sokoia kaie akiraua ruona fakauhsore ropena kai. Rosiviakea a kiri taro ma fatu toro ma, nororigiakea i ta tafa koupa. Kai eia konoiawia a nera noroikaina. Nopogi ma nopogi eia noikaina a kaikai araua.

Samaine

Samaine was the child of Sina and Puga. The two of them begat him and then rejected him. They two abandoned him at Nakiroa. And so he lived all alone. He lived all by himself, but those two, his parents would prepare food. They would skin taro corms and (break off) sugar cane joints and prepare other things and spill the waste over outside the fence. Then Samaine would gather everything and eat

Tasi a nopogi eia kokateage i araua a vere, kokanieni foki i ai. Eia koiawia a fatu torora koroitanumia. Pena kai kohsomo korokake anorau nifatu torora kohsomo rufie kage. Uaia koipena foki tiana vere i ai kohsomo rufie kage a toronei. Kohpu a toro. Korufie eia koiragona. Koiragona kohpalo a toronei. Korufie kage Nakiroa i ai. U ai nonofo i ai.

Tasi a nopogi kai kohmai ta fesao pe a tagata ka fakatupu i Pau. 'E rufie pe avau kafano ki ta fakatupuga.'

Nihmai ta nopogi kai eia kohmai i ta fakatupuga. Eia nopuku, nofakarogo i a takau hsore notavenaga i ta fakatupuga. Kirea nitavenaga tavenaga korava ta tavenaga. Kai a tama Pau nifujia e kirea ta worukogo kirea komoriage mana.

5. Avage mana ta worukogo.

U aia koiamoa ta worukogora

it. Day after day he would eat their foods.

One day he looked over at his parents' gardens, and he yearned for his own. So Samaine gathered sugar cane joints and he planted them. He did that and the cane grew tall and the sections of that sugar cane multiplied growing really well. And so he made another garden there and the sugar cane grew very well. The sugarcane burst forth. It was doing well so he secured it with poles. He staked it and the cane grew tall. All was well in Nakiroa. And so he continued to live there.

One day a message arrived that the people would meet in Pau. 'It would be good for me to go to the meeting.'

When the day came he did attend the meeting. He sat and listened to the senior men exchanging views during the meeting. They all talked and talked until the conference was finished. Then the people of Pau went deep sea fishing and they pulled in a tuna which they presented to him (Samaine).

5. (They) gave the tuna to him.

So he accepted that tuna and

koforimai ki ta hne tei i a Kamkaveni. Kai ko po ko po hmafi. Neifarigoina pe ai kafano ana ruono vae serorikofia ma i Nakiroa kai kopouri pouri.

came round toward the place, over there at Kamkaveni. By then it had begun to get very, very dark. He knew that if he were to return only by walking he would not reach Nakiroa but would be confused and lose his way in the dark.

Eia koikavajia ta sinu i a Kamkaveni. Ituai a sinu e jikai i ta hnena. Ta sinu nikavajia e Samaine. Kohnofo a sinu i ta hnera.

So (Samaine) magically conjured up a *sinu* tree at Kamkaveni. Originally there was no *sinu* tree there. The *sinu* tree was called forth magically by Samaine. The *sinu* tree would stay in that place.

Kavajia ta sinura kohgaro hgarokea i a rakau oji. Eia koiamoa ta worokogora kohkavakake ta sinura. Eia nihkava, hkava, hkava pe karorikofia tan tauru pe eia kafeka ta tauru sinura. Kaia kosopoifo ki Nakiroa.

Having been called forth that *sinu* tree grew high, higher than all the other trees. Samaine picked up that tuna and climbed up that *sinu* tree. He climbed and climbed and climbed until he reached the crown from where he could bend back the branches of that *sinu* tree (to act as a catapult to launch him into the air). Then he (would sail over the cliffs and) could jump down into Nakiroa.

Eia nihkava hkava nirorako hluga ma ta worukogara. Eia kosopoifo ki Nakiroa. Kaie korosopo ki ta mrae i ta ragi, Tavavanea. Ta mraenei, a Ta Kofukofu ma a Ti Auauau nonofo i ai. Ta Kofukofu ma Ti Auauau

Samaine climbed and climbed with that tuna in order to reach the highest branches. (And then launched himself) so that he could jump down into Nakiroa. But instead he jumped into a place in the sky, ru fafine. Ti Auauau e pori.

10. Kiraua nohnofo i ta mraenei, Tavavanea. Jikai foki tasi a tagata nofano ki ai. Sokoia ana nifano ki ai i tano fajaganei. Aia nifenage kai a Ta Kofukofu no i ta mrae noseri-mrae. Eia ta hfinenei pempena ta fare noseri-mrae nokira ta mrae. Notutu penu nofori ta mrae i a nofajaga oji.

Kai a Samaine korofakea ma ta worukogora. A Takofukofu koifakauiage pe, 'Auei, auei akoe nifakea i?'

Samaine saitukage pe, 'E ta ne nifakea i ta fakatupuga i Pau kaie ko po u avau ta pe kanoafe ki tioku a mrae. Avau ta pe ka sopokea i ta sinu. Kaie nipuhpusi pe au nikua kai avau nikohmai ki ta mraenei.'

Ta Kofukofu koitukage pe, 'U akoe nomentua pe akoe kaafe mo jikai? Akoe morefuma nomentua..., mentura pe akoe kaafe, kai nikopo kaie

Tavavanea. This residence, Ta Kofukofu (Mist and Fog) and Ti Auauau (Sea Foam) live there. Ta Kofukfou and Ti Auauau are two women (of the spirit world). Ti Auauau is blind.

10. The two of them reside in this place, Tavavanea. Not another soul went to that place. Only he himself, alone, went there at this time. He went about (and found) Ta Kofukofu at her home sweeping her place of residence. She was a woman who fixed up her house, sweeping and keeping the grounds clean. Everyday she went round her place burning any waste.

Then Samaine just appeared with that tuna. Takofukofu asked him, 'Whoa, whoa where did you come from?'

Samaine replied, 'Well, the thing is I left from the meeting at Pau while it was getting dark and I wanted to return to my home. I thought I could launch myself from a *sinu* tree. Then I don't know what happened to me but I came to this place.'

Then Ta Kofukofu asked, 'And do you hope to go back, or not? You probably think..., your idea may be that you should continue on, but since akoe konofo. Kaie a Ti Auauau sekihmai ana. Avau e puhpusi pe kahmai kakali mo jikai? Kaie kokua? Au karofuna akoe.'

its dark you should stay. Still, Ti Auauau hasn't yet come home. I don't know whether when she comes she'll be upset or not? So what should we do? I am going to hide you.'

Eia koiarafia Samaine koroifuna i fare, koiapojia i ta siegi roru. Eia no i ai nikohisana kai Ti Auauau konohmai.

She leads Samaine away to conceal him in the house, covering him under a grass skirt of roru leaves. He stays there until he is startled by Ti Auauau's arrival.

15. Nikoafiafi a Ti Auauau tera. Eia nimeihfasikea neitu pe, 'Auei, auei, auei konamnamu tagata sa!'

Kaie Ta Kofukofu koitukage pe, 'Hme:, senamnamu tagata mana. I a nopogina kaie a tagata karokea i?'

Eia kopuku pukukage kai eia koitu pe, 'Konamnamu tagata hmafi. Akai nihmai tei ta mrae i ranei?'

Ta KofuKofu koitukage pe, 'Sekatea mana e kitaua ta hmari sa tagata i a nopogina. Kaie a tagata karokea i?'

U akiraua pe hpuku, hpuku hpukukage, kaie a Ti Auauau koinamuia foki. Koitukage ki a Ta Kofukofu pe, 'Ei, konamnamu tagata sa.'

15. Come late afternoon, Ti Auauau appeared. She came bursting forth saying, 'Oh wow, oh wow, oh wow, does it ever stink of people!'

But Ta Kofukofu said, 'Nah..., it never smells of people. These days, from where would people come?'

Ti Auauau sits for quite a while and then she repeats, 'It smells strongly of humans. Who came to the village today?'

And Ta Kofukofu replies, 'We've not seen a real person any time recently. And besides, where would people come from?'

So the two of them just sat and sat and sat, while Ti Auauau continued to detect a strong smell. Finally, she says to Ta Kofukofu, 'Phew, it really reeks of people.'

20. Ta Kofukofu koitukage pe, 'Ei, kai ka i ai sa tagata kai kitea ka feifei rufie mo ka feifei sa.'

Ti Auauau saitukage pe, 'Ei, ka feifei sa iaha?'

U a Ta Kofukufo kolahkage koiamkea ta siegi i ta souiara. Koiarafiamai. Arafiamai. Koiamkea ta ika koitukage pe ta souia ana ni hmai. Ta ika ana tenei.

Kirato koputoiaifo ta ikara. Kai kiratou nohtari notataria kamoa.

Kai a Ti Auauau kofakea koinagkage ano siegi. Fasiegiage. Tera kolakalakakea. Komeijihjikiviniakea eia tata ta vetoka fafora. Kai kotakavini koafekage ki fare pe karoinage kaie kaifasiegiage te ke foki.

25. Kaie Ta Kofukofu ta ne neitukage oji ki Samaine pe, 'Ai rohmai roiavage ona karoa kai akoe kaukanienia, Kanienia pe e rufie, kosoutukua pe e sa.'

20. Ta Kofukofu says, 'Well, if there were a person, then would we feel good or would we feel bad?'

And Ti Auauau says, 'Huh, why would we feel bad?'

So Ta Kofukofu strides over and takes the grass skirt off that boy. She leads him toward Ti Auauau. She leads him toward her. She picks up the fish (and) she says that the boy has come alone. This other is just a fish.

So the three of them wrap that fish and place it down on hot stones. And they three wait and wait and wait until it is done.

Then Ti Auauau steps out from where she has stored her grass skirts. She dons a skirt. And that one goes prancing and marching all about. She turns and spins about near the door going outside there. She pirouettes out and returns back to the house to take off (one skirt) and model another.

25. Ta Kofukofu had already warned Samaine, 'If she comes to (show off and) give you her ornamental skirts you must appreciate this. Appreciate them for their beauty, don't disparage thcm.'

U aia niavage tera karoa nimeilahkea.

Kaie Samaine koitu pe, 'Auei, auei, e rufie hmafi. Numpa wan kea. Takau! Auei! Takau! Niotatou.'

U aia koiveteakea tera kaia koinagkage tera te hkanuhkanu sa feipe sa tagaroa ma.. Ta ne nifatua ta siegi koifasiegiage kofakea komeifori koijihjikiviniage eia i akiraua fafora.

Kai a Samaine saitukage pe, 'Auei, auei ta ne kanioku. Tenei e rufiekea. Tasi foki i ai mo jikai? Tano funa. Tena koniotatou foki.'

30. Eia koiveteakea kai koifasiegiage tera. Nilahkea foki. Kai a Samaine koitu pe akirea, 'Nokaṇieni avau feipe tena. Koniotatou.'

Eia koiveteakea oji koinage i raro. Kaie eia saitukage i a Samaine pe, 'E rufie, akitatou mari kahnofo.'

Kiratou kohnofo. Kiratou

And then Ti Auauau did offer him a skirt in which she had been parading about.

And Samaine said, 'Oh wow, oh wow, how beautiful! It's the best. Fantastic! Wow! Great! It belongs to the three of us!'

So Ti Auauau takes off that one and then she put on one all striped like a sea snake or something similar. She prepared the waist band and then she donned that skirt and came out to circle and spin about around the two of them outside.

Then Samaine says, 'Oh my, oh wow, I want that one to be mine. It's more beautiful than the last. Is there another or not? The most perfect. That one should become ours, encompassing all three of us too.'

30. And so she loosened (that skirt) and she donned yet another grass skirt. She modeled it too. And Samaine exclaimed to them, 'I like the one you have on. It is going to belong to (encompass) the three of us.'

And so (Ti Auauau) took off (that one) too and put it down. Then she announced to Samaine, 'Yes, it is right that we three live together.'

So the three of them lived

nihnofo hnofo. Kaie akiraua koamoa ta kere kopena tasi a hfine. Kiraua nipena ta hfinenei. Kopena i ta tagata. Feipenei, ta tagata kai ta hfine, ta hfine. Kiraua nikopena ma a Samaine.

together. They went on living day to day. Eventually the two Spirit women took up some earth and made a woman. The two of them made a woman. They made her as a human. It's like this, she was a person and she was a woman, a real woman. The two spirit women made her for Samaine.

Kosore ta hfinenei kai kiraua ma Samaine kohnofo. Kiraua nihnofo koamoa tiaraua tama. Kiraua niamoa tiaraua tama, kai akiratou nei ta mrae.

When this woman came of age, she and Samaine lived together. The two of them lived together and begat their own child. They two had a child of their own, and the three of them stayed in the village.

Kai kiraua nigkororo karovere, kai a Samaine ma tiana hfine ma ta tamara, kiratou nei i ta mrae.

The two spirit women would go to garden, while Samaine and his wife and child, all three would remain in the village.

35. Kai akiraua nigkororo karovere. Kiraua nirovere. Kai kofousia fousia fousia kiraua a koupa i ta mrae kohpiri. Kiraua rovere vere roafemai afiafi. Kai akiraua koveteakea vava ta feipa koromai ki ta mrae.

35. And so the two spirit women would go to garden. The two of them went gardening. The two women would make fast the fences around the village securing them tightly. They would go to garden all day and return in the evening. Then the two spirit women would unloose the roped gates and come into the village.

Akiratou kohnofo hnofo hnofo kohtuai. Tasi a nopogi akiratou kotukua pe, 'Akitataura

The family of three just remained living there a long time. One day the three of nohnofo ana i ta mraenei.'

them complained, 'The three of us just stay in this place of residence.'

Kai a Ta Kofukofu ma a Ti Auauau nitukage mana pe, 'Akoutou kanohnofo ana i ta mraenei. Koutou koisorokage i ta hne tei warana. Koisovetea koutou a koupanei kororokea. Koutou kahnofo ana i ta mraenei.'

Ta Kofukofu and Ti Auauau replied to them, 'You three must (content yourselves) with staying in this place of residence. Don't you-three go out into the area over there. Don't untie these fences, you three, in order to go out. The three of you must just stay in this place of residence.'

Kiratou nohnofo ana i ta mrae i nopogi ma nopogi.

So the three stayed within the residence day after day.

Tasi a nopogi ta hfine ma Samaine ma tiaraua tama, kiratou kotu pe, 'Akitatou nikohnofo i ta mraenei nikogahga. Kaie kitatou kaakona mana karokea pe ta ne taha tenopojina kiraua i a kitatou.'

One day the woman with Samaine and their child, the three of them together said, 'We three have been living in this village until we're fed up. Let's try to get out of here in order to (discover) what the two of them are keeping from us.'

40. Kiratou koveteakea vava nifousia i a feipara. Kiratou kovetea oji a vava i a feipara korokea uai tafa ta koupa. Kiratou niroro nirosirakea.

40. The three of them untied the rope wound around those gates. They three unloosed the ropes around the gates and went out beyond the fence. The three of them went out to have a look.

Pe sireifo kai a gatama i marae Mouga nokofura ta raugasau. Kaie faru nopena tapalia. Ta tama araua koikateaifo. Kokanieni hmafi pe eia kafano

As they look down the children in the village of Mouga are playing tag with stalks of cane. And some are playing touch tag. The child of the two foki karoipena a penaganea gatama.

of them stared down. He really wanted to go too and do things children do.

Eia nikokanieni pe kafano karotere nanoa foki. Kotagi tagi pe eia kafanoifo ki mrae Mouga. Eia koitukage i a tamana ma a jinana pe akiratou kahtoifo karoro ki a gatamara. Kaie jikai. Kiratou sekitoifo ana. Kiratou kotagi pe kahtoifo.

He yearned to go and run about also. He cried and cried to go down to the village of Mouga. And so he said to his father and his mother that the three of them should descend to join those children. But it was not to be. The three of them couldn't descend yet. They wept because they (hoped) to descend.

Niromai te afiafi Ta Kofukofu ma a Ti Auauau kosafea kiratou notagi. Kiraua kofakauiage pe, 'Akoutou nitagi iaha?'

In the evening Ta Kofukofu and Ti Auauau find the three of them weeping. The two spirit women ask, 'Why are you three crying?'

Kai akiratou kotukage pe, 'Ei, akimatou nirosafeaifo a gatama i marae Mouga u akimatou kokanieni pe karoro ki akirea.'

And the three of them reply, 'Well, the three of us have looked down and seen the children in the village of Mouga and the three of us want to go to be with them.'

45. Kiraua kotukage pe, 'E rufie. I ranei akimaua katufokina ta vaka i a kai kafujiaifo mautou. Kotau foki kosopoifo ta vakara, kimea kafujiaifo."

45. So the two (spirit women) said, 'Alright. Today the two of us will fill a canoe with food to lower down for you three. When its fully loaded, (you three can) jump into the canoe as well, and we'll lower you down.'

Nihmai ta nofajaga kai kiratou kohsopoifo ta vakara ta ne nifakauteina i a kai. Nifonu.

The time came when the (family of) three jumped down into that canoe which had been

Kiraua, Ta Kofukofu ma Ti Auauau, kofujiaifo kiratou ki Ravaru. Fujiaifo ta vakara.

loaded with food. It was stuffed. The two of them, Ta Kofukofu and Ti Auauau, lowered down the family of three to Ravaru. (They) lowered down that canoe.

Kai akiraua kotukage pe, 'Akoutou, tasi a nopogi pe akoutou ro jikai a kai mautou kai akoutou koromai kameihtoro, htoro nanoa u ai raro nei. Pe kimau rosafea kai kofujiaifo foki mautou faru a kai.'

The two (spirit women) said, 'You three, (when) the day (comes) that you have no more food then you three come and crawl, crawl about down below here. When we see you then we'll lower down some more food for you three again.'

Kiratou koamoa era kai norohnofo nokaina. Kaina, kaina, kaina nipuni kai kiratou koromai i ta nohnea ara nomeihtoro htoro nanoa u ai raro i Ravaru. Akiratou nomeihtoro htoro u ai raro. Kai kiraua kosafeaifo. Akiraua kosara era a kai kofakauteina ta vaka kofujiaifo. Fujiaifo maratou.

So the (family of) three took that food and they lived by eating it. (They) ate and ate and ate until it was gone and then the three of them came to that place to crawl and crawl about down there at Ravaru. They three came to crawl about down below. Then the two spirit women saw them down there. The two of them searched for food with which to load up the canoe to be lowered down. They lowered it down for the three of them.

Akiratou pe tanoa tanoa tanoa pera i nopogi ma nopogi.

They three busied themselves like that day after day.

50. Ta pasiesi koisafea kiratau. Segapu ta meiamo kai tahnera komatahtu i ai. Kosafea kiratou noamkea a kai i ta vakara.

50. Then a monstrous ogre spied the three of them. Without stopping, food kept coming at that place and that one watched closely. He watched the three

of them take out food from that canoe.

Akiratou nikaina kai era sekipuni ana tasi a nopogi kai ta pasiesi niviri i ta hpo ana.I tera nopogi kai kohmai kamihtoro htoro nanoa i Ravaru. Eia nihtoro htoro nanoa i raro kai akiraua kosafeaifo.

They three (the family) had not yet finished eating a batch of their food when one day the ogre awoke just at dawn. On that day he came and crawled and crawled around at Ravaru. He kept crawling about and the two spirit women spied him down below.

Kiraua komentua pe morefuma a takafeitamanara. Kiraua kofujiaifo ta vakara. Ta ne fonu i a kai. Akiraua nifujiaifo nirorako i raro.

The two of them thought probably that was the three family members. The two of them lowered down that canoe. It was full with food. The two of them lowered it down until it arrived below.

Kai ta pasiesi kofenage koroiamkea. Amkea a kai nihpuni ta vaka. Kai aia koitujiakea foki ta vava te nofujiaifo ta vakara. Koitujiakea ta vavara kai eia kofano ki tiona mrae.

Then the ogre went over there and unloaded it. He unloaded the food until the boat was empty. Then he also severed the rope that they used to lower that canoe down. He cut off the rope and then he went to his place.

Tasi a nopogi kiratou nipuni a kai niromai kai ta vaka notakape. Ta gaja vaka. Nigkojikai a kai i ai.

When the day arrived and the family of three had finished their food they came (to Ravaru) but the canoe was (already) lying there, an empty canoe. There was no food in it.

55. U akiratou konolus, kotataruana kojikai maratou a kai. U akiratou konohnofokageana

55. And so the three of them lost out, they became like everyone else with no

pera. Konofijikau i ta vere foki ma ta sara-kai maratou ma kai ta vaka nigko jikai a kai i ai.

food for themselves. They three will have to live just like they are. They will work·in the garden again and seek food for themselves and do everything because the canoe no longer has no food in it.

Nimotu foki ta vava. Koravageana ta fesaoganei.

The rope is broken once again. This story has just ended.

Notes

1 Capell indicates an absence among the West Futunese of Sky World beliefs cognate with other Polynesian cosmologies (1958:36-7).

2 Monberg (1991:114) notes a similar but inverted practice remarked by the Bellonese regarding the movement of the '*ata* of deceased individuals to the spirit world'. On arrival at the homes of the deities, the '*ata* presented their spiritual hosts with offerings of necklaces – just as did the Bellonese paying formal visits to one another'.

3 This theme appears in *The Island of the Dolphin Girls*, a story from Chuuk published by Flood, Strong and Flood (1999:59-63), and also in the Yapese story of Haluwai mentioned in the text (Lessa 1980).

10
Tiata / Tiata

This is a humorous song about a man named Tiata, although his name is never mentioned in the verses. Tiata is a lonesome fellow going from place to place seeking a wife. The verses here trace his path and ridicule his lack of success with women. His journey starts at Hsia village in the northwest district of greater Mouga. Tiata circles the *marae* at Hsia going successively to various neighborhoods around the perimeter and then proceeding along a circuitous route to a series of places in Taroumara. At the final area mentioned, Tupaieri, which is out on the northwest peninsula called Tamouga, Tiata is said to hear the sound of the trumpet shell calling him back to Hsia.

This song was performed in 1973 by Waka Sore, Nawali and Naparau, among others. I recorded the music and lyrics at that time. Napausi Teifisou of Pelitamoko was my primary guide in the initial translation process. Takaronga and I have discussed the song but have found no reason to alter the lyrics as originally transcribed in West Futuna or as translated into English. A musical transcription appears in Figure 31.

Thematic Development and Tone

This song highlights Tiata's plight as a single man seeking companionship. It is appreciated as humorous, evoking laughter throughout its performance. But the laughter is biting and the lyrics fit the style of ridicule in musical compositions identified

***Tiata* / Tiata**

Figure 31: Opening verse and chorus line with musical transcription for *Tiata*.

for a few other Polynesian outliers (Donner 1987: 204, 209-10 for Sikaiana; and McLean 1999:238 for Ontong Java/Luangiua). One wonders whether the original composition was meant as social commentary or intended perhaps as advice through ridicule for Tiata himself (see Basso 1996). The search for love and a jeering tone are also noted by Firth and McLean as characteristic of Tikopia music. However, it seems that among the genres of Tikopia the elements of love and mockery are more often evidenced independently rather than co-occurring in musical compositions (1990:190-233).

Cultural Geography

While this song uses place names as a way to recount Tiata's actions and recall his plight (Basso 1996), we found it impossible to map the narrative trajectory precisely. In general terms it appears that he circles the *marae* in Hsia and then goes on to Taroumara moving out toward land's end on the northwest peninsula before being called back. However, uncertainties plagued people's memories with respect to exact locations of places mentioned relative to one another. Many of the place names designate *mrae*s or residential neighborhoods no longer in existence or overgrown and less salient than in the past. As Takaronga and I considered the significance of this song, we spoke with many community elders originally from Hsia in an attempt to clarify locations. We worked in detail on separate occasions with three knowledgeable residents or descendants of families from Hsia, but their memories of the named locales were idiosyncratic. As we attempted to retrace Tiata's route it became clear that neighborhood names in Hsia had changed significantly since the verses of this song were composed. Over generations, as residents have died or moved away and new families established home sites, or as churches and schools were constructed, neighborhoods have been renamed. Some places including Puga Puga, Taniwihi, Farea, Sepua, Ta Ra ma ta Rama, Safoe and Tupaieri can be located with confidence today establishing an orientation for Tiata's path. Intervening places, however, were subject to conflicting recollections regarding location precluding the completion of a consensual map.

In fact, the difficulties we experienced in locating named places for *Tiata* led us to recognize fluidity typical of residential landscapes and their appellations (Rodman 1985). Neighborhood place names are replaced as elders pass away and the next generation reshapes locales. As home sites are renamed places take on a continually presentist character while simultaneously a residential history is at least potentially preserved in culture memories of past designators. This linguistic productivity, noticeably evidenced for neighborhood appellations, is not so apparent with respect to specific landmarks associated with supernatural events. The names and precise locations of these latter sites have been conserved over generations and still at the end of the second millennium were widely shared among the people of West Futuna.

Tiata

Jino Tasi
Tuapo mau tenei
Nokohnofo kitea
Kaia aia saitukatu akoe sautu-
kuamai
Pe kapena i sa hgoro
tano ata: i e ake ho waiwa, i e
ake ho waiwa
i e ake ho waiwa, i e ake ho
waiwa
i e ake ho waiwa

Jino Rua
Kapena i sa hgoro
Rofori i marae sore
Rotoifo i Pugapuga rofori
Taniwihi
Sarorako i Farea
tano ata: i e ake ho waiwa, i e
ake ho waiwa
i e ake ho waiwa, i e ake ho
waiwa
i e ake ho waiwa

Jino Toru
Sarorako i Farea
Fori Taganawo

Tiata

Verse 1
Midnight it is now
We are all living as we do
Then someone speaks to you
and you in turn reply
That a song will be sung
chorus: i e ake ho waiwa, i e
ake ho waiwa
i e ake ho waiwa, i e ake ho
waiwa
i e ake ho waiwa

Verse 2
A song will be sung
You go round the village center
Descending to Pugapuga. Go
round to Taniwihi
Until you reach Farea
chorus: i e ake ho waiwa, i e
ake ho waiwa
i e ake ho waiwa, i e ake ho
waiwa
i e ake ho waiwa

Verse 3
You arrive at Farea
Go round Taganawo

Fori Serakitoga rofori Karitoru	Round Serakitoga. Go round Karitou
Sarorako i Sepua	To arrive at Sepua
tano ata: i e ake ho waiwa, i e ake ho waiwa	chorus: i e ake ho waiwa, i e ake ho waiwa
i e ake ho waiwa, i e ake ho waiwa	i e ake ho waiwa, i e ake ho waiwa
i e ake ho waiwa	i e ake ho waiwa
Jino Fa	**Verse 4**
Sarorako i Sepua	You arrive at Sepua
Rofori Tutusoro	Go round Tutusoro
Fori ta Ra, ta Mrama, nirotoifo i Safoe	Round ta Ra (the Sun), ta Mrama (the Moon), to descend at Safoe
Rorako i Tupaieri	And arrive at Tupaieri
tano ata: i e ake ho waiwa, i e ake ho waiwa	chorus: i e ake ho waiwa, i e ake ho waiwa
i e ake ho waiwa, i e ake ho waiwa	i e ake ho waiwa, i e ake ho waiwa
i e ake ho waiwa	i e ake ho waiwa
Jino Rima	**Verse 5**
Rorako i Tupaieri	When you arrive at Tupaieri
Sapuia mau i ta pu	(They) are trumpeting for you on the conch
Ropuia i ta pufatu, ropuia ta puariki	Blowing on the stone conch, blowing the royal conch
Tagi fakatautau	Calling you to hurry
tano ata: i e ake ho waiwa, i e ake ho waiwa	chorus: i e ake ho waiwa, i e ake ho waiwa
i e ake ho waiwa, i e ake ho waiwa	i e ake ho waiwa, i e ake ho waiwa
i e ake ho waiwa	i e ake ho waiwa

(tano ata tano fakarava)

i e ake ho waiwa, i e ake ho waiwa,
i e ake ho waiwa, i e ake ho waiwa,
i e ake ho waiwa
i e ake ho waiwa, i e ake ho waiwa,
i e ake ho waiwa, i e ake ho waiwa

(extended and accelerated final chorus)

i e ake ho waiwa, i e ake ho waiwa,
i e ake ho waiwa, i e ake ho waiwa,
i e ake ho waiwa
i e ake ho waiwa, i e ake ho waiwa,
i e ake ho waiwa, i e ake ho waiwa

11
Nahjeji / Lobster Trap

This song recounts an episode of nineteenth century evangelical history for West Futuna, Vanuatu, from the vantage point of islanders present during the encounter. The composer imagines religious conversion as a process of lobster trapping where the people of West Futuna constitute prestigious prey. The central story recounts carefully planned attempts by recent converts from a neighboring island to capture new members for a foreign church. The people of West Futuna see themselves identified as prestigious prey in the eyes of their reinvented neighbors. Vulnerable to entrapment they turn to one among their own leaders for direction. He offers inspiration in the form of a proposal to end the strife by recreating the visitors as *kastom* men respectful of the ways of the land.

Nahjeji was sung by Waka Sore, Nawali and Naparau, with others, late one night in 1973. Figure 32 provides a transcription of the musical line. Lyrics were accompanied by the *kafa* sounding board and *tafiri*, or customary dancing. I first translated the text literally over several months in 1973 and 1974 but without developing a sense of the figurative meaning or *hkano*. The initial performance and subsequent enactments, however, were so striking for the enthusiasm with which this piece was performed that my curiosity regarding its associations persisted for decades. Although I revisited the translation many times over the intervening years it was not until the late 1990s that a coherent sense of the significance of the text emerged. Working with Takaronga, we interviewed a number of people around the island who gave us clues to the song's interpretive import and directed us to those who might best be able to contextualize the lyrics for us. Interviewing those most knowledgeable we were eventually given entrée into tropic forms linking early evangelism with lobster trapping.

With the guidance of Napausi of Pelitamoko, Taroumara and Naparau of Matagi we came to understand *ru fua*, 'two fruits', mentioned in the second verse as an expression for 'Christian converts', specifically applied to Waihit and Josefa, native evangelists from Aneityum. This expression is confirmed in mission references to Waihit and Josefa (Morgan 1854:645; Steel 1880:135) while the more general equation of *fua* and 'convert' appears in Miller's history of the mission in the New Hebrides (1986:168).

Subsequently *fij*, a Bislama or English loan replacing *ura* or *ika* and referring to 'lobsters' sought by the trappers, was associated in our conversations with the 'people of West Futuna'. Figure 33 is a photograph of the *nahjeji* or lobster traps in use on West Futuna from the early 1970s into the turn of the millennium. We suspect these are the same traps referred to by the song lyrics. With the two tropes, *ru fua* and *fij*, deconstructed we were able to unravel at least some of *Nahjeji*'s significance. The potential remains for the past *hkano* of these verses to be further developed and for the lyrics to be re-accentuated in contemporary performances (Bakhtin 1981; Petersen 1992). We look forward to the insights readers may offer after reviewing what we have been able to surmise here.

Nahjeji opens with quasi-ritualized lines drawing the listener's attention toward what is to come. The opening is in the first person, the voice of the composer who acts as narrator. He sets the stage pointing out that he was casually wandering about when a villager, Taina, approached him with news that shattered his plcasant meandering and turned him to more serious thoughts.

Figure 32: Verse 4 and chorus line with musical transcription for *Nahjeji.*

The second verse initiates Taina's complaint and subsequently Taina's voice is carried through into the sixth stanza. Accusations against two converts, Waihit and Josefa of Aneityum, *ru fua* of the second verse, are developed in Taina's voice. The text implies that the two converts have come to stay in the districts of Matagi and Iakana, where they did indeed settle historically after landing at Severaro Bay (Gunn 1914:9-10; Miller, J.G. 1978; Miller, R.S. 1975). Taina accuses the converts of fishing for lobsters on the reef, Segau, which lies at the border of these districts. Segau, photographed from the cliffs above, is shown in Figure 34. Trapping on the local reef without permission would have been a presumptuous act violating customary etiquette requiring

Figure 33: *Nahjeji* 'lobster trap'. Janet Dixon Keller 1998.

requests and permission for access to resources. Indirectly, however, Taina has accused the evangelists of fishing for converts, another presumptuous act. Taina suggests to them that they go back to Hsia and Mouga where they came ashore. If they are to preach then they should preach to people who accepted them to the island.

In the third and fourth verses the lobster trapping metaphor continues implicitly structuring the narrative through Taina's reported speech. He has, he says, pointed out to the evangelists that they made all the preparations for lobster trapping and then awaited low tide to set their weir. When the time was right they placed their traps at a rock formation known locally as Ta Vaka, The Canoe, for its resemblance to the shape of an outrigger. Metaphorically the suggestion is that the evangelists have come to the community (also *vaka*) to implant their new religion. There remains nothing left but to wait and concentrate on a successful 'catch'.

The fifth and sixth verses, still in reported speech, literally recount the results of an unsuccessful fishing venture. Taina has indicated to the converts that when they dove for their traps

Figure 34: Segau showing the surf at Ragragi. Janet Dixon Keller 1998.

expecting to return with lobsters enough for the first of season sacrifice and sustenance for a feast as well, they failed. The lobsters (*ika*), symbolizing the people of West Futuna, were afraid of the traps and shied away, leaving Waihit and Josefa empty-handed and discouraged.

In the fourth and fifth lines of verse six the voice of a chief enters the text, still as reported speech. The chief's words are recalled, 'Why are you two upset? We will fill my canoe.' Perhaps this leader is the song's composer, perhaps someone else. Whoever he may have been, his words began to articulate a resolution to heal the resentment felt by villagers like Taina and re-encompass the missionaries in local contexts.

In the final verse the leader explains his proposal. 'We will fill my canoe', serves by implication to invite Waihit and Josefa to step into the chiefly canoe, or metaphorically to become part of the local community. The second line posits a literal and metaphoric return to West Futuna. The canoe will go to sea, crossing the reef only to return to the island with the south wind. Once on shore again the converts will visit a spring of local knowledge where they will drink the waters of *kastom* ways. This action would reinvent the evangelists as islanders. The proposal would result in healing wounds and offers a plan for incorporating the outsiders into West Futuna communities, but on local terms. As far as history reveals, the possibility was never enacted.

Background and Connections

This song offers a rare glimpse of indigenous sentiment during a tumultuous time. Reactions to early evangelism are typically preserved only from the viewpoint of those bringing the Gospel. Unwritten traditions seldom endure to allow us a more diverse reading of the past. *Nahjeji* is exceptional in this regard and we are not aware of other versions, or of other compositions developing a theme or tropic lyrics similar to *Nahjeji*.

However, we do find that Maroi Sore collaborating with the Reverend William Gray of Tanna, and an individual named Natshia, recorded a song from Aniwa that opens with the same line as *Nahjeji* and continues throughout the initial verse with similar lyrics (Sore 1909:41). This may be a reflection of ritualized passages that served as openings for the *tagi* genre of traditional songs. It is reassuring to note similarities in our translation of the initial verse of *Nahjeji* with the English rendering of the first verse of the song published by Gray, Maroi Sore and Natshia approximately a full century earlier. We reproduce a segment of their work below.

Niotean ta fanua. (A)vau noko-fano	_______. I was going
Tiavagerapu ana, ni-viri avau	Aimlessly only, scared was I
Iatakoi, nimei-fasao mou-pakia-	At thee, come to talk, and you slap
Mai iavau, moufurusia (a)vau iangoro.	on me, and turn round for me the song.

Nahjeji is frequently performed today in festive and tourist contexts in Vanuatu, where the exuberant rhythm, music and accompanying dancing are displayed for appreciative, multi-ethnic ni-Vanuatu and expatriate audiences. Traveling musical groups, particularly the well-known *Futuna Fatuana*, include this composition in their repertoire of traditional genres presenting music and dance for audiences throughout the Pacific. The original composer of the song was most likely a man of influence living in Iakana or Matagi in the 1850s. It would have been during late 1853 or 1854 that tensions developed between evangelists and the local populace creating the context for this song.

In October 1853, Wahit and Josefa, converts from Aneityum appointed to introduce the Gospel to Futuna, arrived on West Futuna and were stationed in Iakana and Matagi. 'They were the FIRST NATIVE EVANGELISTS in the Western Pacific' (emphasis as in Gunn 1914:9; see also Murray 1876; Steel 1880). Initially they were welcomed in these communities, but increased incidence of disease and rumors of harmful consequences to result from conversion created an atmosphere in which the evangelists found themselves unwelcome and spurned.

In December of 1853 a sandalwood vessel called in at West Futuna and the passengers from Tanna terrified the local residents by reporting on misfortunes that would befall any who accepted Christianity. An influenza epidemic had been raging and this heightened suspicions with the result that Waihit and Josefa were blamed (R.S. Miller 1975). Conflicting experiences with neighbors from Aneityum where Christianity had reputedly taken hold caused concern as well. Reports of travelers to Aneityum extolled the changes that had taken place since conversion, but those visiting West Futuna from Aneityum during this era conducted themselves with ungoverned abandon, apparently undermining values that might otherwise have been associated with Christianity. When Waihit attempted to account for the poor character of the seaman in their personal choices he was derided and his life threatened.

During this period Waihit and Josefa were hungry and often unable to care for or feed themselves. Their gardens were raided and threats against their lives were made openly (Gunn 1914; Miller 1975; Steel 1880). Gunn reports that Waihit, in his distress, used to follow pigs to the bush and eat the roots they dug up (1914:10). Again and again Waihit's life was threatened; once, for example, when he attempted to intervene in plans for a human sacrifice, and again when the respected Chief Navaeka, too long away from the island, was feared dead. In this latter case it was assumed that Waihit, a master of the seas and storms before his conversion (Gunn 1906:118; Lawrie 1895), had created impassable conditions at sea that had taken the West Futuna leader's life.

The arrival of the mission vessel returning Chief Navaeka was perhaps just in time to prevent an assassination. It was in this climate that we suspect the song *Nahjeji* was composed perhaps specifically to pose a resolution for difficult and stressful times. I have wondered if the composer might not be Chief Navaeka, who is mentioned in mission reports as particularly influential during the time of Waihit and Josefa's stay on West Futuna (Gunn 1906; Inglis 1860; Lawrie 1895). But no one we asked remembered or was willing to reveal the original composer's identity. Additional information on Waihit and West Futuna history of this time period can be found in Geddie (1855:especially 108-9), Gunn (1914:especially 9-11), Inglis (1860), J.G. Miller (1978, 1981 and 1986) and R.S. Miller (1975).

Cultural Geography and The Canoe

Figure 35 maps the significant places and directions employed in *Nahjeji*. After arriving in Mouga district, the evangelists Waihit and Josefa would have moved southward toward the villages of Iakana and Matagi, where they were to be stationed. At the outset perhaps this journey was auspicious. But things quickly soured and the evangelists found themselves in precarious circumstances. The resolution for the unhappy situation involving the missionaries was the proposal of a voyage by canoe out over the reef, beyond the local shores, to be followed by a return to land directly from the south.

The resolution voyage was to be exceptionally brief. The chief seems to suggest going out just beyond the reef and then awaiting the proper wind conditions for a return to land. The return trip is to symbolize both a fresh start for the evangelists and a compromise. Waihit and Josefa would forego their missionizing ways and relearn local practices and knowledge while the residents of Matagi and Iakana would accept them as members of their communities. The reef plays a particularly significant role here. It is as though crossing its width frees the converts from any transgressions they may have committed and offers them the opportunity to return and begin their engagement with the people of West Futuna anew. The lyrics draw on the symbolism of the reef as a protective fringe surrounding the island. In crossing this boundary moving inward, travelers are required to acknowledge and respect *kastom*s of the land.

Evoking the reef in this way also recalls and emphasizes the circular geography of the island. This circular imagery is reinforced by the shape of *nahjeji*, as depicted in Figure 33. The trap, itself, is roughly hemispherical, circular in top view, with a central hole for the lobsters to enter. This replicates the idealized three-dimensional shape of the island of West Futuna with its circular outline, elevated interior and *tapu* center on the plateau. The lobster trap as an image of evangelism suggests again the fear of confinement, ideological and physical, so prominent in island lore.

Finally, like *Samaine* this song draws on the polysemy of *vaka*, the West Futuna word for 'womb, canoe, community and generation'. Fusing these meanings in the final verses of *Nahjeji* simultaneously proposes a voyage and envisions the reformation of a community living in harmony.

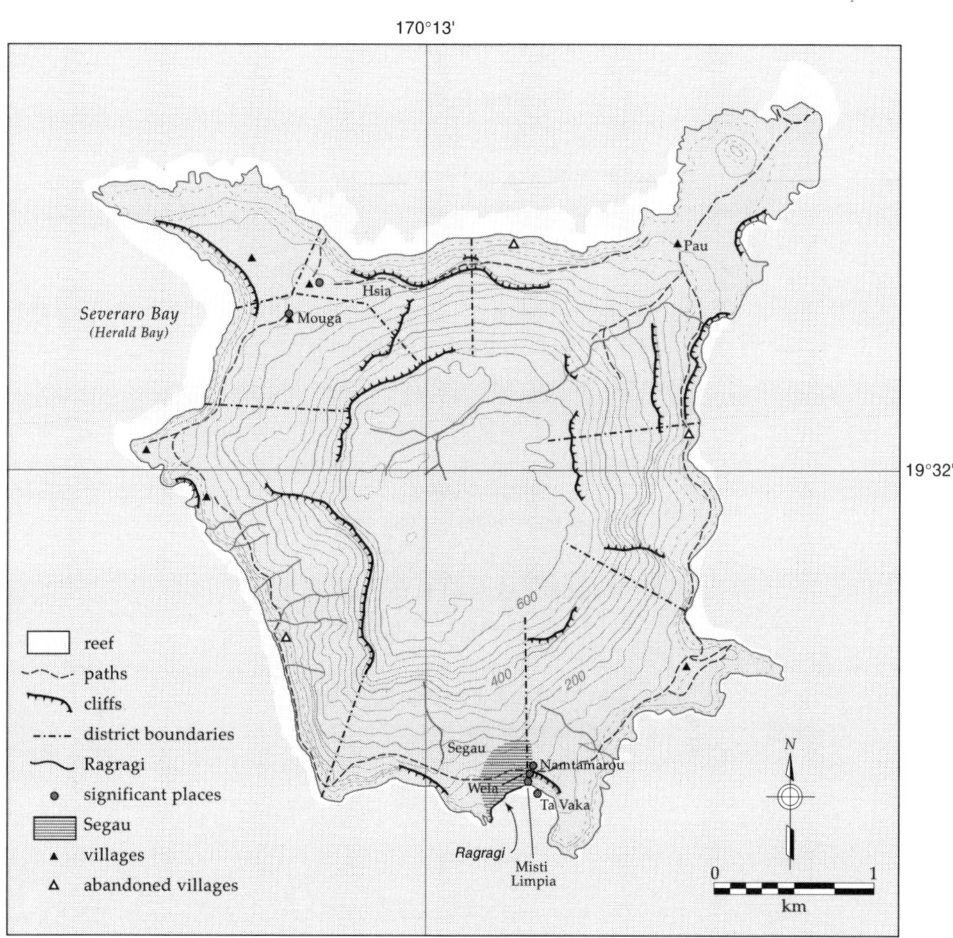

Figure 35: Locations where episodes transpire or are envisioned to take place in *Nahjeji*.

Nahjeji

Nojino Tasi

Niotean ta fanua avau nokofano
Tavage rapuana niviri avau i a Taina
Nokofasao nokofakauia avau
Sa tafuri tuk finagaro

tano ata: yei hei a ho ho yei hei hei ao
ei o yei hei hei ao, yei hei a ho ho
yei hei hei ao, a hei ho yei hei hei ao

Nojino Rua

Kaie segaro nimeitukua Taina
Pe, 'korua ru fua komeihnofo.'
'Koveteakea korua i ta tai Segau.'
'Kofakairoa i Hsia ma i Mouga'

tano ata: yei hei a ho ho yei hei hei ao
ei o yei hei hei ao, yei hei a ho ho
yei hei hei ao, a hei ho yei hei hei ao

Nojino Toru

'Kofakairoa i Hsia ma i Mouga.'
'Korotujia koamoa uagatai.'
'Koronage uai Ragragi kopempena.'
'Nokoraga tou soa kai nokotahri tai
hma i ai.'

Lobster Trap

Verse 1

I was just going out in this land of ours
To wander casually about when I was surprised by Taina
He spoke questioning me
And suddenly my daydreaming was turned around

chorus

Verse 2

However, I won't forget what Taina had come to say,
'You two fruits have come to stay'
'You two cast out (lobster traps) in the sea at Segau.'
'Go and preach to the people of Hsia and Mouga'

chorus

Verse 3

'Preach to the people of Hsia and Mouga'
'(You) cut (pandanus) and took it to the sea.'
'You soaked (the pandanus) at Ragragi and prepared it.'
'Your brother does the weaving

Lobster Trap

Verse 1

I was just going out in this land of ours
To wander casually about, when I was surprised by Taina
He spoke questioning me
And suddenly my daydreaming was turned to other thoughts

chorus

Verse 2

However, I won't forget what Taina had come to say,
'You two converts have come to stay'
'You reach out into our community trying to convert us.'
'Go away, back to preach to the people of Hsia and Mouga (the communities that let you land)'

chorus

Verse 3

'Preach to the people of Hsia and Mouga'
'You took advantage of our resources.'
'And prepared carefully to set your traps.'
'You have each done your

tano ata: yei hei a ho ho yei hei hei ao
ei o yei hei hei ao, yei hei a ho ho
yei hei hei ao, a hei ho yei hei hei ao

Nojino Fa

'Kai nokotahri tai hma i ai.'
'Rohma ta tai koronage i ta hmiji.'
'Korotomia i Ta Vaka akoe kafiji'
'Nokomementuana a fij nigkoto i ta
nahjeji'

tano ata: yei hei a ho ho yei hei hei ao
ei o yei hei hei ao, yei hei a ho ho
yei hei hei ao, a hei ho yei hei hei ao

Nojino Rima

'A fij nigkoto i ta nahjeji.'
'Kai ta pohpo kai korosuruia.'
'Korotugia i ta mara mara kaie jikai!'
'Nigkohlika a-ika i ai, akoe kotagimai koafe.'

tano ata:yei hei a ho ho yei hei hei ao
ei o yei hei hei ao, yei hei a ho ho
yei hei hei ao, a hei ho yei hei hei ao

and (you both) await the low
tide there.'

chorus

Verse 4
'You await the low tide there.'
'When the tide receded you
placed (traps) down in the
current.'
'Made them fast at Ta Vaka
(The Canoe) and you came
back ashore'
'Concentrating on the lobsters
that would fall into the trap.'

chorus

Verse 5
'Lobsters should fall into the
trap.'
'Come dawn you dive for them.'

'They will be first of season offerings, but there is not a one!'
'The lobsters were afraid
(of the trap), you return
discouraged.'

chorus

jobs and you bide your time
together.'

chorus

Verse 4
'You awaited the proper time.'
'When the time was right you
put your traps in place.'

'You placed them well in our
community and waited'

'Concentrating all the while on
harvesting those who would
convert.'

chorus

Verse 5
'People should be converted.'

'As the light dawns you seek
them out'
'In order to begin a new era,
but no one falls into your trap!'
'The people avoid the trap and
you are discouraged.'

chorus

Nojino Ono

'Akoe kotagimai koafe.'
'Akoe koafemai kai ru umu nokotu'
'Kai ru nasipi o ru nahjeji, kai saitukatu,
Kahmate akorua i aha? Kautaina ta vaka oku'

tano ata: yei hei a ho ho yei hei hei ao
ei o yei hei hei ao, yei hei a ho ho
yei hei hei ao, a hei ho yei hei hei ao

Nojino Fitu

'Kautaina ta vaka oku
makaafe i ahe rotumai sau Ritoga.'
'Reijikijia Mis(t)i Limpia, rofano uauta
Rofijikake i Weia kai nimeiinu i a Namtamarou'
(Alternatively Namtanarau/Namtamataga.)

tano ata: yei hei a ho ho yei hei hei ao
ei o yei hei hei ao, yei hei a ho ho
yei hei hei ao, a hei ho yei hei hei ao
yei hei a ho ho yei hei hei ao
ei o yei hei hei ao, yei hei a ho ho
yei hei hei ao, a hei ho yei hei hei ao
yei hei a ho ho yei hei hei ao
ei o yei hei hei ao, yei hei a ho ho
yei hei hei ao, a hei ho yei hei hei ao
yei hei a ho ho yei hei hei ao
ei o yei hei hei ao, yei hei a ho ho
yei hei hei ao, a hei ho yei hei hei ao
yei hei a ho ho yei hei hei ao
ei o yei hei hei ao, yei hei a ho ho
yei hei hei ao, a hei ho yei hei hei ao

Verse 6
'You return discouraged.'
'Back on land you find two ovens waiting'
'For two lobster portions from the traps, then he (the chief) says to you,
"Why are you-two upset? We will fill my canoe."'

chorus

Verse 6
'You are discouraged.'
'Others are counting on you'

'To make your contribution, then the chief addresses you,

"Why are you-two upset? We will bring you into our community."'

chorus

Verse 7
'We will fill my canoe
And return with the south wind.'
'When the wind makes white caps at Mis(t)i Limpia, then we'll go shoreward
To ascend at Weia and drink from Namtamarou'
(a spring and source of local knowledge).

Chorus repeated several times with increasing tempo each time and ending in a loud crescendo

Verse 7
'We will bring you into our community
Letting you join us anew'
'As you are re-encompassed by our land

We offer access to the wisdom of our ancestral ways.'

Chorus repeated several times with increasing tempo each time and ending in a loud crescendo

12
Ano Hkano / Deep Readings and Contemporary Connections

With stories of the supernatural and histories set to musical verse, ancestors have bequeathed discursive clues to right living to the people of West Futuna. These clues are far from explicit plans. Whether those who came before were supernatural or mortal, they seldom conveyed their truths directly. Yet their words offer windows on the past and tender wisdom for those eager to orchestrate their own changing circumstances (LiPuma 2000; Mueggler 2001; Orta 2004).

This chapter proffers initial interpretations. We take the mythical *hkai* first to establish narrative elements of cultural logic and perspective, autochthonous principles subject to strategic manipulation (Keller and Keller 1996; Feinberg 2002). Subsequently *tagi* offer an opportunity to explore the use of these supports as imaginal potentials for reorganizing messy circumstances or muddled situations. Together the logics of *hkai* and circumstances of *tagi* constitute conjunctures where transformations perhaps unwittingly emerge (Holland 1992; Lugo 1990; Sahlins 1981, 1985, 1991). In the very composition and performance of *tagi*, the status quo is put at risk and generative principles are tested. As we develop the meaningful frameworks of oral literature and song lyrics we simultaneously look more broadly at social process and envision a place for narrative inspiration in contemporary practices.

Taken as a whole this collection of oral literature and musical lyrics discloses parameters for social life, offers a landscape in constant dialogue with identities, provides a cosmology that gives meaning to existence, and poses historical examples of what might go wrong in wayward happenings. Examination of possibilities for the transport of these frameworks to new environments and for the application of ideas implicated in the narratives to emerging dilemmas, motivates our search for ties among narrated worlds and contemporary lived experience. Ultimately we seek to test Glassie's promise that bodies of literature like that compiled here are capable of unsettling the spaces we inhabit and stimulating initiatives within them (1982:13).

Hkai / Mythical Tales

Supernatural Genealogy

The earliest inhabitants of West Futuna are supernatural heroes, heroines and villains whose actions establish ethics for human occupants of the land. They are often thought of as half human and half otherworldly. Unlike humans these characters have extraordinary powers, both physical and mental, and it is these attributes that enable the remarkable events of the distant past. Like humans these supernatural characters are related. Majihjiki and Sina, an original brother and sister, marry and have children, who in turn marry and continue the reproductive cycle, until, it is argued, descent gradually produces human offspring with responsibility for themselves and for the land, reef and seascapes they have inherited. A partial genealogy of the supernatural derived from textual accounts and inter-textual comparisons is presented in Figure 36. Not shown in the chart are the monster, *pasiesi*; or the spirit women, Ti Auauau and Ta Kofukofu. These characters are likewise part of the original supernatural state but their relationships to humankind are not those of direct descent. Ti Auauau and Ta Kofukofu seem to stand apart from the earliest ancestors as perennial advisors. They act as guardians for the gradual process through which island communities are established. *Pasiesi*

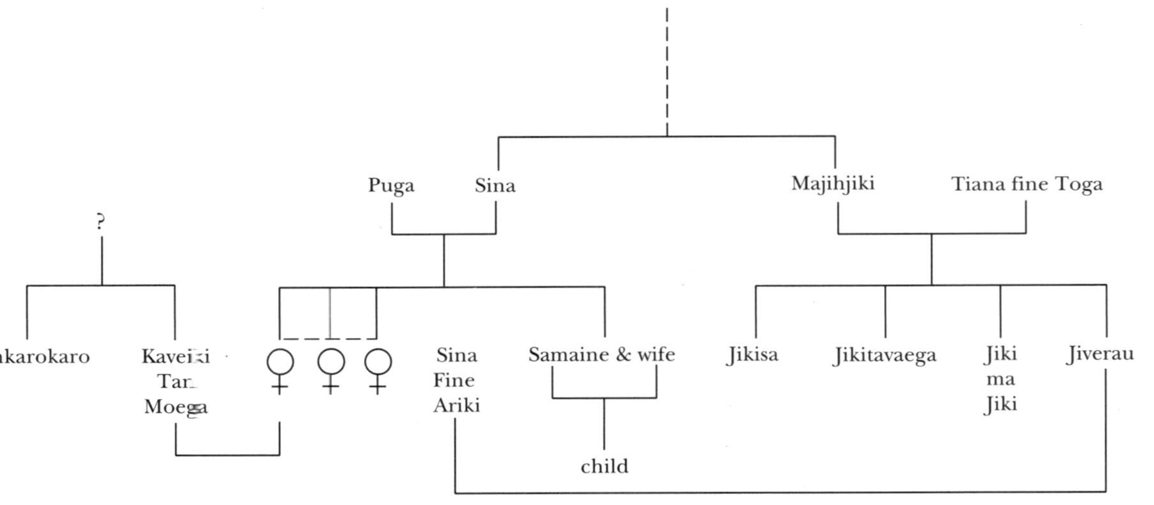

Figure 36: Supernatural genealogy of the *hkai*.

and his ilk embody pernicious forces that challenged the formation of social life and still threaten to tear communities apart.

The kinship outlined in Figure 36 does not reflect all of the relationships among supernatural characters. For example, Majihjiki has other wives and children in stories not presented here. Nonetheless the connections summarized by the chart are familiar to West Futuna audiences and were made apparent in discussions of textual significances. Recognizing these genealogical links enriches understanding of the narratives. For example, Jiverau's return to take Sina Fine Ariki as his wife acquires moral value in light of their parental ties and the real world cultural preference for cross-cousin unions. We suspect there is an even larger supernatural family surrounding the core we have presented, one that would be more fully revealed by examining additional tales. In a continuing spiral such tales and the relationships implicated in them would add new insight into the meanings of the familiar stories already collected.

Still we offer a cautionary note on the inter-textual process of analysis for on first seeing the genealogical chart of the supernatural Takaronga's reaction was one of uncertainty. Accustomed to thinking of kinship ties among those of the spirit world as pertinent to individual narratives, he paused to reflect when presented with the derived chart. In the end he found it stimulating. Still, he pointed out, the relationships developed within individual texts are immediately verifiable while the more inclusive genealogy presented here must remain tentative.

Text and the Social World

The most oft-repeated theme among the *hkai* is that of making the transition from a situation of nurturing care to one of reciprocal engagement with others. We see this theme in the episodes of confinement and escape (Gifford 1924:187-90; Kirtley 1971:154; Lessa 1980:8-11). Children of the land, a beloved daughter, and an abandoned son find themselves, through rather different circumstances, imprisoned within the *fare ariki* of the *pasiesi*, or fenced within a refuge, or held within a gated abode in the clouds. In each case those confined are well provisioned by their keepers. Yet the state of confinement imperils social life-ways. It is only through escape from the exclusive protection of others that the reciprocity essential for human life can be realized.

Responsibility entails separation from original keepers, and accomplishing this separation exacts a price. The children captured by *pasiesi* flee from him only to become embroiled in an extended chase. They must accept a principle of moderation in order to succeed in their escape. Sina Fine Ariki leaves her sanctuary to begin married life, but her departure is a source of fatal grief for her parents. Samaine and his family leave their supernatural guardians to live with humans, ultimately sacrificing absolute security for mature responsibility within a village community.

This theme is indexed although not fully developed in *Majihjiki ma FaFine Toga* and *Rufei Soa*. In the former a confining proscription is the condition for complete provisioning. Eventually the situation proves untenable. Majihjiki's wife escapes the terms of her marriage presumably to assume full responsibility and participation in the social life of her homeland. In *Rufei Soa* death and confinement within the underworld are specters of entrapment by a clam and betrayal by a brother. It is spousal loyalty that reverses the narrative trajectory enabling a return from a fate of confinement within the underworld to sustained, married life.

In the end, in all the stories the characters establish appropriate social ties. Survival is insured by interchange in the context of mutual, not asymmetrical, relationships with others. Equivalence and difference become intertwined in reciprocity. Sustenance comes to depend upon sharing and exchange among distinctive but equal participants. The gift that cannot be returned, the stories warn, is dangerous. Perhaps it is no coincidence that these tales are among the most salient for the contemporary populace of West Futuna and their descendents. Surely in the construction of individual resilience and the formation of interactive bonds are the principles for an independent nation-state that has transcended dependencies of the colonial era and emerged as an equal but unique co-participant with others in the global scene. Might we not see in the traditional narrative *ata* new indexes with contemporary relevance as their *hkano* are transformed to encompass dilemmas of the post-colonial era?

A second common theme revolves around tensions associated with post-marital residence. A typically gendered distinction between enforced and strategic possibilities for movement (Jolly 1999) is destabilized in the episodes of *Majihjiki ma Fafine Toga* and *Sina Fine Ariki*. Both men and women travel in these tales. Jiverau travels to find his bride and Sina Fine Ariki travels to a foreign land to reside with her new husband, in an ideal patrilocal pattern. Majihjiki's Tongan bride moves freely from place to place as an unmarried woman. Forced by marital circumstances to settle with her spouse she eventually regains the possibility of movement and returns to her homeland. Majihjiki, originally rooted to his place in Pau, ultimately follows his wife and they raise a family in her place. In these stories men and women travel, characters of each gender selectively initiate movement or follow one another. Residential options grow out of the exigencies of circumstance and flexibility seems to be an inter-textual message. Displacement of a woman from her natal community to that of her husband is not presented as inevitable but as a choice complemented by other options.

In inverting the residential norm *Majihjiki ma Fafine Tonga* is exceptional. The suggestion of a feminist voice arises with the narrative denouement. In all other versions of this ni-Vanuatu tale of which I am aware (Codrington 1891; Jolly 1999; Thieberger pers. comm.), the marriage is dissolved by the residential crisis and a woman's rejection of patrilocal precedent. Only in interpretations of the West Futuna versions does the couple reunite and only via an addendum to the West Futuna tale does the husband make the move to his wife's home.

This gaze, perhaps from a woman's perspective, resonates with the interlaced outcomes, both personal and cultural, attendant upon Sina Fine Ariki's departure from her home. In the demise of the parents of the Princess Sina her narrative seems to chastise the system for hardships created by the male residential bias. And yet there are mitigating circumstances that run against the critique as well. Inter-island travel, like inter-village associations, becomes a source of alliance, communication and common history among communities that would otherwise be isolated, their populations eternally separated by the arbitrary accident of emplacement via birth.

Proper residence is a theme indexed by *Ta Pasiesi ma Majihjiki*. One of the main objects of the tale is to insure the island is resettled appropriately, one boy and one girl returning to each village site around the perimeter. The outcome is a pattern of villages punctuating the paths along the island circumference. The presumption is that each couple represents a future family, the sons and daughters of which will become interlinked through marriage and exchange relations. Loss of a daughter's immediate presence will be a sacrifice but one that will bring access to diverse resources. As accentuated in the narrative situations of inter-island travel, the imagined mosaic, in this case of inter-village marriages, creates an enduring social fabric of reciprocal dynamics that ensures continuity of people and their life-ways.

Such issues are not only of the imagined worlds of narrative but infuse lives of the people of West Futuna today. Mobility is increasingly the enabling foundation of life. Sacrifices of co-presence facilitate life-long relationships of exchange that preserve family integrity over distances. And the new community mosaics emerging in the context of mobility for both men and women are the source of fresh identities for the people of Vanuatu. Unquestionably, the traditional anchors of narrative speak to possibilities for the future.

A third focus in the *hkai* revolves around the proper character of relationships among kin: brothers, spouses, parents and their children. Character struggles in the stories test alternatives and posit oppositional and imaginal developments for proper and improper canons of lived experience (Burke 1966; LeRoy 1985). As Firth has indicated traditional tales are not so much 'a reflection of the social structure itself as of organizational pressures within the social structure' (1961:179) and traditional West Futuna narratives are no exception. The clearest cases of contests illustrating such pressures are developed in the narratives of *Rufei Soa* and in the contrast between *Sina Fine Ariki* and *Samaine*.

Rufei Soa is grounded in a struggle between *soa* or 'brothers', who by normative practice should cooperate effectively for the support of their extended families. Jealousy intervenes, however, and one brother aims to destroy the other. Were it not for the resistance of Kaveiki Tan Moega's wife, Vahkarokaro, the jealous one, might have succeeded. Her loyalty preempts his plan. Evil is denied its purchase and the story moves toward restoration of the original marriage. Impossible in actuality is the consequence faced by the evil brother who is forever ostracized to a life of isolation for his deeds. The cooperative kin-based ethic is reinforced by contrast with this drastic narrative outcome.

Struggles between parents and children are depicted in *Sine Fine Ariki* and perhaps assumed in *Samaine*. In the former tale, the princess and her parents are put in contention over her marriage and departure. Initially in control the parents confine their youngest daughter hoping to preserve their natal family forever. Sina Fine Ariki's maturity, represented by her escape, is their loss. Exaggerated by the episodes of the tale, parental grief is depicted as unbearable. The daughter's marriage entails her parents' death. A rift between the generations that narrative cannot heal, marks a challenge of real life that must with regularity be overcome. In *Samaine* by contrast, it is parental abandonment that threatens survival. Taken together the narratives depict opposing risks for the reproduction of family units and perhaps conjointly point to the possibility of a middle road, one in which early nurturance is replaced by life-long reciprocity and cooperation.

Via these narratives traditional relations of brotherly support and guidelines for generational transitions are carried into the present as inspiration. Issues of how to navigate modern circumstances and urban lifeways are infused with questions of reconstructing kin relations in social milieus where individuality challenges ties of birth. The process seems to be one of expanding the relevance of kinship rather than relinquishing this mode of being in the world. In the service of the success of each individual, interpersonal networks are formed out of increasingly diverse relations modeled on those of earlier times. Exchange has proved a persistent mode for maintaining ties though goods themselves and means of transporting them are constantly revised. Sisters reside or travel together much as they would have cooperated in weekly excursions to the plateau gardens in earlier times. Collateral ties among a variety of cousins and across generations provide opportunistic access to resources and labor augmenting agnatic traditions. Intermarriage bridging communities provides unprecedented affinal arrangements that are recognized as expansions of the original mosaic. Even as nuclear families take shape, households are open to incorporating extended kin or outsiders in the pursuit of professional or educational goals. The contemporary scene constituted by increasingly mobile and self-directed individuals is simultaneously an arena where kin-based obligations, responsibilities and support inspired by possibilities from the past create flexible and enabling foundations in the present.

A final thematic device of the stories uses character traits to shape possibilities for personhood (LiPuma 2000). For example, *Ta Pasiesi ma Majihjiki* juxtaposes proper and improper ways of being. Central to right living are the qualities of cooperation and conservation that contrast with the evils of self-indulgence and gluttony. Cooperation is also contrasted with self-gratification in the dynamics of *Rufei Soa*. Today in the face of growing materialism and rising practices of conspicuous consumption, ideals for right living are in flux. Narrative lessons may have an enduring relevance for the ongoing process of shaping persons and creating citizens of the new republic.

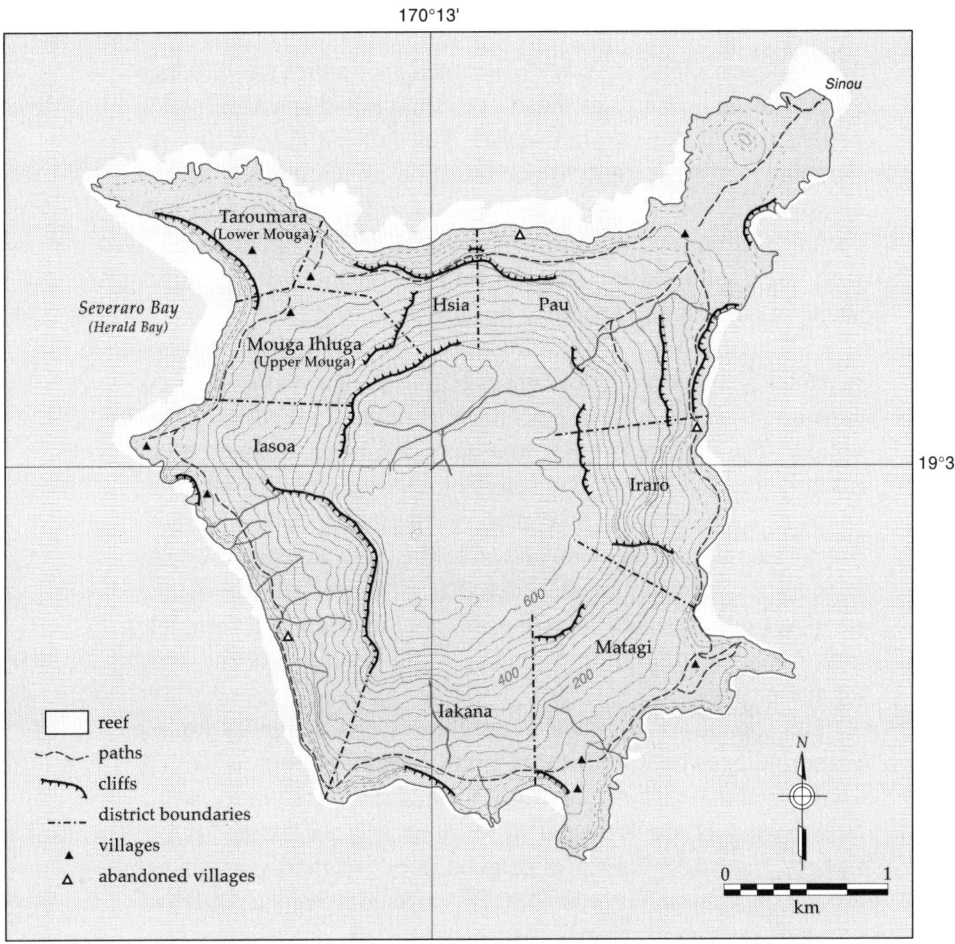

Figure 37: Political districts and village sites for West Futuna, Vanuatu.

Cultural Geography and Cosmology

The *hkai* collected here take-for-granted and in turn (re-)produce a cultural geography, an idealized, constructed space in which people and the supernatural reside. The full outlines of this geography gradually came to our attention as we worked among ethnographic and narrative maps considered in conjunction with social practices and spatial metaphors of the tales. Within each story we found partial clues to a larger cosmology that takes shape in circular and spherical imagery.

We start from real life circumstances depicted in Figure 4 (Chapter 3) and reproduced here as Figure 37. Recall that districts surround a central plateau, which itself contains a revered central hollow. The plateau extends to a hazy perimeter, unmarked but roughly coexistent with the island's highest circuit of cliffs. Political districts begin to take shape at the precipices and radiate out into the sea. Villages are placed exclusively around the larger, concentric perimeter of the land. The main path on the island of West Futuna connects these residential districts in a complete circuit that re-presents the boundary of the central plateau but on a grander scale.

The spatial arrangement of neighborhoods or family homes within villages may reflect this larger circular pattern as well. A sacred, public *marae* is centrally located within a village while neighborhoods are arranged in sections radiating from its periphery. Figure 38 illustrates neighborhoods primarily organized around the central *marae* in Pau. This village reflects a pattern of circular order more clearly than many others, but even as residential areas expand beyond primary, radiating neighborhoods, as has occurred on the western edge of Pau, or where the terrain makes it difficult to discern a circular pattern on the ground, an ideal arrangement for living is imagined and homes are said to ring a central, public space.

Settings in the narratives recurrently accentuate prominent *marae* at Pau, Ravaru, Mouga and Nakiroa creating a mutual

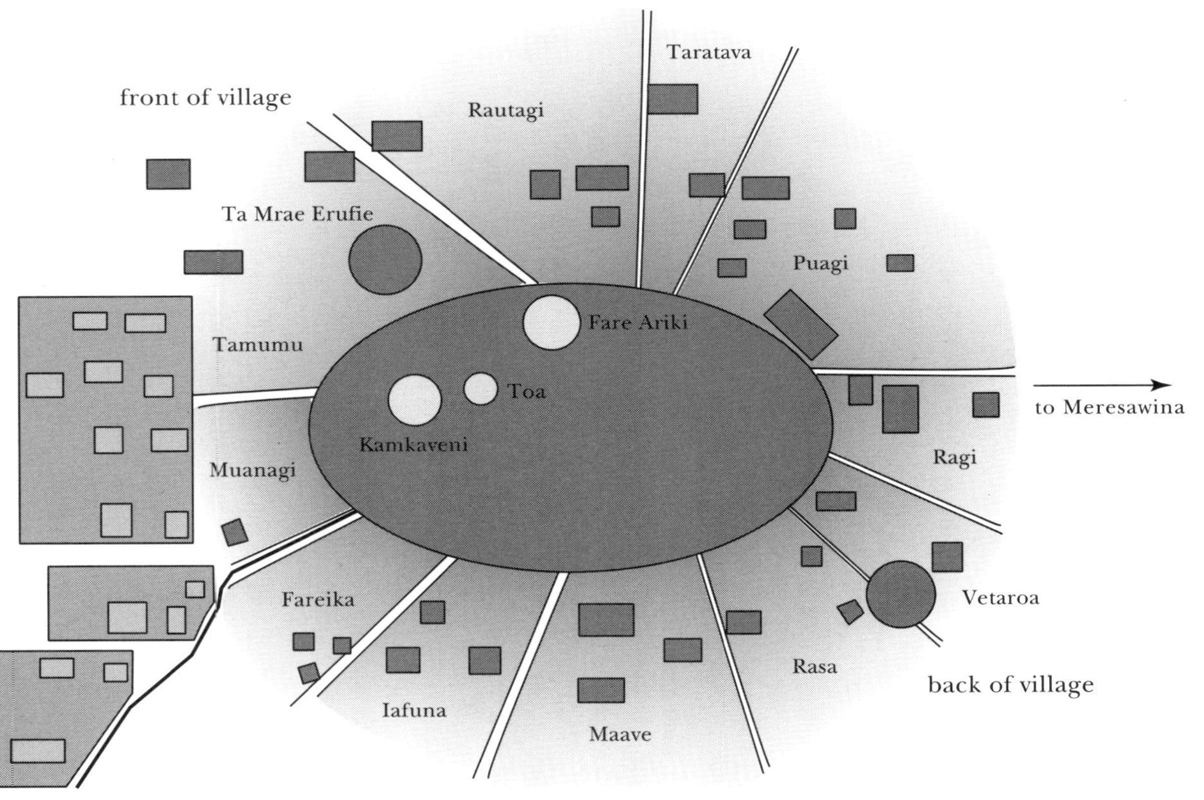

Figure 38: Home sites around the central *marae* in Pau.

interchange of recounted and lived significances in these places. A series of metaphors highlight the circular geometries further. In *Ta Pasiesi ma Majihjiki* the children and their hero disguise themselves within a large breadfruit, the children becoming its seeds and *Majihjiki* its core. The imagery conjured by this trope is that of the breadfruit sliced in half to reveal seeds distributed around the central portion of the fruit, a pattern mimicking the arrangement of neighborhoods around their *marae*, villages around the island interior, or gardens surrounding the hollow within the high plateau.

In *Majihjiki ma Fafine Toga*, Majihjiki's wife is restricted from entering a room where her wings have been hidden beneath *ta foi niu furi sore*, 'a special, big, round stone'. The stone under which her wings are buried evokes a plan view of the island of West Futuna where the woman herself has become rooted. Circles are evident again in the fences surrounding confining spaces. The narrator of *Sina Fine Ariki* explicitly gestures with his hands to recreate rounded outlines of concentric restraints. And Samaine's family is similarly confined within encircling fences surrounding a misty abode.

Siegi, a women's grass skirt, appearing prominently in the tale of *Samaine,* also participates in this imagery of circular forms. Grass skirts envelope their wearer. As used in *Samaine* an analogy between *siegi* and *karoa* 'necklets, ornamentation' emphasizes the encircling property of both.[1] Perhaps in encircling an individual these articles of adornment figuratively demarcate and mediate boundaries of personhood. *Samaine* witnesses a series of remarkable grass skirts modeled by a spirit woman into whose world he has accidentally intruded. Affirming the conspicuous and protective splendor of the grass skirts may be a symbolic act reaffirming boundaries accidentally crossed in his journey while acknowledging an ontological divide separating him from the spirit women.

The fringing reef, roughly circular in the course it makes around the island, accentuates the importance of encompassment. Neither land nor sea, the coral fringe occupies a transitional space in island topography and captures the narrative imagination. The north shore reef is created initially by Majihjiki, wishing to forestall a pursuing monster. It thus serves at its inception to protect islanders and challenge evil. The full encircling form is evoked in the final episode of *Sina Fine Ariki,* when Puga, fraught with grief, jumps to his death. Transformed into a massive protrusion of brain coral in the band that rings the land he will forever stand vigil protecting the islanders as he watches for the approach of strangers. Yet the narratives remind us that the reef is not impassable. Jiverau, Majihjiki, the brothers (Vahkarokaro and Kaveiki Tan Moega), and the women from Tonga find ways to transgress its width. In this the narratives mimic real life where border crossings are also frequent. A tension between protection and interaction so important in the thematic structure of the tales is reinforced by the tropic use of the encompassing yet permeable coral fringe reminding readers that the land itself can be a place of confinement if not subject to the enrichments of travel and engagement.

This significance for the reef's circular form recalls again the cultural geography of village and neighborhood layouts and resonates with the symbolic impact of narrative fences, breadfruit seeds, the circular form of the *sinu* tree, and grass skirts. Each figurative trope is an analogue of the others and each embodies the tension between protection and reciprocity, confinement and escape. These literary devices double back on themselves repeatedly. As it rings the shore, for example, the coral takes on the import of a protective fence or grass skirt around the waist of the land, just as the concentric fences restraining characters in turn resonate with the risks of boundary crossings at the reef.

This significance for the coastal margins of islands has been recognized by Pacific scholars. Anthropologists, archaeologists and historians of the Pacific have argued that coastal zones reflect conjunctions and disparities of island life. Artistic renditions of the period of European exploration frequently depict encounters at shorelines. The beach, it has been argued, bore witness to cultures in contact and ultimately harbored material evidence of those meetings (Dening 1980; Kirch 1997; Sahlins 1985). In the eloquent prose of Greg Dening (1992:177):

> Beaches are beginnings and endings. They are the frontiers and boundaries of islands. ... history is more likely to be born on beaches, marginal spaces between land and sea ... where everything is relativised a little, turned around, where tradition is as much invented as handed down, where otherness is both a new discovery and a reflection of something old.

It is this theme of frontiers and boundaries that reappears in the West Futuna *hkai*. Yet our tales suggest it is not at the site of beaches precisely where transformative power is located, but rather at the coral perimeter in the geographical region where land and sea overlap. The geography of the reef serves as repository for the interpenetrating dualities of place and travel, identity and alliance, encompassment and crossing. In everyday life dualities merge here too. Male and female share this space, jointly exploiting resources nurtured by the coral ecology.

However, this two-dimensional analysis of the reef and its symbolic associations falls short of recreating the full cultural geography and associated cosmology implicated by the *hkai* at issue. Completing the analysis requires attention to three-dimensional space. In *Rufei Soa*, the reef is significant for its depth. *Kaveiki Tan Moega*'s journey to the underworld is initiated at *Ta Toka*, conspicuously centered in the reef formation at Severaro Bay.[2] The deceased's path continues along the reef moving toward the depths of the underworld. As his wife follows she repeatedly calls down into the crevices and crannies of rock and coral seeking information about her husband. In these episodes the reef constitutes yet another border zone, one between the world of the living and the world of the dead.

A world below the land raises the question of a world above the land and in the story of Samaine this possibility is instantiated. The spirit women, Ta KofuKofu and Ti Auauau, introduced in *Rufei Soa* where they inhabit the entryway to the underworld, are also found residing in the misty realm above the island cliffs. This parallelism constitutes a spiritual encompassment of the land emphasizing a third dimension of the cultural geography and positing an ontological divide between the landed world of humanity and surrounding abodes of the supernatural.

Reflecting on the narratives further it is clear that many examples of the circular imagery we identified are intimately embedded within spherical forms. The breadfruit in which the children and Majihjiki conceal themselves is a spherical fruit. The *sinu* tree of Samaine's tale recreates in inverted form the three dimensions of the island geography, and *pasiesi*'s grotesque embodiment of a compass mimics the three-dimensional contour of the land. The shape of the *fare ariki,* the giant clam shell responsible for Kaveiki Tan Moega's death, and the brain coral imagery in *Sina Fine Ariki* further suggest three-dimensional hemispheres that serve as inspiration for narrative tropes. Even the grass skirt encircling a woman's waist evokes a three-dimensional human form.

A final allusion in this vein emerged with respect to West Futuna's horizon. The names of the spirit women of the tales evoke the horizontal plane. Mist, fog and sea foam are elements of sky and sea that merge in the distant haze encircling West Futuna on the plane of the land (see also Bonnemaison 1994:36; Codrington 1891:11). Their homes too, underworld and Ta Vavanea, merge at the horizon. Yet, we realized, it is not spirits who importantly reside at the periphery of the landed plane, but other beings, *tama toga* 'children from afar' or *maivaka* 'those who come by ship'. Conceptually centered in the horizontal plane, the island of West Futuna is surrounded on its horizon by other, real world lands and peoples less well understood than consociates at home. Supernatural engagements in the narratives connect West Futuna with these genuine margins. The travels of Majihjiki, Jiverau and the women of Tonga reflect real life encounters where continuity and change are forever counterpoised in interactions with others at the edge of the visible sphere. Figure 39 imagines the spherical

Figure 39: A view of the universe as it takes shape in West Futuna narratives.

cosmology derived from the entangled circular and spherical images constructed in and referenced by the collected *hkai*.

This conception places humans, foreigners and ancestral spirits in concentric worlds of spherical contour centered on the island of West Futuna itself. The people of West Futuna find themselves surrounded by a horizon of others. Likewise they are embraced by spirit worlds above and below, places they may venture to only briefly while living. These ontological distinctions are emphasized by the narrative concern with boundaries symbolized in the images of the reef, fences, clouds, grass skirts, and the risks attendant upon their crossings.

Centripetal and centrifugal movements are significant in this cosmology. An absence of a meaningful opposition between up and down as symbolic anchors for the *hkai* puzzled us for some time (M. Rodman raised this concern in Canberra in 2000). This gap in expectations for symbolic potential became particularly troubling as the importance of elevation and three-dimensional imagery began to emerge. Eventually it became clear that movements of interest in the narratives were valued according to their inward/outward trajectory along the radii of the cosmological sphere or the circular spaces encompassed by it rather than along a two-dimensional vertical axis. Connecting inner and outer in the narrative discourses are trajectories to and from the sky and tracks to and from the reef. Following a centrifugal course away from land and toward the underworld or the cloudy upper home of the spirits is fraught with danger, while returning to the land is the West Futuna version of a happy ending. Up and down are, in fact, unified rather than contrasted within the narrative world. Their significance is that of directional orientations toward and away from land or supernatural abodes.

Movement to and from the distant horizon might have been captured by the symbolism of opposing centripetal and centrifugal forces, but are not. Contact with human others seem to carry more conflicted associations than movement between the mortal and supernatural realms. Whether directed outward or approaching West Futuna, involvements with the periphery are filled with trepidation. Such movements entail multiple boundary crossings. Breaches of fenced or walled spaces, *mraes* or villages are compounded by reef crossings of both departures and arrivals. The imagined entanglements that result are narrative reminders of the unpredictable yet essential reciprocity that sustains self and other whether in the worlds of familiar tradition or emergent innovation (Lugo 1997).

Also embedded within the narratives are directional contrasts, rightward and leftward, that create nuanced and shifting moods reflective of real life. Episodes of the stories oriented in a rightward direction as one faces the plateau are perceived as auspicious. *Fori fakamatau* or 'to go around in the right way' is the appropriate linguistic expression for such actions. Movement in the opposing direction is associated with apprehension, even threatening or sinister possibilities. The linguistic expression is *fori fakamasui* or 'traveling in the wrong or left moving way as one faces land'. This directional logic is captured ethnographically in the *uka* or proper lines of communication. The contrast is said to be based upon associations with the winds. The mild prevailing easterlies that enable life's activities are perceived as moving rightward, while detrimental gale-force storms are associated with westerlies and experienced as leftward moving in their trajectory (see Blust 1997:47).[3]

The cosmology thusly envisioned places foreigners and the supernatural in concentric realms centered on the island and people of West Futuna who themselves must wrestle with the simultaneously bounded and porous spaces of their lives and their stories. This is not the vision of the Polynesian pantheon of gods and multileveled heavens (Feinberg pers. comm.; Goodenough 1986; Handy 1927:76-7; Herdrich 1991). It is closer to the cosmology reconstructed by Monberg for Bellona where the island is centered with underworld below and abodes of the gods above, although in Bellona the heavens are differentiated by quadrants that we haven't found in evidence for West Futuna (1991:26-7). Critical to the West Futuna perspective are the successive modes of encompassment that require repeated transgression of safe and familiar realms in the achievement of engagement with others: kin, foreigners and supernatural ancestors, who inhabit the imagined spaces of narrative as they do the real spaces of life. Such transgressions are carefully governed in narrative as in life by etiquettes for border crossings.

Tagi / Historical Songs

We turn now to examine the relations between text, the social world, cultural geography and cosmology in another narrative genre, the musical compositions referred to as *tagi*. The songs we have translated do not draw on the supernatural explicitly so that genealogy is not pertinent to this discussion. Nor is a process of allegorical cues to right living directly relevant. The texts, instead, are immediate products of lived experiences. The initial challenge to the audience is to decode figurative tropes in terms of actual events, personalities and perspectives. In the cases of both *Tiata* and *Nahjeji,* linking texts with the encounters they depict calls on the same cultural principles embodied by the *hkai* and therewith enables judgments on the past and comparative assessment of the unfolding present.

Tiata is the simpler of the two songs. It is a musical critique of a man unlucky in love. Place constitutes the symbolic framework for the lyrics. Without mentioning Tiata by name the verses successively note the neighborhoods he has frequented in search of a mate. Mention of a circuit of places is sufficient to recall his plight and ridicule his poor fortune. For those who knew Tiata or have learned of his life from others, perhaps his personality and details of his encounters with women also come to mind. In the end he is no better off than when the song began. He is called home with no expectation that his solitary circumstances will change. Beyond the evaluation of one man's situation, the song and its mocking tone emphasize the importance of marriage in providing ties to neighborhoods and villages in the residential circuits of local life, a theme woven into several of the *hkai* and emphasized in non-narrative, spatial symbolism as well (Keller 1988).

Nahjeji, 'Lobster Trap', propounds the difficulties of foreign intrusions into a local scene, a process constitutive of past encounters as of present conditions. The lyrics are deeply embedded in historical events. Of particular concern is the violation of West Futuna norms by visiting outsiders bent on changing rather than respecting a status quo. Composed as it was during the mid-nineteenth century at the height of tensions between community members and Aneityumese evangelists the lyrics were constructed in tropic form. A perceived similarity between lobster trapping and religious conversion creates the primary symbolic framework.

The composer employs other themes made apparent in the *hkai* to convey his message. A concern with confinement is a primary organizing feature of the song. The lobster trap is equated with the Church, its teachings and its personnel, a metaphor that plays on a general fear of stagnation associated with confinement in this case in evangelical traps. A feared loss of self-determination and of continuity with local life-ways was associated with conversion and led people (*fij, ika*) to shy away from Christianity (*nahjeji*).

This song also takes advantage of cultural geography and cosmology. Primary events of the narrative are situated at the island perimeter. The reef is particularly significant as the site where lobster traps are set. As in the *hkai*, traditions are at risk at the coral margins of the land. The final verse of *Nahjeji* presses this significance further, contrasting the island's center with its risky surrounds. Although *Namtamarou*'s precise location is debated today, the local font of knowledge is consistently located up and inland, approaching if not within the central plateau. The spring represents local custom and value, presumably a supernatural gift from time before. It is a place with the power to convey wisdom and thereby transform strangers into consociates. Reaching this resource requires auspicious, inward or centripetal movement from the sea.

Border crossing is an essential element of the song. The composer's solution to discordant circumstances is to remove offenders, proposing to take them beyond the reef to the open sea from whence they can return to West Futuna to start their stay afresh. The disharmony they have engendered can be repaired only by transforming their objectives and their practices. To achieve this the evangelists must receive and respect local knowledge. And to make this possible they must leave the land where their presence has been disturbing. By crossing the reef moving outward they become symbolically neutral again. A subsequent return to land by traversing the coral border inward provides an opportunity to enter the community of West Futuna on local terms.

Imagery associated with *ta vaka*, 'canoe', and hemispherical or spherical forms bolster the logic of the proposed solution. As in *Samaine*, the polysemous linking of 'womb, canoe, community and generation' by mention of *ta vaka* in *Nahjeji* repeatedly alludes to possibilities for encompassing the foreigners within the local. The challenge in the *Nahjeji* lyrics as in life is for the people of West Futuna to receive yet control the impact of outsiders by shaping novelty to their purposes (Peterson 1992:20). Indeed it is hard to imagine an historical event with greater impact on contemporary life in Vanuatu than early evangelism. Initially resisted, history demonstrates that ideas from afar were ultimately received and domesticated. The lessons from this musical recounting and its historical aftermath couldn't be more pertinent to ongoing processes of assessment as islanders receive, challenge and transform global forces that reach their shores today.

There is a deep 'deliberate ambivalence about dealing with foreigners' (Petersen 1992:20) symbolized in the tropic forms of *Nahjeji*. Novelty and stability hang in the balance. The lobster trap is a hemispherical form reproducing the shape of the land itself even to its central depression. Island and entrapment are symbolically equated in this imagery suggesting not only islanders' vulnerability to outsiders' evangelical traps but also an awareness that island ways too can confine. Spiritual and geographical encompassment may filter the foreign but the same qualities make islanders vulnerable to isolation, cut off from the reciprocity so essential to survival. A doubly valenced logic and equivocal stance toward encompassment pervade *Nahjeji* as these tensions have pervaded all of the narratives herein encountered, motivating a concern with interactions involving the horizon.

In this connection the argument for filtering the strange, of course, may also imply its own inversion. Ideologies and practices from West Futuna that reach communities on the horizon will inevitably be reconfigured in the alternative terms of those places. The processes envisioned by boundary crossings and converging spheres of influence are mutual ones that enable forces from within and without Vanuatu to insure the vitality associated with exchange amidst both persistent, enduring differences, and transformations of those differences in each locale.

Past Words in Present Ways

In his recent book, *Catechizing Culture*, Orta (2004) argues that the past is an 'unclosed chapter'. We conclude in similar vein by examining particular circumstances in Vanuatu from the vantage point of narrative discourses of earlier eras. We have argued herein that traditional stories and songs go unnoticed by the people of West Futuna for their contemporary relevance. Narratives are not often interrogated for sage or pertinent perspectives on immediate events. Perhaps it is all the more surprising then to find echoes from the *hkano* of *hkai* and *tagi* underlying specific strategies for adapting in contexts of global influence. Perhaps, but our ethnographic gaze at recent practice offers evidence for the resilience of ancestral wisdom. This perception of lasting influence ultimately returns us to examine oral literature and musical lyrics as resources for envisioning roads to viable Pacific life-ways.

We start several decades after World War II, when children of West Futuna families, including Takaronga, typically attended boarding schools following their early elementary education. These schools, patterned on British or French institutions, were located on Tanna or Efate. While some families followed their children, providing a home away from home, many remained on West Futuna reuniting with their offspring only during holidays or interim breaks. Welcoming the boarders back was a festive occasion but one colored by unease. I witnessed one occasion in the 1970s. A scheduled day for the students' return began with the island community rising early. People were restless and involved in anticipatory discussions of the ship's arrival. Parents stood on cliff tops peering into the distance for visual cues of a vessel they could already track by the *muuu* of the engine. Yet when the progress of the launch was certain, the watchers gradually dispersed. The boat anchored off Ta Fasua. The children were brought to shore in canoes and climbed the path to Pau, but no crowd waited to greet them. Neither family nor community immediately enveloped the young. Instead people had returned circuitously to neighborhoods and kitchens to focus on a feast in preparation. Children slowly gravitated to their family homes, but parents and offspring did not embrace. Seldom did they acknowledge one another with more than a glance. Only haltingly were conversations initiated. Those who had stayed behind re-engaged but in abbreviated exchange with those who had gone away. Yet in the hours after the children's coming ashore, talk gained momentum and controlled emotions surfaced with increasing confidence. Bonds of affection and respect were reaffirmed. As the feast was readied, the village was renewed. West Futuna was still home.

When asked about their dispersal from the cliff tops just as the children were to disembark, adults whispered of their uncertainty. Would the pupils have been seduced by the ideas of others? Fears that foreign influence might transform the hearts and minds of the next generation while abroad unsettled the process of re-engagement. As the narrative tales would predict border crossings are hazardous. And as *Nahjeji* implies, travelers risk entrapment during episodes of encompassment by foreign ways. Effects of real life excursions require assessment. Reconstituting community is always uncertain. In this, life and narrative are mimetic.

However, the lived experience of travelers including students returning home to West Futuna transcends an opposition of continuity and change by folding these polar extremes into one another. Those who go abroad are emissaries who return with bits and pieces of other worlds for local consumption. Fashion, food, a turn of phrase, play and ideology infiltrate and interact with established repertoires inevitably altering practice and reconstructing significance.

This process of domesticating the foreign is not the only trajectory possible. Broached in the tales, by contrast, is identic reproduction of community. In *Ta Pasiesi ma Majihjiki* it is assumed that given opportunity, children taken from their homes can return to recreate a social fabric that replicates original conditions. Knowledge gained during narrative adventures represents traditional wisdom that would normally have been learned at home and will serve the children well, as it did their ancestors, in (re-) establishing continuing principles for social order. Or as *Rufei Soa* suggests, novelty may augment but not transform tradition. Kaveiki Tan Moega and his wife return to Moega with new information to enhance a repertoire of right principles. The cure they have acquired represents accretion rather than fundamental modification of the local font of wisdom.

However, in the dynamics of *Nahjeji* words seem to come closer to a critical perspective on much of real life experience. At the heart of the poetic lines are conflicting desires to incorporate others while avoiding the potential for foreign ideas to destroy the familiar. This conflict presages the plight of the returnee conversant in alternative and inexplicably attractive possibilities. The sung verses hint at a resolution via nativizing alterity. That such strategies have materialized is obvious. And while vital, transformative consequences of the process are not envisioned explicitly in lyrical form, they are demonstrable in everyday life. Christianity has been shaped by Pacific tenets. Children educated abroad have come home to lead their new republic along versions of paths worn smooth by tradition. Continuing emphasis on encompassment and circular order echoes in recurrent strivings to discover those indigenous principles that serve to reinforce community while enabling individuals to partake of consonant potentials from their horizons (Keller n.d.; Rakau n.d.).

As people of West Futuna engage in nativizing the foreign and reshaping tradition, facets of cultural geography so richly implicated by narrative are invoked. The communities of West Futuna once conceived of as neighborhoods surrounding their *marae*, or as villages encircling an interior plateau are now conceived of as a larger perimeter surrounding the island of West Futuna itself. Home sites established in Tanna, Port Vila and even Noumea or Fiji dot what was the regional horizon of the past and what is now the new circuit of indigenous communities. Young women root their foreign husbands within ni-Vanuatu cities they themselves have only recently inhabited or follow spouses to lands only imagined a generation ago. Relative to this enlarged perimeter, the island of West Futuna is a center. Gradually as people have established residential alternatives overseas, the home island has taken on ancestral overtones. It is conceived of as a common site for respite and recovery, for learning traditional knowledge and practices of the land, for meeting obligations through ritual and celebratory activities. The homeland and those who remain resident there constitute a customary resource where both productive and iniquitous elements of past practice and belief survive and intermingle. Under conditions of emigration West Futuna has become a *tapu marae*. Emerging communities abroad constitute the protean periphery of human engagement. In some places residential neighborhoods even take the circular shape of villages at home. But even where patterns for living are distorted the mosaic of connections remains. The scale is larger than, yet analogous with, that shaped in the lines of mythological, historical and spatial discourses, contributing an undercurrent of familiarity and rightness to diasporic expansion.

This geographical ideology resonates with indigenous conceptions shared by islanders throughout the archipelago and even in Melanesia more broadly. Expanding horizons are repeatedly seen to bring the world within reach of local centers. The Republic of Vanuatu, for instance, is frequently conceived of as positioned at the heart of a global landscape (Miles 1998:191, 193). And LiPuma's discussions of regional Melanesia envision island locales encompassed by global structures of Christianity, 'capitalism, the nation-state and internationalized Western culture' (2000:12) in the manner of previous encompassment by local wisdom. Critical to this center-periphery imagery is the porous quality of intermediate boundaries and the dynamics of both centripetal and centrifugal forces. Influence radiates from island centers to their peripheries as well as from the more metropolitan margins inward (Bennardo 1996, 2002; Herdrich 1991; Herdrich and Clark in preparation; Lehman and Herdrich 2002). Local confidence in the power of familiar ideologies and practices to receive and mold external influence while disseminating their own, recalls the promise suggested in the lyrics of *Nahjeji*.

As Vanuatu struggles with new nation-state status, those in positions of leadership as well as the interested public are constantly engaged in debating the best roads to avoid dependency and foreign exploitation while shaping their country in a Melanesian Way invigorated by global potential (Reganvanu 1999). One road emphasizes *kastom* as a 'dominant unifying symbol' (Tonkinson cited in Miles 1998:73-4), a platform from which the voices of ni-Vanuatu can be raised in harmony and projected out into the world. Yet a danger lurks with the use of *kastom* as a rallying call for unity. In a republic of over one hundred ethnic and linguistically distinguished communities, drawing on specific *kastoms* for collective practice is as likely, it is said, to evoke difference as to engender commonality. The utility of *kastom* as a symbol of national identity to date has rested precariously on the magical power of the label itself (Malinowski 1948, 1978[1935]).

We suggest, however, that nuanced and substantive comparisons of narrative discourses promote rather than undermine ni-Vanuatu identity. As community ethnography demonstrates, complementarity constitutes effective social glue. Projects already conducted by fieldworkers with the Vanuatu Cultural Center have explored local cultural practices and encouraged examination of differences as well as similarities. Narrative, we suggest, while a part of *kastom* in the grand sense, is well suited to this sort of disentangling. The preliminary comparisons begun in this volume indicate overlapping episodes and themes among stories told throughout Vanuatu. The commonalities raise questions of prevalent values, of borrowings and of divergent uses for common forms. Tales and histories unique to a single community pose vantage points on diversity and suggest interlocking pieces of a puzzle yet to be completed. Such issues need not be divisive. Inter-textual analysis of narrative discourses can serve to inform expanding community mosaics and open conversations among complementary partners to the republic by creating a critical dialogism that will enrich awareness of common ground and shared heritage while also offering a vocabulary for understanding difference. (Re-)accentuating the arts of oral narrative and musical composition creates an opportunity to appreciate diversity and yet celebrate belonging within Vanuatu.

Notes

1 A special status for grass skirts was first suggested in the 1970s when I noticed a small class of items, which I thought of provisionally as property that were marked distinctively in possessive constructions to indicate a close or inalienable relationship to their possessor. Such items include shoes, cloth, grass skirts, homes, canoes, one's residential neighborhood, belts, the island itself, the sea, land parcels and the notion of place (Dougherty 1983:58-61). I came to appreciate that these entities are classed together because they encompass or envelop their possessors. Shoes cover one's feet. Cloth, skirts and belts are worn around the body. One's home, neighborhood, segments of land, designated places and the sea envelop a person. The expression *ta fanua oku* 'my land' indicates encompassment by a larger land mass and positions one not only within the land but also within the family associated with it. This conceptual encompassment is a fundamental element in the construction of the local cosmology.

2 Independent suggestion of the association of the reef with spiritual forces comes from the lingering belief among the people of West Futuna that dynamiting of a passage through the reef at Ta Fasua during World War II, by the Americans, angered the ancestral spirits who continue to this day to attack humans who frequent the place, exacting retribution for the original offense.

3 An imaginary line running northeast (*tamtagi raki*) to southwest (*ruitoga tane*) divides the wind compass of West Futuna such that currents originating west of this line are associated with the gale force potential of the westerlies

in contrast with the milder breezes associated with the winds originating east of the line. See Mueggler 2001:205 for a mention of the symbolic significance of the winds for the people of Zhizuo, southwest China. See Blust 1997 for comparison with other Austronesian systems and especially the axis of the west/northwest and east/southeast monsoons.

Aia Oji Tera

That's All There Is

14
A Pepa Uai Ta Koro / References Cited

Aaron, Daniel Bangtor, Paiaporou Antfalo, Frank Din, James Gwero, Simon Karae, Pakoa Mala, Leisale Mangawai, William Mete, Allen Nafuki, Dick Joel Peter, Kami Shing, George Tabeva, Shadrack Vulum, Wilson Wayback. 1981. *Yumi Stanap: Leaders and Leadership in a New Nation*. Institute of Pacific Studies, The University of the South Pacific and Lotu Pasifika Productions. Christchurch: Whitcoulls Ltd.

Agar, Michael. 1980. Stories, Background Knowledge and Themes: Problems in the Analysis of Life History Narrative. *American Ethnologist* 7(2):223-39.

Anderson, Benedict. 1983. *Imagined Communities: Reflections on the Origins and Spread of Nationalism*. London: Verso Books.

Anderson, Johannes C. 1995 [1928]. *Myths and Legends of the Polynesians*. New York: Dover Publications.

Ashby, Gene (compiler and ed.). 1989. *Never and Always: Micronesian Legends, Folktales and Folklore*. By the students of the Community College of Micronesia. Illustrated by Thomas Joel. Second Expanded Edition. Pohnpei: Rainy Day Press.

Bakhtin, M.M. 1981. *The Dialogic Imagination*. Edited by Michael Holquist. Translated by Caryl Emerson and Michael Holquist. Austin: University of Texas Press.

Ballard, C. 1998. 'The Sun by Night: Huli Moral Topography and Myths of a Time of Darkness' in *Fluid Ontologies: Myth,*

Ritual and Philosophy in the Highlands of Papua New Guinea. Edited by L.R. Goldman and C. Ballard. Westport: Bergin and Garvey. pp. 67-85.

Basso, Keith. 1979. *Portraits of 'the Whiteman': Linguistic Play and Cultural Symbols among the Western Apache*. Cambridge: Cambridge University Press.

———. 1996. *Wisdom Sits in Places*. Albuquerque: University of New Mexico Press.

Bauman, Richard. 1986. *Story, Performance and Event: Contextual Studies of Oral Narrative*. Cambridge: Cambridge University Press.

Bauman, Richard and Charles L. Briggs. 2003. *Voices of Modernity: Language Ideologies and the Politics of Inequality*. Cambridge: Cambridge University Press.

Bayard, Donn. 1976. *The Cultural Relationships of the Polynesian Outliers*. Otago University Studies in Prehistoric Anthropology. Dunedin: University of Otago.

Beaglehole, J.C. (ed.) 1961. *The Journals of Captain James Cook. Vol II: The Voyage of the Resolution and Adventure 1772-1775*. Cambridge: Cambridge University Press for the Hakluyt Society.

Beckwith, Martha W. 1970 [1940]. *Hawaiian Mythology*. New Haven: Yale University Press.

Bedford, R.D. 1973. *New Hebridean Mobility: A Study of Circular Migration*. Research School of Pacific Studies, Department of Human Geography. Publication HG/9. Canberra: The Australian National University.

Bellwood, P. 1979. Settlement Patterns. *Prehistory of Polynesia*. Edited by J. Jennings. Cambridge: Harvard University Press. pp. 308-22.

Bennardo, Giovanni. 1996. A Computational Approach to Spatial Cognition: Representing Spatial Relationships in Tongan Language and Culture. Ph.D. thesis, Department of Anthropology, University of Illinois, Urbana.

———. (ed.) 2002. Representing Space in Oceania: Culture,

Language and Mind. *Pacific Linguistics* 523. Canberra: Research School of Pacific and Asian Studies, The Australian National University.

Besnier, Niko. 1998. 'Polynesian Outliers' in *Garland Encyclopedia of World Music*. Vol. 9. Edited by A. Kaeppler and J.W. Love. New York: Garland Publishing Co. pp. 833-36.

Biersack, Aletta. (ed.) 1991. *Clio in Oceania: Toward a Historical Anthropology*. Washington: Smithsonian Institution Press.

———. 1998. 'Sacrifice and Regeneration among the Ipilis: The View from Tipinini' in *Fluid Ontologies: Myth, Ritual and Philosophy in the Highlands of Papua New Guinea*. Edited by L.R. Goldman and C. Ballard. Westport: Bergin and Garvey. pp. 43-66.

Blust, Robert. 1997. 'Semantic Change and the Conceptualization of Spatial Relationships in Austronesian Languages' in *Referring to Space: Studies in Austronesian and Papuan Languages*. Edited by Gunter Senft. Oxford: Clarendon Press. pp. 39-52.

Bolton, Lissant. (ed.) 1999. Fieldwork, Fieldworkers: Developments in Vanuatu Research. *Oceania* 70(1):1-108.

Bonnemaison, Joël. 1984. The Tree and the Canoe: Roots and Mobility in Vanuatu. *Pacific Viewpoint* 25(2):117-52.

———. 1994. *The Tree and the Canoe: History and Ethnogeography of Tanna*. Honolulu: University of Hawai'i Press.

Borofsky, Robert. (ed.) 2000. *Remembrance of Pacific Pasts: An Invitation to Remake History*. Honolulu: University of Hawai'i Press.

Bott, Elizabeth, with the assistance of Tavi. 1982. *Tongan Society at the Time of Captain Cook's Visits: Discussions with Her Majesty Queen Salote Tupou*. Wellington: The Polynesian Society (Incorporated).

Braudel, Fernand. 1958. Histoire et sciences socials: la longue durée. *Annales: Économies, Sociétiés, Civilisations* 13:725-53.

Brewer, William F. and G.W. Nakamura. 1984. 'The Nature and

Functions of Schemas' in *Handbook of Social Cognition*. Vol. 1. Edited by R.S. Wyer and T.K. Srull. Hillsdale: Erlbaum. pp. 119-60.

Burke, Kenneth. 1966. *Language as Symbolic Action*. Berkeley and Los Angeles: University of California Press.

Capell, Arthur. 1938. The Stratification of Afterworld Beliefs in the New Hebrides. *Folklore* 49:51-85.

———. 1958. Anthropology and Linguistics of Futuna-Aniwa, New Hebrides. Sydney: *Oceania Linguistic Monographs,* No. 5.

———. 1960. The Maui Myths in the New Hebrides. *Folklore* 71:19-36.

———. 1984. Futuna-Aniwa Dictionary, with Grammatical Introduction. Canberra: *PL*, C-56.

Codrington, R.H. 1891. *The Melanesians: Studies in the Anthropology and Folklore*. Oxford: The Clarendon Press.

Connerton, Paul. 1989. *How Societies Remember*. Cambridge: Cambridge University Press.

Corr, Rachel E. 2000. Cosmology and Personal Experience: Representations of the Sacred Landscape in Salasaca, Ecuador. Ph.D. thesis. University of Illinois, Champaign-Urbana.

Crowley, Terry. 1990. *Beach-la-Mar to Bislama: The Emergence of a National Language in Vanuatu*. Oxford: Clarendon Press.

Dening, Greg. 1980. *Islands and Beaches: Discourse on a Silent Land, Marquesas 1774-1880*. Honolulu: The University Press of Hawai'i.

———. 1992. *Mr. Bligh's Bad Language: Passion, Power and Theatre on the Bounty*. Cambridge: Cambridge University Press.

Donner, William W. 1987. Don't Shoot the Guitar Player: Tradition, Assimilation and Change in Sikaiana Song Performances. *Journal of the Polynesian Society* 96(2):201-23.

———. 1992. It's the Same Old Song but with a Different Meaning: Community and Ethnicity in Sikaiana Expressive Culture in *The Arts and Politics*. Edited by Karen Nero. *Pacific*

Studies 15(4):67-82.

Dorney, Sean. 2002. Interview with Prime Minister Edward Nipakei Natapei. *Radio Australia*, May 23.

Dougherty, Janet W.D. 1977. Reduplication in West Futuna. *Journal of the Polynesian Society* 86:207-21.

———. 1983. *West Futuna-Aniwa: An Introduction to the Language of a Polynesian Outlier*. Publications in Linguistics 102. Berkeley: University of California Press.

Drummond, Lee. 1981. The Serpent's Children: Semiotics of Cultural Genesis in Arawak and Trobriand Myth in *Symbolism and Cognition*. Edited by Clark Cunningham et al. *American Ethnologist* 8(3):633-60.

Duranti, A. 1994. *From Grammar to Politics: Linguistic Anthropology in a Western Samoan Village*. Berkeley: University of California Press.

———. 1997. Universal and Culture-Specific Properties of Greetings. *Journal of Linguistic Anthropology* 7(1):63-97.

Eisenman, Stephen F. 1997. *Gauguin's Skirt*. London: Thames and Hudson.

Elbert, Samuel H. 1949. Uta-matua and other Tales of Kapingamarangi. *Journal of American Folklore* 62:240-46.

Elbert, Samuel H. and Torben Monberg. 1965. *From the Two Canoes: Oral Traditions of Rennell and Bellona Islands*. Honolulu: University of Hawai'i Press in cooperation with the Danish National Museum, Copenhagen.

Facey, Ellen E. 1988. *Nguna Voices: Text and Culture from Central Vanuatu*. Calgary: University of Calgary Press.

Farnell, Brenda. 1995. *Do You See what I Mean: Plains Indian Sign Talk and the Embodiment of Action*. Austin: University of Texas Press.

Feinberg, Richard. 1988. Socio-spatial Symbolism and the Logic of Rank on Two Polynesian Outliers. *Ethnology* 27(3):291-310.

———. 1989. Possible Prehistoric Contacts between Tonga and Anuta. *The Journal of the Polynesian Society* 98(3):303-18.

———. 1998a. *Oral Traditions of Anuta, A Polynesian Outlier in the Solomon Islands*. NewYork and Oxford: Oxford University Press.

———. 1998b. 'Anuta' in *Garland Encyclopedia of World Music*. Edited by A. Kaeppler and J.W. Love. Vol. 9. New York: Garland Publishing Co. pp. 856-61.

———. 2002. Elements of Leadership in Oceania. *Anthropological Forum* 12(1):9-44.

———. 2003. *Anuta*. Mt Prospect: Waveland.

Feld, Steven. 1990. *Songs and Sentiment: Birds, Weeping, Poetics and Song in Kaluli Expression*. 2nd Edn. Philadelphia: University of Pennsylvania Press.

Firth, Raymond. 1961. *History and Traditions of Tikopia*. Wellington: The Polynesian Society.

———. 1985. *Tikopia-English Dictionary: Taranga FakaTikopia ma Taranga FakaInglisi*. Auckland: Auckland University Press.

———. 1998 'Tikopia' in *Garland Encyclopedia of World Music*. Edited by A. Kaeppler and J.W. Love. Vol. 9. New York: Garland Publishing Co. pp. 852-56.

Firth, Raymond and Mervyn McLean. 1990. *Tikopia Songs: Poetic and Musical Art of a Polynesian people of the Solomon Islands*. Cambridge: Cambridge University Press.

Flood, Bo, Beret E. Strong and William Flood. 1999. *Pacific Island Legends: Tales from Micronesia, Melanesia, Polynesia and Australia*. Honolulu: The Bess Press.

Foale, Simon and Martha Mcintyre. 2000. Dynamic and Flexible Aspects of Land and Marine Tenure at West Nggela: Implications for Marine Resource Management. *Oceania* 71:30-45.

Forman, Charles. 2001. Finding Our Own Voice: The Reinterpreting of Religion by Pacific Island Theologians. Paper presented at the Annual Meeting of the Association for Social Anthropology in Oceania, Muskogee, Florida.

Forster, George. 2000. *A Voyage Around the World*. Vol. II. Edited by Nicholas Thomas et al. Honolulu: University of Hawai'i Press.

Futuna – the Rock Island. *Quarterly Jottings of the New Hebri-*

des, South Sea Islands. No. 98 (October):1-2. 1917. Issued by the John G. Paton Mission Fund. Edited by A.K.L.

Gauguin, Paul. 1997 [1921]. *Gauguin's Intimate Journals*. Translated by Van Wyck Brooks. Preface by Emil Gauguin. Mineola. New York: Dover Publications, Inc.

Geddie, John. 1855. Mission to Tanna and Fortuna written from Aneityum, December 8th, 1854. *The Missionary Register of the Presbyterian Church of Nova-Scotia*. April.

Geertz, Clifford. 1980. *Negara: The Theater State in Nineteenth Century Bali*. Princeton: Princeton University Press.

Gifford, Edward Winslow. 1924. *Tongan Myths and Tales*. Bernice P. Bishop Museum Bulletin 8. Honolulu: Bernice P. Bishop Museum. Kraus reprint New York 1971.

———. 1929. *Tongan Society*. Bernice P. Bishop Museum Bulletin No. 61. Honolulu: Bernice P. Bishop Museum.

Glassie, Henry. 1982. *Passing the Time in Ballymenone: Culture and History of an Ulster Community*. Philadelphia: University of Pennsylvania Press.

Goldman, L.R., J. Duffield and C. Ballard. 1998. 'Introduction. Fire and Water: Fluid Ontologies in Melanesian Myth' in *Fluid Ontologies: Myth, Ritual and Philosophy in the Highlands of Papua New Guinea*. Edited by L.R. Goldman and C. Ballard. Westport: Bergin and Garvey. pp. 1-14.

Goodenough, Ward H. 1986. Sky World and This World: The Place of Kachaw in Micronesian Cosmology. *American Anthropologist* 88(3):551-69.

Goodwin, Majorie Harness. 1990. *He-Said-She-Said: Talk as Social Organization Among Black Children*. Bloomington and Indianapolis: University of Indiana Press.

Goody, Jack. 2000. *The Power of the Written Tradition*. Washington: The Smithsonian Institution Press.

Gray, Rev. W. 1891. Letter to Reverend William Gunn, December 24.

———. 1909a. Four Aniwan Songs. *Journal of the Polynesian Society* 3:93-7.

———. 1909b. Aniwan Folklore. *Journal of the Polynesian Society* 3:162-64.

Green, Roger. 1967. 'The Immediate Origins of the Polynesians' in *Polynesian Culture History*. Edited by G.A. Highland et al. Honolulu: Bernice P. Bishop Museum. pp. 215-40.

Grey, George. 1855. *Polynesian Mythology and Ancient Traditional History of the New Zealand Race*. London: J. Murray.

Gunn, Rev. William. (Trans.). n.d. *Tabuk Tapu*. Suva: The Bible Society in the South Pacific.

———. 1903. The Story of Amoshishiki and Pasiesi. *The New Hebrides Magazine*. December, pp. 23-4.

———. 1906 'Trials and Triumphs in the New Hebrides' in *The Pacific Islanders: From Savages to Saints*. Chapters from the Life Stories of Famous Missionaries and Native Converts. Edited by Delavan L. Pierson. New York and London: Funk & Wagnalls Company.

———. 1914. *The Gospel in Futuna*. London: Hodder and Stoughton.

———. 1924. *Heralds of the Dawn*. London: Hodder and Stoughton.

Handy, E.S. Craighill. 1927. *Polynesian Religion*. Bernice P. Bishop Museum Bulletin No. 34 and Bayard Dominick Expedition Publication Number 12. Honolulu: Bernice P. Bishop Museum.

Hanks, William. 1989. Texts and Intertextuality. *Annual Review of Anthropology* 18:95-127.

Hereniko, V. 1997. 'Pacific Cultural Identities' in *The Cambridge History of the Pacific Islanders*. Edited by D. Denoon et al. Cambridge: Cambridge University Press. pp. 428-36.

Herdrich, David. 1991. Towards an Understanding of Samoan Star Mounds. *Journal of the Polynesian Society* 100(4):381-435.

Herdrich, David and Jeffrey Clark, in preparation. *Spatial Concepts in Samoa: Implications of a Point-field Model for Ethnology and Prehistory*.

Herzfeld, Michael. 1982. *Ours Once More: Folklore, Ideology and the Making of Modern Greece*. Austin: University of Texas Press.

Hill, Jonathan. 1988. *Rethinking History and Myth: Indigenous South American Perspectives on the Past*. Urbana: University of Illinois Press.

Holland, Dorothy. 1992. 'The Woman Who Climbed Up The House: Some Limitations of Schema Theory' in *New Directions in Psychological Anthropology*. Edited by Theodore Schwartz et al. Cambridge: Cambridge University Press. pp. 68-82.

Hooper, Anthony and Huntsman, Judith. (Translation). 1991. *Matagi Tokelau*. Apia: Office for Tokelau Affairs, and Suva: Institute of Pacific Studies, University of the South Pacific.

Howe, R. 1984. *Where the Waves Fall: a New South Sea Islands history from First Settlement to Colonial Rule*. Pacific Islands Studies Program. Center for Pacific and Asian Studies. Honolulu: University of Hawai'i Press.

Hutchins, Edwin. 1995. *Cognition in the Wild*. Cambridge: MIT Press.

Hymes, Dell. 1981. *In Vain I Tried to Tell You*. Philadelphia: University of Pennsylvania Press.

Inglis, Rev. John. 1858. *The Reformed Presbyterian Magazine*, May.

———. 1859. Sixth Annual Report of the Reformed Presbyterian Synod's Mission to the New Hebrides written from Aneityum, New Hebrides, July 29.

———. 1860. Sep. 17, 1858 – Visit of the *John Knox* to Fotuna. Entry from Rev. Inglis' Journal in *The Missionary Register of the Presbyterian Church of Nova Scotia*. April. pp. 57-8.

———. 1890. *Bible Illustrations from the New Hebrides*. London: Thomas, Nelson and Sons.

Jolly, Margaret. 1997. 'Women-Nation-State in Vanuatu: Women as Sign and Subjects in the Discourses of *Kastom*, Modernity and Christianity' in *Narratives of Nation in the South Pacific*. Edited by Ton Otto and Nicholas Thomas. Amsterdam:

Harwood Academic Publishers.
———. 1999. Another Time, Another Place. *Oceania* 69(4):282-300.

Kaeppler, A., P. Crowe, W. Chenoweth and L. Lindstrom. 1998. 'Vanuatu' in *Garland Encyclopedia of World Music*. Edited by A. Kaeppler and J.W. Love. Vol. 9. New York: Garland Publishing Co. pp. 688-709.

Kaeppler, A. and J.W. Love. (eds). 1998. *Garland Encyclopedia of World Music*. Vol. 9. New York: Garland Publishing Co.

Kapferer, Bruce. 1988. *Legends of People, Myths of State: Violence, Intolerance and Political Culture in Sri Lanka and Australia*. Washington: Smithsonian Institution Press.

Kaufman, Michael T. 1999. Walter Lini, 57, Clergyman Who Led Nation of Vanuatu. Obituaries. *New York Times,* February 23.

Keller, Charles and Janet Keller. 1996. *Cognition and Tool Use: The Blacksmith at Work*. Cambridge: Cambridge University Press.

Keller, Janet Dixon. 1988. Woven World: Neotraditional symbols of unity in Vanuatu. *Mankind* 18(1):1-13.

———. n.d. Confronting Transformations in Urban Landscapes. Paper presented at the Annual Meetings of the American Anthropological Association, 2005. Washington, D.C.

Keller, Janet and Lehman, F.K. 1991. Complex Concepts. *Cognitive Science* 15:271-91.

Kenzo and Associates. 1992. *Visions of the Pacific*: Video of the 6th Festival of the Pacific Arts, Rarotonga, Cook Islands. Prepared for the New Zealand Ministry of Cultural Development, Wellington, New Zealand.

Kirch, Patrick Vinton. 1994. *The Wet and the Dry. Irrigation and Agricultural Intensification in Polynesia*. Chicago: University of Chicago Press.

———. 1996. *Legacy of the Landscape: An Illustrated Guide to Hawaiian Archaeological Sites*. Honolulu: University of Hawai'i Press.

———. 1997. *The Lapita Peoples*. Cambridge [MA]: Blackwell Publishers.

———. 2000. *On the Road of the Winds: an Archaeological History of the Pacific Islands before European Contact*. Berkeley and Los Angeles: University of California Press.

Kirch, Patrick Vinton, and Marshall Sahlins. 1992. *Anahulu: The Anthropology of History in the Kingdom of Hawai'i*. 2 vols. Chicago: University of Chicago Press.

Kirtley, Basil F. 1955. *A Motif-Index of Polynesian, Melanesian and Micronesian Narratives* (Dissertation: 2 Vols.). Indiana University Bloomington. Publication number 14,600, University Microfilms, Ann Arbor, Michigan.

———. 1971. *A Motif-Index of Traditional Polynesian Narratives*. Honolulu: University of Hawai'i Press.

Kirtley, Basil F., and Samuel H. Elbert. 1973. Animal Tales from Rennell and Bellona. *Journal of the Polynesian Society* 82:241-65.

Kuschel, Rolf, and Torben Monberg. 1977. History and Oral Traditions: A Case Study. *Journal of the Polynesian Society* 86(1):85-96.

Lawrie, Rev. J.H. 1895. 'Waihit of Aneityum' in the Missionary Review of the World. *Quarterly Jottings issued by the John G. Paton Fund*, Number 10, October.

Lehman, F.K. 1980. 'On the Vocabulary and Semantics of "Field" in Theravada Buddhist Society' in *Essays on Burma*. Edited by J.P. Ferguson. (Contributions to Asian Studies 16.) Leiden: E.J. Brill.

Lehman, F.K., and David Herdrich. 2002. On the Relevance of Point Fields for Spatiality in Oceania in 'Representing Space in Oceania: Culture in Language and Mind'. Edited by Giovanni Bennardo. *Pacific Linguistics* 523. Canberra: Research School of Pacific and Asian Studies, The Australian National University.

LeRoy, John. 1985. *Fabricated World: An Interpretation of Kewa Tales*. Vancouver: University of British Columbia Press.

Lessa, William A. 1980. More Tales from Ulithi Atoll: A Content

Analysis. *Folklore and Mythology Studies,* Number 32. Berkeley: University of California Press.

Lindstrom, Lamont. 1986. Kawmera Dictionary: N+kukua sai Nagkiariien N+nin+fe. *Pacific Linguistics Series C* Number 95. Canberra: The Australian National University.

———. 1990. *Knowledge and Power in a South Pacific Society.* Washington: Smithsonian Institution Press.

———. 1992. *Cargo Cult: Strange Stories of Desire from Melanesia and Beyond.* South Sea Books. Honolulu: University of Hawai'i Press.

———. 1997. 'Chiefs in Vanuatu Today' in *Chiefs Today: Traditional Pacific Leadership and the Postcolonial State.* Edited by Geoffrey White and Lamont Lindstrom. Palo Alto: Stanford University Press. pp. 211-28.

———. 1998. 'John Frum Music of Vanuatu' in *Garland Encyclopedia of World Music.* Edited by A. Kaeppler and J.W. Love. Vol. 9. New York: Garland Publishing Co. pp. 211-12.

———. 1999. Cargo Cult 2000. Keynote Address. *Cargo, Cult and Critique.* Workshop Sponsored by the Frobenius-Institute and Aarhus University, Aarhus, Denmark.

Lindstrom, Lamont, and James Gwero. (eds.) 1998. *Big Wok: Storian blong Wol Wo Tu long Vanuatu.* Suva: Institute of Pacific Studies and The University of the South Pacific.

Lipuma, Edward. 2000. Encompassing Others: The Magic of Modernity in Melanesia. Ann Arbor: University of Michigan Press.

Lord, Albert B. 1982. 'Oral Poetry in Yugoslavia' in *Memory Observed: Remembering in Natural Contexts.* Edited by Ulric Neisser. San Francisco: W.H. Freeman and Company.

Love, J.W. 1998. 'Performing Arts' in *Garland Encyclopedia of World Music.* Edited by A. Kaeppler and J.W. Love. Vol. 9. New York: Garland Publishing Co. p. 836.

Lugo, Alejandro. 1990. Cultural Production and Reproduction in Ciudad Juárez, Mexico: Tropes at Play among Maquiladora Workers. *Cultural Anthropology* 5(2):173-96.

———. 1997. 'Reflections on Border Theory, Culture and the Nation' in *Border theory: The Limits of Cultural Politics*. Edited by Scott Michaelsen and David E. Johnson. Minneapolis: University of Minnesota Press.

Luomala, Katharine. 1955. *Voices on the Wind: Polynesian Myths and Chants*. Illustrated by Joseph Feher. Honolulu: Bernice P. Bishop Museum.

Lynch, John. 1998. *Pacific Languages: A History*. Honolulu: University of Hawai'i Press.

Lynch, John and Kenneth Fakamuria. 1994. Borrowed Moieties, Borrowed Names: Sociolinguistic Contact Between Tanna and Futuna-Aniwa, Vanuatu. *Pacific Linguistics* 17(1, March):79-92.

McLean, Mervyn. 1999. *Weavers of Song: Polynesian Music and Dance*. Honolulu: University of Hawai'i Press.

McLendon, Sally. (ed.) 2003. Linguistics Forum. *American Anthropologist* 105(4).

Mageo, Jeannette Marie. 2001. *Cultural Memory: Reconfiguring History and Identity in the Postcolonial Pacific*. Honolulu: University of Hawai'i Press.

Māhina, 'Okutsitino. 1992. *The Tongan Traditional History Tala-e-Fonua: A Vernacular Ecology-Centered Historico-Cultural Concept*. Ph.D. thesis. Canberra: The Australian National University.

Malinowski, Bronislaw. 1948. *Magic, Science and Religion*. New York: The Free Press.

———. 1978 [1935] *Coral Gardens and Their Magic*. Vols. 1 and 2. New York: Dover Publications, Inc.

Memmott, Paul, and David Trigger. 1998. 'Marine Tenure in the Wellesley Islands Region, Gulf of Carpentaria' in *Customary Marine Tenure in Australia*. Edited by Nicolas Peterson and Bruce Rigsby. Oceanic Monograph 48. Sydney: Oceania Publications.

Merlan, Francesca. 1998. *Caging the Rainbow: Places, Politics and Aborigines in a North Australian Town*. Honolulu:

University of Hawai'i Press.
Miles, William F.S. 1998. *Bridging Mental Boundaries in a Postcolonial Microcosm: Identity and Development in Vanuatu*. Honolulu: University of Hawai'i Press.
Miller, J. Graham. 1978. *Live: A History of Church Planting in the New Hebrides to 1880. Book One*. Lawson: Presbyterian Church, Mission Publications of Australia, and Sydney: Bridge Printery.
———. 1981. *Live: A History of Church Planting in the New Hebrides Now the Republic of Vanuatu to 1880. Book Two*. Lawson: Presbyterian Church, Mission Publications of Australia, and Sydney: Bridge Printery.
———. 1986. *Live: A History of Church Planting in the Republic of Vanuatu 1881-1920. Book Four.* Port Vila: Presbyterian Church of Vanuatu, and Lawson: Presbyterian Church, Mission Publications of Australia.
Miller, R.S. (ed.) 1975. *Misi Gete: John Geddie, Pioneer Missionary to the New Hebrides*. Presbyterian Church of Tasmania, Australia.
Monberg, Torben. 1974. Poetry as Coded Messages: The Kananga of Bellona Island. *Journal of the Polynesian Society* 8(4):427-41.
———. 1991. *Bellona Island Beliefs and Rituals*. Honolulu: University of Hawai'i Press.
Morgan, Captain. 1854. Fotuna. A communication from Captain Morgan of the 'John Williams' to the London Missionary Society. *The Reformed Presbyterian Magazine,* August. p. 645.
Moyle, Richard. 1981. *Fagogo: Fables from Samoa in Samoan and English*. Auckland: Auckland University Press and Oxford University Press.
———. 2003. Nā Kkai Takū: Takū's Musical Fables. Collected by Richard M. Moyle. English Translations by Natan Nake and Tekaso Laroteone. Boroko: Institute of Papua New Guinea Studies.
———. n.d. Songs from the Second Float: A Musical Ethnogra-

phy of Takū Atoll, Papua New Guinea. Pacific Islands Monograph Series. Monograph No. 20. Center for Pacific Islands Studies, University of Hawai'i at Manoa. Honolulu: University of Hawai'i Press.

Mueggler, Erik. 2001. *The Age of Wild Ghosts: Memory, Violence and Place in Southwest China*. Berkeley: University of California Press.

Murray, Rev. A.W. 1876. *Forty-Years Mission Work in Polynesia and New Guinea*. London: James Nisbet & Co.

Myers, Fred. 1986. *Pintupi Country, Pintupi Self: Sentiment, Place and Politics Among Western Desert Aborigines*. Canberra: Australian Institute of Aboriginal Studies/Washington: Smithsonian Institution Press.

Neisser, Ulric. 1976. *Cognition and Reality: Principles and Implications for Cognitive Psychology*. San Francisco: W.H. Freeman and Company.

———. 1998. 'Stories, Selves and Schemata: A Review of Ecological Findings' in *Theories of Memory*. Edited by Martin A. Conway et al. Vol. II. East Sussex: Psychology Press. pp. 171-86.

Nero, Karen L. (ed.) 1992. The Arts and Politics. Special Issue of *Pacific Studies* 15(4):1-349.

Orta, Andrew. 2004. *Catechizing Culture: Missionaries, Aymara and the 'New Evangelization'*. New York: Columbia University Press.

Ortner, Sherry B. 1989. *High Religion: A Cultural and Political History of Sherpa Buddhism*. Princeton: Princeton University Press.

——. 1995. The Case of the Disappearing Shamans, or No Individualism, No Relationalism. *Ethos* 23(3):355-90.

Perez, Isabel Maria. 1999. *Chiriboga Ideology, Cosmology and Illness: A Miskitu Ethnography in Time of War*. Ph.D. thesis, University of Illinois, Department of Anthropology.

Petersen, Glenn. 1992. 'Dancing Defiance: The Politics of Pohnpeian Dance Performances' in *The Arts and Politics*. Edited by Karen Nero. Special Issue of *Pacific Studies* 15(4):13-28.

Peterson, Nicholas and Bruce Rigsby. 1998. *Customary Marine Tenure in Australia*. Oceania Monograph 48. Sydney: Oceania Publications.

Pinkser, Eve. 1992. 'Celebrations of Government: Dance Performance and legitimacy in the Federated States of Micronesia' in *The Arts and Politics*. Edited by Karen Nero. Special Issue of *Pacific Studies* 15(4):29-56.

Poignant, Roslyn. 1967. *Oceanic Mythology*. London: Paul Hamlyn Ltd.

Prout, Rev. E. 1843. *Memoirs of the Life of Rev. John Williams*. London and Andover.

Rakau, Fiama n.d.(c. 1997). 'Background Paper IV' in *The Cross and the Tanoa: Gospel and Culture in the Pacific*. Suva: South Pacific Association of Theological Schools. pp. 80-98.

Rawlings, Gregory E. 1990. 'Foundations of Urbanisation: Port Vila Town and Pango Village, Vanuatu' in Fieldwork, Fieldworkers: Developments in Vanuatu Research. Edited by Lissant Bolton. *Oceania* 70(1):72-86.

Ray, Sidney H. 1901. Stories from the Southern New Hebrides, with Introduction and Notes. *Journal of the Anthropological Institute* 31:147-54.

Reganvanu, Ralph. 1999. Afterword: Vanuatu Perspectives on Research. *Oceania* 70:98-100.

Rice, William Hyde. 1971 [1923]. *Hawaiian Legends*. Honolulu: Bernice P. Bishop Museum Bulletin 3. 2nd edn. Kraus reprint co. New York.

Robbins, Joel. 2001. God is Nothing But Talk: Modernity, Language and Prayer in a Papua New Guinea Society. *American Anthropologist* 103(4):901-12.

Rodman, Margaret. 1985. Moving Houses: Residential Mobility and the Mobility of Residences in Longana, Vanuatu. *American Anthropologist* 87(1):56-72.

——. 1992. Empowering Places: Multilocality and Multivocality. *American Anthropologist* 94:640-55.

Rossen, Jane Mink. 1998. 'Bellona' in *Garland Encyclopedia of World Music*. Edited by A. Kaeppler and J.W. Love. Vol. 9. New York: Garland Publishing Co. pp. 848-52.

Sahlins, M. 1981. *Historical Metaphors and Mythical Realities: Structure in the Early History of the Sandwich Islands Kingdom*. Association for Social Anthropology in Oceania Special Publication No. 1. Ann Arbor: University of Michigan Press.

———. 1985. *Islands of History*. Chicago: University of Chicago Press.

———. 1991. 'The Return of the Event Again: with Reflections on the Beginnings of the Great Fijian War of 1843-1855 between the Kingdoms of Bau and Rewa' in *Clio in Oceania: Toward a Historical Anthropology*. Edited by Aletta Biersack. Washington: Smithsonian Institution Press. pp. 37-100.

Salmond, Anne. 1991. *Two Worlds: First Meetings Between Maori and Europeans 1642-1772*. Auckland: Viking Books.

Senft, Gunter. 1997. (ed.) *Referring to Space: Studies in Austronesian and Papuan Languages*. Oxford: Clarendon Press.

Sherkin, Samantha. 1999. *Forever United: Identity Construction across the Rural-Urban Divide*. Ph.D. thesis, Department of Anthropology, University of Adelaide, South Australia.

Shore, Bradd. 1996. *Culture in Mind*. Oxford: Oxford University Press.

Shutler, R. Jr. 1971. New Hebrides Radio Carbon Dates, 1968. *Asian Perspectives* XIV:84-7.

Sore, Maroi (Maroi the Elder). 1909. A Song of Aniwa. *Journal of the Polynesian Society* 3:41-5 (2nd edition printed at Leipzig, Germany).

Steel, Robert. 1880. *The New Hebrides and Christian Missions with a Sketch of the Labour Traffic and Notes of a Cruise through the Group in the Mission Vessel in 1874*. London: James Nisbet and Co.

Stewart, Kathleen. 1996. *A Space by the Side of the Road: Cultural Poetics in an 'Other' America*. Princeton: Princeton University Press.

Strathern, A. 1998. 'Sacrifice and Sociality: A Duna Ritual Track' in *Fluid Ontologies: Myth, Ritual and Philosophy in the Highlands of Papua New Guinea*. Edited by L.R. Goldman and C. Ballard. Westport: Bergin and Garvey. pp. 31-42.

Sullivan, Lawrence E. 1988. *Icanchu's Drum: An Orientation to Meaning in South American Religions*. New York: Macmillan Publishing Co.

Sutton, David. 1998. *Memories Cast in Stone: The Relevance of the Past in Everyday Life*. New York: Berg.

———. 2001. *Remembrance of Repasts: an Anthropology of Food and Memory*. Oxford and New York: Berg.

Taylor, John. 2001. Personal Communication. Canberra: Research School of Pacific and Asian Studies, The Australian National University.

Tedlock, Dennis. 1983. *The Spoken Word and the Work of Interpretation*. Philadelphia: University of Pennsylvania Press.

Thieberger, Nicholas. 2000. Walking to Erro. Paper presented to a cross-disciplinary conference, Walking About: Travel, Trade, Migration and Movement in Vanuatu. Canberra: The Australian National University.

Thomas, Allan. 1992. Songs as History. *Journal of Pacific History* 27(2):29-36.

———. 1998. 'West Futuna' in *Garland Encyclopedia of World Music*. Edited by A. Kaeppler and J.W. Love. Vol. 9. New York: Garland Publishing Co. pp. 861-64.

Thomas, Allan, and Takaroga Kuautoga. 1992. HgoroFutuna: Report of a Survey of the Music of West Futuna, Vanuatu. *Occasional Papers in Pacific Ethnomusicology* No. 2.

Tonkinson, Robert. 1982. Vanuatu Values: A changing symbiosis. *Pacific Studies* 5:58.

Tyler, Stephen. 1978. *The Said and The Unsaid. Mind, Meaning and Culture*. New York: Academic Press.

UNESCO. c. 1996. *Vanuatu: The Music Tradition of West Futuna/ La Musique Traditionnelle de Futuna Occidental*. Musiques

Traditionnelles d'Aujourd'hui/Traditional Music of Today.

Van Trease, Howard. 1987. *The Politics of Land in Vanuatu*. Suva: University of the South Pacific.

Wagner, Roy. 1972. *Habu: The Innovation of Meaning in Daribi Religion*. Chicago: University of Chicago Press.

Wan Smolbag Theater and Pacifika Communications. 1996. *Things We Don't Talk About*. Produced jointly with Pasifika Communications and funded with contributions from British Aid. Port Vila, Vanuatu.

———. 1997. *Kasis Road*. Produced jointly with Pasifika Communications and funded with contributions from British Aid, Canada Fund, Government of Japan GGP Programme, Aus Aid and New Zealand Official Development Assistance. Port Vila, Vanuatu.

Ward, Gerard, John W. Webb, and M. Levison. 1973. The Settlement of the Polynesian Outliers: A Computer Simulation. *Journal of the Polynesian Society* 82(4):330-42.

Weiner, James. 1991. *The Empty Place*. Bloomington: Indiana University Press.

White, Geoffrey and Lindstrom, Lamont. (eds.) 1997. *Chiefs Today: Traditional Pacific Leadership and the Postcolonial State*. Palo Alto: Stanford University Press.

Index of selected names, narrative titles, concepts, words and phrases